REPUBLICAN AND FASCIST GERMANY

Themes and Variations in the History of Weimar and the Third Reich 1918–45

John Hiden

Longman
London and New York

Longman Group Limited,
Longman House, Burnt Mill,
Harlow, Essex CM20 2JE, England
and Associated Companies throughout the world.

Published in the United States of America
by Longman Publishing, New York

First published 1996

ISBN 0 582 49209 2 CSD
ISBN 0 582 49210 6 PPR

British Library Cataloguing in Publication Data

A catalogue record for this book is available from the British Library

Library of Congress Cataloging-in-Publication Data

Hiden, John.
  Republican and Fascist Germany : themes and variations in the
history of Weimar and the Third Reich 1918–1945 / John Hiden.
    p. cm.
  Includes bibliographical references and index.
  ISBN 0–582–49202–2. -- ISBN 0–582–49210–6 (pbk.)
    1. Germany--Politics and government--1918–1933. 2. Germany-
-Politics and government--1933–1945. 3. Fascism--Germany.
4. National socialism--Germany. 5. Germany--Economic
conditions--1918–1945. 6. Germany--Social conditions--1918–1933.
7. Germany--Social conditions--1933–1945. 8. Right and left
(Political science) 9. Political culture--Germany. I. Title.
DD240.H478   1996
943.085--dc20
                                                    95–41857
                                                        CIP

Set by 7 in 10/12 Bembo
Produced by Longman Singapore Publishers (Pte) Ltd.
Printed in Singapore

Contents

Contents

Acknowledgements

I have benefited enormously from the work of numerous fine historians of modern Germany and from my discussions with a good many of these. I can only regret that I am unable to acknowledge them all individually. The footnotes are reserved largely for studies to which I make direct reference in the main text. Any specialist in the field will recognize the extent of my indebtedness, but I hasten to add that if errors have nonetheless crept into the book they are all my own work. The Department of European Studies granted me a period of study leave during 1995 to complete the writing. I am very grateful indeed for this. I am also happy to record my thanks to the British Academy for the Small Grant which it gave me at an earlier stage of my work on this volume. It is a particular pleasure to acknowledge the stimulus I have enjoyed from working and teaching with my fellow Germanist and younger colleague at Bradford, Dr Martyn Housden. Finally – and as always – I am thankful for the indispensable support of my wife and my dear friend, to whom this book is dedicated.

John Hiden   Guiseley, July 1995

For Juliet

Abbreviations and Acronyms

AA	German Foreign Office	(*Auswärtiges Amt*)
ADB	General German Civil Servants' Association	(*Allgemeiner Deutscher Beamtenbund*)
ADGB	General Federation of German Trade Unions	(*Allgemeiner Deutscher Gewerkschaftsbund*)
AFA	General Free Federation of Salaried Employees	(*Allegemeiner freier Angestelltenbund*)
AO	Foreign Organization	(*Auslandsorganisation*)
APA	Foreign Policy Office	(*Aussenpolitisches Amt*)
BDI	League of Industrialists	(*Bund der Industriellen*)
BVP	Bavarian People's Party	(*Bayerische Volkspartei*)
DAF	German Labour Front	(*Deutsche Arbeiter Front*)
DBB	German Civil Service Association	(*Deutscher Beamtenbund*)
DDP	German Democratic Party	(*Deutsche Demokratische Partei*)
DNVP	The German Nationalist People's Party	(*Deutschnationale Volkspartei*)
DVP	German People's Party	(*Deutsche Volkspartei*)
Gestapo	'Secret State Police'	(*Geheime Staatspolizei*)
HSSPF	Higher SS and Police Leaders	(*Höhere SS und Polizeiführer*)
IMCC	Inter-Allied Military Control Commission	

KAPD	German Communist Workers' Party	(*Kommunistische Arbeiter Partei Deutschlands*)
KPD	German Communist Party	(*Kommunistische Partei Deutschlands*)
NSBO	National Socialist Factory Cells	(*Nationalsozialistische Betriebszellen-Organisation*)
NSDAP	National Socialist German Workers' Party	(*Nationalsozialistische Arbeiter Partei*)
OHL	Army High Command	(*Oberste Heeresleitung*)
OKW	High Command of the Armed Forces	(*Oberkommando der Wehrmacht*)
RDB	Reich Association of German Civil Servants	(*Reichsbund der Deutschen Beamten*)
RDI	Reich Association of German Industry	(*Reichsverband der deutschen Industrie*)
RHB	Reich Association of Higher Civil Servants	(*Reichsbund der höheren Beamten*)
RKVD	Reich Commissioner for the Strengthening of German Nationality	(*Reichskommissar für die Festigung deutschen Volkstums*)
RLB	[Agrarian League renamed]	(*Reichslandbund*)
RNS	Reich Food Estate	(*Reichsnährstand*)
RSHA	Reich Security Main Office	*Reichssicherheitshauptamt*)
RVK	Reich Coal Association	(*Reichsvereinigung Kohle*)
SA	Storm Detachment	(*Sturmabteilung*)
SPD	Social Democratic Party	(*Sozialistische Partei Deutschlands*)
SS	Protection Squads	(*Schutzstaffel*)
USPD	Independent German Social Democratic Party	(*Unabhängige Sozialdemokratische Partei Deutschlands*)
VDA	Association for Germandom Abroad	(*Verein für das Deutschtum im Ausland*)
VOMI	Ethnic German Liaison Office	(*Volksdeutsche Mittelstelle*)
ZAG	Central Working Association	(*Zentralarbeitsgemeinschaft*)

Introduction

The present volume spans the period between 1918 and 1945, years witnessing among other things the historic peacemaking at Versailles, the rise of fascism, the early stages of co-existence between communist and capitalist societies, the advent to power of Adolf Hitler, the path to the Second World War, the brutal onslaught on the Jewish peoples and the final high drama of Germany's defeat and partition. Momentous enough in themselves, these events have had the most fundamental impact on Europe and have become the object of renewed and mounting public interest since the re-unification of Germany in 1990. There are of course general histories of modern Germany which include coverage of the Weimar Republic and the Third Reich, but they are often understandably short of detail. At the other extreme are studies concentrating either on National Socialist or Weimar Germany. Of the latter, however, many also turn out in fact to be largely concerned with Hitler, his movement and his rise to power. Bookshelves holding volumes on the Nazi state positively groan beneath the weight.

One of the central aims of this book is to tilt the balance more towards the Weimar era, giving due and necessary attention to National Socialism but emphatically not at the expense of observing potentially constructive developments during the 1920s. Thus, to take one example, the early history of the National Socialist German Workers' Party (*Nationalsozialistische Arbeiter Partei* – NSDAP) is set in the context of a full and critical consideration of the major German political parties and against the backdrop of some rather interesting but often overlooked progress in the Reichstag. However, the historiographical imbalance between the 1920s and 1930s is only redressed in the larger interest of promoting an informed, structured and critical discussion of the period as a whole. To this end the book deliberately focuses on major themes and debates and follows them in most cases right through from the 1920s to the 1930s and indeed into the war years. It does not purport to be a complete history of Germany between 1918 and 1945. Moreover, the multi-layered approach shows more clearly than the narrative format how much effort was required and on how many different fronts before the Weimar Republic could be destroyed and with it some of its promising policies. The resilience of the Weimar Republic is not something which is commonly stressed, partly because it was for so long treated as a mere antechamber to the Third Reich.

Monocausal explanations for the final end of Weimar have admittedly long been out of favour but the deterministic gloom hovering over the republic's life has not been wholly dispelled. The German republic proclaimed in November 1918 was not 'doomed from birth' in the very obvious sense that – in contrast to 1945 – it was neither invaded nor partitioned. Its economic power was still great and, the Versailles peace treaty notwithstanding, its influence on the international scene was likely to remain weighty. Politically, the abdication of the Kaiser had sealed the fate of monarchy in Germany and with it that of the other rulers in the federal German states prior to the Republic's declaration. Thus although Germany's first parliamentary governments had to function under adverse conditions – dealing with domestic revolution and completing the acceptance of the peace treaty – even the opponents of the republican state form were compelled to work within a democratically elected Reichstag.

The thematic approach adopted in this book also seeks to promote a loosening of the rigid periodization still quite often imposed on German history after 1918 – a practice which diverts attention from the underlying socio-economic structures and the mundane continuity of daily life. From this vantage point the respective 'births' of the Weimar Republic in 1918–19 and of the Third Reich in 1933–34 do not mark complete breaks in the development of modern Germany. Does this also mean that these were not 'revolutionary' happenings? The Marxist view that bourgeois revolution opened the road to democracy, whilst a proletarian revolution paved the way to a classless society, produced a paradigm of a 'good' revolution. Examples of the latter were believed to be the revolutions in France in 1789 and in Russia in 1917. These were instances where a conjunction of ideas and events had by and large taken a consistent course and where their 'objective reality' was confirmed by their permanence.[1] Against such a

---

1. E. Weber, 'Revolution? Counter revolution? What revolution?', in W. Laqueur (ed.), *Fascism. A reader's guide* (London, 1979), pp. 488ff.

stern test the 'revolutions' in Germany were judged to have failed. Rather than pursuing the arguments for and against this judgement for the moment it might be more helpful to make brief *comparisons* between the upheavals marking the beginning and end of the 1920s. In devoting the rest of the introduction to this task the temptation to adopt a Hitler-centric approach to interwar Germany is reduced at the outset whilst at the same time central themes can be identified prior to their detailed analysis in subsequent chapters.

Tackling the mountain of literature on the revolution of November 1918 and the National Socialist seizure of power in 1933 demands a sturdy constitution. Yet even the casual reader will discern a major contrast between the general historical treatment of the two events. In the case of 1918–19 the emphasis is on the spontaneous nature of the political reaction impelling the German socialists into power in the dying days of the war. The National Socialist *Machtergreifung* is seen, however, as the outcome of an orchestrated and ruthless pursuit of office by the Hitler movement during the Weimar Republic's final years. In reality both the proclamation of the Weimar Republic on 10 November 1918, under an all-socialist provisional government, and Hitler's assumption of the chancellorship on 30 January 1933, came in essentially unpredictable crises. In neither case was it possible to calculate odds and plan strategies with complete certainty.

This is obviously not to deny the existence of socialists and National Socialists following the bright light of ideology. Yet the victories of socialism in 1918 and of National Socialism in 1933 were both sustained by powerful and broad public pressure for change. Even in 1918 distaste with the existing system was not by any means confined to the left. There was for a while popular appreciation of the need for reforming the old order. Admittedly, the sentiment evaporated fairly quickly. There was not, for example, much good will towards the Weimar Republic at the end of the 1920s amongst the German elites – the leaders of the armed forces, the civil servants, businessmen and landowners. Not even these, however, were all bent on destroying the Republic at the outset. In 1918, and in 1933, the recognition by the German establishment of the inevitability of change was tempered by attempts to control the governments of first Friedrich Ebert and subsequently Adolf Hitler.

There are obvious parallels between, on the one hand, the activities of the military/political clique in the last weeks of the Weimar Republic, culminating in Hitler being offered the crown, and, on the other hand, the events of 1918, when parliamentary democracy was supposedly 'granted' by the military establishment, in the forms of the celebrated wartime generals, Paul von Hindenburg and Erich Ludendorff. In both instances, however, placing too much emphasis on 'revolution from above' and on the conspiratorial nature of the German establishment's role in the Republic's final crises tends, apart from underestimating the pressure for change, to exaggerate the cohesion within the German elites. It is a matter of record that their indifference to the Republic did not spare them shivers of apprehension about the NSDAP. Their attempt to contain someone of Hitler's ilk smacked at least as much of desperation as of cunning. Yet desperation was also in the air in November 1918, when German social democracy was regarded by the elites as the lesser evil and at any rate preferable to full-blown communism. In this respect the essential idea behind the 'containment' of Hitler, namely to swing his movement behind the government and then to control it, was perhaps anticipated in the words of Prince Max Baden, as the head of Germany's first representative government. In October 1918 he pronounced: 'In a word, collaboration with the people, but away with the rule of the masses.'[2] Thinking for the moment not only of 1933 but also of 1918 in terms of 'containment', makes it easier to appreciate that the policy can never have been entirely one of calculated and rational choice. In 1918 and 1933 Germany's anxious elites collaborated with what they perceived as 'moderates' in the threatening mass movements in order to ward off something worse.

That was a prime consideration of General Groener in making his celebrated telephone call to President Ebert on 10 November 1918. Groener and his fellow officers persuaded themselves that by their offering support to Ebert the political cart would at least not 'slide further to the left'.[3] Similarly, by 1933 an important group in the army, centring on Field Marshal Werner von Blomberg and Field-Marshal Walther von Reichenau, backed Hitler's chancellorship so that a new government coalition of the right could rein in extremists in the National Socialist German Workers' Party (NSDAP). The immediate rationale of the army's working understanding with the Social Democratic Party (*Sozialistische Partei Deutschlands* – SPD) in 1918 was to ensure the orderly return of the German troops from the front, although in honesty the soldiers' councils which had sprung up could probably have achieved this on their own. More importantly, the arrangement facilitated the transmission to the Weimar Republic of the old army's system of values, together with many of its officers. As early

2. E. Matthias and R. Morsey (eds), *Die Regierung des Prinzen Max von Baden* (Düsseldorf, 1962).
3. F. L. Carsten, *Reichswehr und Politik* (Cologne–Berlin, 1964), p. 12.

as December 1918 the military was therefore able to check the formation of a democratic fighting force (*Volkswehr*), foreshadowed by units formed in Baden, Württemburg, Thuringia and elsewhere, and based on the principles of the so-called Hamburg programme. The latter – adopted by the all-German Congress of Workers' and Soldiers' Deputies in December 1918 – affirmed the control of the units and discipline by the soldiers' councils, as well as the election of officers by the men and the abolition of all insignia of rank.[4] Notwithstanding this, by early 1919 the old army leaders had consolidated their hold over the more 'reliable' Freikorps and other diverse elements rapidly being recruited to form the basis of the new German army, the Reichswehr. The Treaty of Versailles unintentionally favoured the process by stipulating for Germany a small but all-professional force of one hundred thousand men. By 1933–4, the army leaders were rewarded for their support of Hitler through the emasculation of their chief rival, the powerful paramilitary wing of the NSDAP, the SA (*Sturmabteilung*). The bloody elimination of SA leader Ernst Roehm gave the Reichswehr control over the pre- and post-military training of a mass of potential recruits to the ranks of the regular forces.

It is plain that the pro-National Socialist sentiments of many of the younger Reichswehr officers in 1933 find very few parallels in the relationship between armed forces and socialism in 1918. Nonetheless, by the very act of countering what they saw as a threat from extreme revolutionary forces, the army leaders effectively ensured the *functioning* of the new political order in the 1920s, just as they did in the 1930s. In both instances the German officers helped to secure the more or less peaceful transition to political systems which were markedly different from the world in which they had been nourished. This very much suggests that for much of the time self-interest may have motivated the military leaders quite as much as conviction. Survival was all. Whilst the armed forces initially escaped the sort of close control demanded by political activists both in 1918 and 1933 there were important differences in the underlying position of the German military in the 1920s and 1930s. The Weimar constitution vested the supreme command of the Reich's military forces in the President of the Republic, although the man actually responsible to the Reichstag was the Defence Minister. Considerable opportunities existed in practice for the Reichswehr to operate in the parliamentary system to further its own interests. After 1933 the situation was much changed. Following Hindenburg's death in 1934, Hitler, already Reich

4. F. L. Carsten, *Revolution in Central Europe 1918–1919* (London, 1972), pp. 72–3.

President, became Supreme Commander of the Armed Forces. He demanded a personal oath of loyalty to the 'Führer of the German Reich and People'. Moreover the decline of the NSDAP's paramilitary force, the SA, was paralleled by the consolidation of a distinct organization for the SS (*Schutzstaffel*). The latter development boded ill for the independence of the German officer corps and ultimately facilitated the blurring of ideological lines between SS and Reichswehr, with brutal consequences during the Second World War.

Georg Grosz's famous painting of the pillars of the German state included, apart from the military and the church, the academics. These were members of the German civil service, itself an essential part of the skein of public life linking Bismarck to Hitler. In November 1918 the installation of 'observers' from the SPD and the Independent German Social Democratic Party (*Unabhängige Sozialdemokratische Partei Deutschlands* – USPD) in the offices of the ministerial bureaucracy signalled plans for radical reform. The task of these men and women was to make sure that the administration functioned in the spirit of the revolution. The nearest counterpart to those early revolutionary watchdogs were the distinctly less appetizing local NSDAP men and SA commissars who, in 1933–4, swept into government offices at various levels. Again, their ill-defined task was to ensure appropriate responses from the German civil service in the new order. However, the bureaucrats had some trump cards up their sleeves.

In the first place they enjoyed a virtual monopoly of administrative and management skills. These were initially in short supply in the socialist ranks in 1918 and in those of the National Socialists in 1933. Professional civil servants could often bypass their revolutionary 'shadows' in 1918–19 in the day to day routines. The most celebrated example was provided by the German Foreign Office, where first Wilhelm Solf and then Count Ulrich Brockdorff-Rantzau asserted their primacy in making policy. After 1933 the same office was defended against National Socialist pretenders, for a while, by Foreign Minister Konstantin von Neurath. The democratization of the bureaucracy threatened in November 1918 failed to materialize in any significant way. However, although the Weimar constitution expressly guaranteed the civil service career structure and privileges, the specific conditions of work during the 1920s did not generate huge job satisfaction. This partly explained the growing appeal of National Socialism. Civil servants' futures seemed assured after the demise of the Weimar Republic and the passage of the *Law For The Re-establishment Of The Civil Service* on 7 April 1933. The price paid by the civil service, as by the army, was that in 1918 and again in 1933 it too was obliged to facilitate the transition to two entirely different systems of government. Explanations of the German bureaucracy's behaviour before 1933 which put too much weight on affinities between the authoritarian tradition of the Reich civil service and the values of National Socialism are therefore open to question. Political preferences naturally played an important part in determining German civil servants' actions during the crises of 1918–19 and 1933–4, but in the last resort a major consideration for them was to remain employed. The bureaucratic drive to preserve career structures and exclusivity of caste must never be underestimated. However, not even pragmatism of this high order could protect the German civil servants for ever after 1933.

The nature and extent of the accommodation described above was naturally also determined by prevailing political realities, by what was *possible* as well as by what was desirable. In reflecting on the accommodation between the German elites and the new political orders of 1918 and 1933 the role of individuals must not be exaggerated. Both Marxist and bourgeois historians writing of interwar Germany have been guilty of this. The former portrayed Ebert as a block to aspirations for 'genuine' socialist changes in 1918, and Hitler as the saviour of monopoly capitalism in crisis. Bourgeois historians blamed Ebert for not exploiting opportunities in 1918 to overhaul society, thereby failing to avoid the conditions which gave rise to Hitler. As to the Führer, western historians have long overstated his control of events during Germany's transition from multi-party to single-party state. We now have a much fuller picture of the complex political and social contexts in which first Ebert and then Hitler operated. Neither of them would have been brought to the threshold of power without their large and frequently undisciplined mass followings. The SPD/USPD coalition comprising Germany's Provisional Government from 10 November 1918 until 29 December 1918, owed its authority not to the *state* (the Wilhelmine state had ceased to exist), but to the network of revolutionary workers' and soldiers' councils formed throughout the land. The meetings in Berlin of the Central Congress of Councils were particularly important. Unlike Ebert in 1918, Hitler was formally appointed Chancellor and had a more obvious base of power in the state. Only at that point, however, did the full effects of the NSDAP combat organizations, the SA and the SS, make themselves felt in the various German regions (*Länder*). Unbridled rank and file action from below softened political opponents and prefaced NSDAP control, first in Prussia on 6 February 1933 and thereafter in the other *Länder*.

In this sense the attempt in 1918, through elements in the council movement, to institute more far-reaching change than the SPD leadership was ready to accept, had its counterpart in the zeal of the 'Brown movement' in 1933–4 for a second, 'proper' revolution, going beyond the mere assumption of state power. Hitler's following was no more homogeneous than that sustaining the council movement in 1918, and neither was subject to easy control and direction. Blunt action was used against the 'wild' SA internment camps of 1933–4, as it was earlier against maverick soldiers' and workers' councils in 1918–19. Yet force alone would not have been enough to defeat such opposition had the prevailing political climate not favoured it. Thus the Congress of Workers' and Soldiers' Councils on 16 December 1918 itself voted to call for parliamentary elections, checking hopes that the council movement would become the foundation of a far more radical order. The disparate elements on the left making up the communist movement, as well as the USPD leaders, were affronted by the decision. The latter showed their displeasure by leaving the government shortly afterwards. But the decision of the Berlin Congress echoed the mood of the population at large. Preparations for a multi-party system followed inexorably from the Congress vote. Additional obstacles to sweeping revolution were soon provided by the re-emergence of political groupings from the old Imperial Reichstag.

It was consistent with the SPD's historical development that in 1918–19 its leaders resorted to parliamentary democracy in order to frustrate more extreme revolutionary plans to extend the control of workers' and soldiers' councils. That great violence was also used against the German communists was, however, a sad and bitter comment on the nature of the relationship developing between Ebert and the German establishment. In that sense, at least, the Weimar Republic may be called the last act of Empire.[5] Nevertheless, the murder of key figures on the far left like Rosa Luxemburg and Karl Liebknecht at the hands of the Freikorps did not prevent the emergence of a communist party in December–January, 1918–19. The German Communist Party (*Kommunistische Partei Deutschlands* – KPD) was anti-republican, but its very existence testified to the way in which divergent political values were to be accommodated within the Weimar system. An elected National Assembly in Weimar in January 1919 demonstrated the fitness and readiness of the German socialists to govern with others. The SPD confirmed in 1918–19 that it was indeed a party which preached revolution but did not make it. Hitler's

5. Cf. E. Kolb, *The Weimar Republic* (London–Boston–Sydney–Wellington, 1988), pp. 138ff.

celebrated 'Enabling Act' of 1933 established by contrast the inherently expendable nature of parties other than the NSDAP. Not only were the remaining, sad remnants of the other bourgeois parties eliminated from the political arena, but even the German nationalists, whose support had been so crucial to Hitler's earlier electoral strategy, were reduced to impotence by 1934. This was in addition to the onslaught against organized socialism. If 1918–19 made it difficult for German socialism to work with its offspring, German communism, then 1933–4 imposed a belated community of interest on the German left. It also provided Hitler with the justification and opportunity, after the Reichstag fire on 27 February 1933, to treat socialism and communism as synonymous and to drive both from public life.

Not only political but economic realities helped in 1918 and in 1933 to shape the transition from one system to another. The quest to survive was perhaps more pronounced and overt in the German business community than it was in the armed forces and bureaucracy, with their habitual references to duty and the interests of the state; capitalists are expected to defend their own interests come what may. In 1918 they were self-evidently against revolution. No more were the SPD leaders exactly committed to draconian social and economic change. It is not therefore surprising to find an equivalent of the Ebert–Groener arrangement in the community of work and business. Such was the agreement made on 15 November 1918 between Hugo Stinnes, a prominent captain of industry, and Carl Legien, spokesman for the unions. In taking this step to secure the continuation of production, German industrialists were also seeking to end the detested state wartime controls over the economy. Reich Economics Minister, Wichard von Moellendorf, had actually been hoping to prolong these.[6] However, the Stinnes–Legien deal compelled employers to accept for the time being some at least of the major long-standing demands of unionized labour. The Provisional Government undoubtedly lost opportunities to exploit differences within industry and finance during the early weeks of the revolution. By spring 1919, when the new SPD Minister for Economics, Rudolf Wissell, was appointed the initiative for a planned socialist economy had been lost. However, the example of other advanced societies, like Britain for instance, showed that the reversion to the free market economy and the abandonment of wartime controls was not something peculiar to Germany. The important point is that the process of industrial compromise in the

6. G. D. Feldman, 'Economic and social problems of German demobilisation, 1918–1919', *Journal of Modern History*, 47 (1975); R. Bessel, *Germany after the First World War* (Oxford, 1993), pp. 99ff.

Reich provided yet another degree of legitimacy for the new political order. Whether this made the SPD itself into a mere 'interest' party or whether the compromise reflected the fact that the SPD had always been such a beast is a question deferred for the moment.

If the commercial world no more rushed to embrace socialism in 1918 than the army and civil service of Germany had done, then at least it managed to work with German labour to restore order in the economy and to crank it back to something approaching normal life. As to National Socialism later, divisions certainly existed on the subject within large scale German industry. Yet no more in 1933 than in 1918 did this prevent big business from indirectly facilitating the transition between different political orders. Disillusionment with Weimar politics spread through the board room long before the late 1920s. The gravity of the slump from 1929 onwards made the effects of the Stinnes–Legien agreement still more difficult for German industrialists to swallow than it had been at the beginning of the decade. Although active support for Hitler's cause was not particularly pronounced in the world of big business, there developed amongst German industrialists a growing disinclination to resist his charms with any vigour. As in 1918–19, the prime concern of big business by 1933–4 was to ensure the day-to-day functioning of capitalism and enterprise. Individual business and indeed agrarian leaders might doubt Hitler's abilities, but they perceived their options to have narrowed after the breakdown of the consensus between labour and industry during the slump. Big business expected, as in 1918, to secure greater influence over the making of economic policy in 1933. It seemed likely, too, with the setting up of the General Council of the Economy in July 1933. Big business was strongly represented on it. Yet, like the other key groups, private enterprise could only ensure its survival in the 1930s at a price and never exclusively on its own terms.

Enough has been said for the moment to see that the relationship between the political upheavals in Germany in 1918–19 and 1933–4 was far more complex than the direct causal link later asserted by Hitler, when he described his movement's successful bid for power in terms of overthrowing the men and ideas of 1918. Both events were, rather, in their different ways pivotal moments in the long process of adjustment and development of German politics and society; both can only be properly assessed by examining what developed from them, and the following pages attempt this task. First it is essential to see how the new Weimar Republic regulated its relations with the outside world, for the solution of foreign policy problems was critical to the viability of German democracy after 1918.

CHAPTER ONE

Policy for the sake of the Republic

The category of 'strangely neglected topics' revered by Kingsley Amis's young history don, Jim Dixon, would not embrace the Treaty of Versailles, the central plank of the peace settlement at the end of the First World War. Bitterness could be expected from the losers but even winners were highly critical of the treaty. John Maynard Keynes's gloomy 1920 diatribe, *The Economic Consequences of the Peace*, is simply one of the more successful titles on the subject jostling for space on library shelves. Leader of the Labour opposition in Britain, Ramsey MacDonald, said at roughly the same time that Europe was 'beholding an act of madness unparalleled in history'.[1] Much later, in 1934, a study made by Gathorne-Hardy for the Royal Institute of International Affairs reported that 'few apologists can now be found for the settlement'. This was partly because mistakes arose from hasty judgements reached in the troubled atmosphere following the Armistice, which militated against 'sober decisions or a durable peace'. Yet the writer also criticized the idealistic aspects of peacemaking, remarking of self-determination that 'the cardinal inherent vice of the doctrine lies in the fact that to apply it in practice inevitably involves its violation'.[2]

The peace treaties came to be seen as a central cause of the Second World War, an idea exemplified by E. H. Carr's description of the interwar period as the 'twenty years crisis'. Carr located unrest in the division created by the settlement between powers who were 'satisfied' – Great Britain, France, the United States – and those who were

---

1. Cited in F. L. Carsten, *Britain and the Weimar Republic. The British Documents* (London, 1984), pp. 27–8.

2. G. M. Gathorne-Hardy, *A Short History of International Affairs 1920 to 1934* (London, 1934), pp. 12, 16.

'dissatisfied'. The latter included Germany, Soviet Russia, Japan and Italy.[3] German resentment against the Versailles terms, as well as the manner in which they were presented, was certainly one factor aiding Hitler's rise to power. So, too, was the absence of a 'timely or far sighted attempt to revise the peace treaties and to continue the necessarily unfinished work of the Paris Peace Conference'.[4] On the other hand the post-war order manifested signs of better health in the mid-1920s, before its immune system was fatally undermined by the Great Depression. In this sense the Versailles peace itself can hardly be said to have 'caused' the Second World War.

THE CONDITIONS OF PEACE

Between the Reich's surrender to superior military force in the autumn of 1918 and the signature of the Treaty of Versailles in the following summer harsh lessons were learned in the new international realities. The first was the Allied refusal to allow the Weimar Republic to negotiate at the peace conference. The German Foreign Minister, Count Ulrich Brockdorff-Rantzau, regarded this as inconsistent with President Wilson's Fourteen Points, on which the Armistice had broadly been based. The throng of German officials and experts geared up to brief Germany's six-man peace delegation shared the frustration, prompting Brockdorff-Rantzau to violate protocol by receiving the draft peace terms on 7 May from a seated position. Among the provisions causing most offence was that charging Germany with responsibility for bringing the war about. The Allies' largely negative response to the German counterproposals of 29 May fell short of the sensitive, but whether there was a tactful way of reminding Germany of its defeat is open to doubt. After heated debates in the National Assembly the new SPD-Centrist coalition under Gustav Bauer announced that 'Surrendering to superior force but without retracting its opinion regarding the unheard of injustice of the peace conditions the government of the German Republic therefore declares its readiness to accept and sign the peace conditions imposed by the Allied and Associated Governments.'

Criticism of the territorial settlement at Versailles evoked rejoinders about the Reich's own harsh settlement with Russia under the terms

---

3. E. H. Carr, *Conditions of Peace* (London, 1942), p. xi.
4. G. Schulz, *Revolutions and Peace Treaties, 1917–1920* (London, 1972), p. 236.

of the Treaty of Brest-Litovsk in March 1918. Yet precisely that remembered image of their dominion made it harder for Germans to face the pruning of the Reich's territory after 1919, particularly where changes benefited Poland. A visible token of the shift in relative power was the creation of the Polish 'corridor' – linking Poland to the Baltic sea at Danzig. It absorbed West Prussia and Posen (Poznan) from Germany and isolated East Prussia. Marienwerder and Allenstein, two districts of West and East Prussia, were allowed to remain with Germany only after plebiscites in 1920. An inconclusive vote on Upper Silesia in 1921 resulted in a partition of the area between Germany and Poland. The German-speaking city of Danzig became a 'Free City' under League supervision. It fell within the Polish customs frontier, however, and its foreign relations were under Poland's direction. Germany had to relinquish control over Memel – which local Germans described as 'our river but not our border'. It, too, was under Allied supervision until its seizure by Lithuania in 1923.[5] The German Foreign Office viewed the cession of the Hultschin district to Czechoslovakia as less worrying. It sought to avoid anything 'which might be construed as partisanship in the conflict between Germans and Czechs in Bohemia', where economic prospects for the German minorities were more favourable than those confronting Germans left in Poland.[6]

In the west the settlement of the new German–Belgian and German–Danish borders was achieved with relative ease. The latter involved the division of Schleswig, the northern part joining Denmark whilst the southern area remained German. The districts of Eupen and Malmedy went to Belgium. The arrangements on the Franco-German border were more problematic. Inevitably, Alsace-Lorraine was returned to France whilst the Saar was placed under an international commission of the League of Nations, with provisions for a plebiscite after fifteen years. Meanwhile the valuable mines fell into France's waiting hands as part of the reparations for damage to French mining during the war. These provisions did not, however, satisfy the government in Paris. It wished to incorporate the Saar and indeed to exclude Germany from the Rhineland by restoring the borders of 1814. This idea was advanced on the eve of the Peace Conference by

5. On Danzig, C. M. Kimmich, *The Free City. Danzig and German Foreign Policy 1919–1934* (New Haven, London, 1968), pp. 1–22. On Memel, V. Zalys, *Ringen um Identität. Warum Litauen zwischen 1923 und 1939 im Memelgebiet keinen Erfolg hatte* (Lüneberg, 1993), p. 37.

6. J. W. Bruegel, *Czechoslovakia before Munich. The German Minorities and British Appeasement before Munich* (Cambridge, 1973), p. 37.

Marshal Foch and a few weeks later by the French cabinet, on the grounds that France could never be secure while Germany controlled the Rhineland militarily.[7] Ultimately, the resistance of the British and American governments ensured the continuation of German sovereignty on both banks of the Rhine, although conditions were attached. One was the Allied occupation of the strategically important bridgeheads of Mainz, Coblenz and Cologne, as well as all German territories west of the Rhine. The Allied troops were to complete their evacuation over a fifteen-year period, possibly earlier if Germany demonstrated its goodwill and offered satisfactory guarantees of fulfilling its treaty obligations. In addition, the whole of the west bank of the Rhine was demilitarized, as well as a fifty-kilometre-wide strip on the east bank of the river.

The strategic weakening of Germany was completed by deep cuts in its armed forces. After 1919 the Weimar Republic was left with a regular army of 100,000 men and a navy of 15,000. The ban on conscription prevented any significant expansion of Germany's military potential. Service in the new Reichswehr involved twelve years for the rank and file and twenty-five for officers, whilst no more than five per cent of effective forces could be replaced each year. The infamous and influential German General Staff, as well as the military academies and cadet schools were abolished. Mobilization measures or preparations for mobilization were forbidden. Severe restraints were placed on German war materials production. No offensive weapons, aeroplanes, tanks or submarines were permitted. With their powers of control and inspection under the Versailles Treaty the Allies had surely done what they could to bottle up Prussian militarism. Houdini himself might have refused the challenge. The rationale for leaving Germany virtually defenceless was, in the dry words of Part V of the peace treaty: 'In order to render possible the initiation of a general limitation of the armaments of all nations.' As if this were not enough, France was given, on 28 June 1919, treaties of guarantee by Britain and the United States, promising military support in the event of a German attack, although these lapsed in 1920. Having so to speak nailed down the coffin lid, the French sought to apply heavy weights too.

Germans felt that their territorial losses were harsh. As a result of the Treaty of Versailles more than 6 million Germans were left outside the new borders of the Weimar Republic. In the process 65,000

---

7. Memo cited in P. S. Wandycz, *France and her Eastern Allies 1919–1925. French–Czechoslovak–Polish Relations from the Paris Peace Conference to Locarno* (Minneapolis, 1962), pp. 37–8.

square kilometres of land were lost to the new Germany. The fact that union between Germany and Austria was expressly forbidden by the Treaty of Versailles was also regarded with great bitterness since popular opinion in both countries was then running in favour of *Anschluss*. The provision reinforced German arguments that the principle of self-determination was not applied fairly by the peace-makers. Territorial debits were completed with the loss of Germany's colonies. The Reich's African holdings were divided in the form of different classes of mandates, under the League of Nations, between Britain, South Africa, France and Belgium. A few small areas were annexed by France and Portugal. The Pacific territories were taken over by Australia, New Zealand, Britain and Japan.

To the reparations burden (considered in Chapter 5) must be added the depletion of Germany's economic base through the loss of territories and possessions. A calculation of lost resources would include 14.6 per cent of Germany's arable land, 74.5 per cent of its iron ore, 68.1 per cent of its zinc ore, 26 per cent of coal production, as well as the potash mines and textile industries of Alsace. German overseas investment was confiscated as was its property in enemy countries. Losses of shipping included all merchant ships in excess of 1,600 tons, half of the merchant fleet between 1,000 and 1,600 gross tons, a quarter of the fishing fleet and large quantities of rail locomotives and rolling stock. There were restrictions on German foreign trade through the imposition of a five-year ban on protective tariffs and the obligation of Germany to give the Allies most-favoured-nation treatment.[8]

A NOTE ON GERMAN 'REVISIONISM'

The debates in the National Assembly prior to 28 June made plain that Germans of every political hue would seek the revision of the peace terms, a process invariably regarded outside the Reich as harmful *in itself*. This arises partly from viewing Weimar foreign policy through the prism of the Third Reich. General accounts of the origins of 'Hitler's war' in 1939 are legion but there are only two 'standard' works on Weimar foreign policy. Both are in German, the first by Ludwig Zimmerman in 1958, the second, some thirty years later, by

---

8. A survey of the Versailles Treaty's text is in J. A. S. Grenville, *The Major International Treaties 1914–1973. A History and Guide with Texts* (London, 1974), pp. 59ff.

Peter Krüger.[9] In between these two volumes interest centred on the 'continuity' of foreign policy aims between Bismarck and Hitler, or more precisely a continuity of aggression. Passing swiftly along an air corridor between the 'nationalist' Bismarckian and Hitlerian empires, historians seemed disinclined to consider the detailed terrain of the Weimar Republic. The charitable point to make – particularly today – is that Germans enjoyed no monopoly of nationalism. It would have been odd had Germany's political leaders not joined those of the other powers in pursuing national interests during the 1920s, preferably with due regard for those of other powers. Moreover, the impact of the peace terms on Germany's foreign and domestic relations was extraordinarily pervasive, so that virtually any move by Weimar governments to recover the capacity to make policy – let alone the ambition to change borders or to reduce the financial burdens of peace – ran up against the treaty.

The Reich's approaches to policy making were already beginning to change before the peace settlement. The German Peace Society (*Deutsche Friedensgesellschaft*), founded by A. H. Fried and the formidable Bertha von Suttner in 1892, admittedly had an uphill struggle as an 'alien body' in imperial Germany.[10] In spite of this its critique of unrestrained power politics was strengthened by the inexorable move towards democratization in the Reichstag. With their celebrated July 1917 'peace resolution' the SPD, the Centre and the Left Liberals staked a claim to a new and more durable European order being achieved in co-operation with Germany's wartime enemies. This very early manifestation of European understanding (*Verständigung*) could not be ignored indefinitely.[11] Even within the hallowed walls of the German Foreign Office (*Auswärtiges Amt* – AA) there lurked officials urging change, who shared the anxiety of the commercial world to see foreign policy become more responsive to Germany's trading needs. Progress was made through the reforms completed in 1920, named after their architect in the AA, Edmund Schuler. As well as merging the consular and diplomatic services, Schuler reorganized the AA into departments which were broadly responsible for regions. Alongside this reformism there was inevitably some continuity of

9. L. Zimmermann, *Deutsche Aussenpolitik in der Ära der Weimarer Republik* (Göttingen–Berlin–Frankfurt, 1958); P. Krüger, *Die Aussenpolitik der Republik von Weimar* (Darmstadt, 1985).

10. D. Riesenberger, *Geschichte der Friedensbewegung in Deutschland. Von den Anfängen bis 1933* (Göttingen, 1985), p. 97.

11. W. Ribhegge, *Frieden für Europa. Die Politik der deutschen Reichstagsmehrheit 1917–1918* (Essen, 1988), pp. 182–92.

personnel and attitudes, but in titling his memoirs *Wanderer Between Two Worlds*, the Republic's very first foreign minister, Wilhelm Solf, testified to the altered realities. The AA – though designated by the constitution as the sole agency for foreign affairs – was now at last under a minister responsible to the Reichstag. In the post-Versailles order the Ministries of Finance and Economics also played a major role in formulating and implementing policy, as did the legal department of the AA under the formidable Friedrich Gaus.

Additional pressures for a 'new' German foreign policy were beginning to come from some of the Reich's business leaders, aware of the profits to be gained from free economic exchange and the peaceful arbitration of disputes.[12] It is therefore fair to say that there was an emergent 'constituency' behind Weimar foreign policy. This included not only the political forces sustaining the 'Weimar coalition', but also trade unionists and industrialists, in so far as they desired a Europe-wide recovery. In this respect it is not quite accurate to describe the period between 1919 and 1923 as one of 'missing conceptions', although party political pressures made it difficult at first to formulate a coherent overall strategy.[13] Adolf Köster, distinguished man of letters and successor to Brockdorff-Rantzau, had ideas enough but little time to implement sustained policy before Hermann Müller's cabinet fell in June 1920. Moreover, in the immediate post-war months key aspects of the peace settlement were still unresolved, notably reparations and the referendums on Germany's borders, so that the AA was aiming at a moving target, and the authority and dominance of Gustav Stresemann had yet to make itself felt. Nonetheless, the angry cries from German nationalists after the war testify to the fact that a policy identified with the Weimar Republic *was* beginning to emerge from the outset. It was one where force had little role to play.

Even Brockdorff-Rantzau accepted this, having failed to split the Allies from the United States by his mantra-like insistence on the application of President Wilson's Fourteen Points.[14] Rantzau's doubts were shared by General Wilhelm Groener, who temporarily took over the direction of the German Army High Command (*Oberste Heeresleitung* – OHL). Some of his brother officers wished to defy the Peace Conference by holding out in the east and their fantasy was briefly nourished when the Armistice insisted that German troops had

12. Krüger, *Aussenpolitik*, pp. 17–23.
13. Ibid., p. 210.
14. In general see U. Wengst, *Graf Brockdorff-Rantzau und die aussenpolitischen Anfänge der Weimarer Republik* (Frankfurt am Main, 1973).

to provide an interim defence of the Baltic front against the Red Army. Germany's ensuing and abortive 'Baltic adventure' served instead to increase Allied anxieties. Groener had long since argued that further resistance endangered the unity of the Reich, which he was 'prepared to make *any* sacrifice' to avoid. He maintained that even if Germany could quite easily gain initial victories in the east, action would 'ultimately be doomed to failure' because of overwhelming Allied military superiority in the west.[15] The enforced evacuation of the Baltic states by the German freikorps in December 1919 confirmed Germany's military impotence. That remained absolutely fundamental to the conduct of Weimar foreign policy for the next fourteen years.

THE ILLUSION OF EAST–WEST CHOICES 1921–23

The Republic's military weakness persuaded many Germans to hope for Russian help in undermining the Versailles system, since Russia had not been party to the peace settlement and had grievances against Poland. As it happened, Polish military action in 1920 eventually forced the Bolsheviks to accept the loss of territory on their western border, under the terms of the Treaty of Riga (March 1921), while Lenin's 'New Economic Policy' (NEP) aimed above all to preserve the revolution at home. Under these conditions of 'peaceful co-existence' Reichswehr Chief, General Hans von Seeckt, favoured illicit collaboration with Russia in order to circumvent the Versailles restrictions and to restore the capacity of German forces. Reichswehr officers developed intermittent contacts with the Soviets in 1919–20 to prepare for military-industrial production and from early 1921 a special section in the Reichswehr ministry, *Sondergruppe R*, was devoted to Russian affairs. Seeckt continued to insist that mutual German and Russian antagonism to Poland gave the two large powers a vital bond and that 'with Poland falls one of the strongest pillars of Versailles, the preponderance of France'.[16]

Seeckt's capacity to control his ideological aversion to communism in the interests of *Realpolitik* was common enough in circles hostile to the Republic. It was not unknown in German industry either. 'The

---

15. Citations from F. L. Carsten, *Reichswehr und Politik, 1918–1933* (Cologne, Berlin, 1964), pp. 46, 48.
16. Memorandum of 11 September 1922, cited ibid., pp. 140–1.

Germans are divided financially into two camps,' a British Foreign Office memorandum observed. The 'businessmen on the Rhine whose factories are working (thanks to the occupation) are largely looking westwards. The rest of Germany is looking East.'[17] Key officials in the Eastern Department of the AA, notably Baron Ago von Maltzan, desired from the outset to develop good working relations with Soviet Russia. So, too, did Chancellor Joseph Wirth, whose administrations spanned the period May 1921 to November 1922. Both men were also perfectly well aware of the advantages of keeping Poland under pressure in this way. However, in considering so-called 'Easterners' in the Weimar Republic it is important to differentiate sharply between those who favoured giving absolute priority to links with Russia after 1919, and those who were anxious to minimize Allied displeasure.

Inevitably, Germany tried to capitalize on the West's fear of bolshevism during 1918–19 to secure better peace terms – exemplified in Brockdorff-Rantzau's argument that the front against the Red Army should be erected on the Weichsel and Memel, rather than on the Rhine.[18] Karl Radek commented bitterly that: 'The corpse of the Soviet republic was meant to be the dowry toward a *mariage de convenance* between Germany and the Entente.'[19] Although Rantzau's strategy failed, the need to observe Allied sensitivities remained paramount. Inter-governmental contacts between Germany and the Soviets in 1920 were largely confined to agencies responsible in each country for repatriating prisoners of war. In spite of huge pressure from German industry it was not until two months after the signature of the British–Soviet trade agreement, on 16 March 1921, that Germany concluded its own trade treaty with Russia (6 May). Contacts with the Soviets were still broadly restricted to the economic field, particularly under Friedrich Rosen, Foreign Minister in Wirth's first cabinet (10 May to 26 October 1921). Keeping Russia on 'hold' in this way preserved Germany's treaty obligation to respect future Allied arrangements while reserving its right to be part of any economic penetration of the new Russia.

The latter consideration was essential to securing Wirth's domestic power base.[20] No German leader could afford to stand aside from the fierce European competition to gain access to the Eldorado that the

---

17. *Documents on British Foreign Policy (DBFP)*, Series 1, vol III, p. 227.

18. H. Helbig, *Die Träger der Rapallo-Politik* (Göttingen, 1958), p. 21.

19. Cited in G. Hilger and A. G. Mayer, *The Incompatible Allies* (New York, 1971), p. 19.

20. E. Laubach, *Die Politik der Kabinette Wirth* (Lübeck–Hamburg, 1968), pp. 110–11.

Russian market was thought (mistakenly) to be. Nevertheless, Wirth had to focus his attention sharply on the West, following the London Ultimatum of 5 May 1921. Apart from presenting the reparations bill, the ultimatum set out to end German prevarication over disarmament and the trials of war criminals. In responding with the policy of 'fulfilment' Wirth made virtue out of necessity, hoping to demonstrate through co-operation that the actual peace terms were in reality unfulfillable. Under these conditions he could hardly – as nationalists urged – play the 'Russian card' against the Allies. Rather, Germany was bound to try to reconcile its *Ostpolitik* with its policy towards the West. An echo of Brockdorff-Rantzau's strategy can be detected in Wirth's warning to the British representative Lord D'Abernon in 1921 that alongside a 'democratic Germany, which sincerely desired peace and work and reconciliation' there existed a Germany of reactionaries and communists, who preferred catastrophe to commerce.[21]

The German Chancellor's reference to communism in Germany fell on fertile ground in Britain, where concern about a German collapse undermining the peace settlement was reinforced by the economic recession of 1921. Before 1914 Germany had been Britain's chief European market, which goes far to account for the view aired in the Foreign Office that the creation of a stable German government remained 'the essential and central requirement of British policy, the first condition to which our national recovery is subject'.[22] How could this aim be squared with Anglo-German rivalry in the Europe-wide race to enter Soviet markets between 1919 and 1922? Lloyd George's preferred solution was to include the Weimar Republic in his proposed European consortium to open up Russia. Britain enjoyed supervisory and even interventionist rights as a Versailles power over German fiscal and trade policy. What better position from which to collaborate with an economic rival? Had British policy succeeded, the United Kingdom would have advanced its pretensions to lead economic relations with the Soviets. In addition, both Germany and Russia could have been implicated in the process of managed change to the post-war order. At the same time it shows that British good will towards Germany did not extend to giving it complete freedom of movement in eastern Europe, notwithstanding Britain's refusal to commit itself to military alliances there.

Britain's oddly persistent involvement with the region is still insufficiently emphasized. Even during the war there developed within

---

21. F. L. Carsten, *Britain and the Weimar Republic*, pp. 74–5.
22. Cited ibid., pp. 81–2.

the British Foreign Office an emotional commitment to the idea of a balance of power when peace came, where the new 'small' states of eastern Europe would have a distinctive role to play. One of the British delegates at Paris, Harold Nicolson, associated like other influential figures with the journal *The New Europe*, testified:

> Bias there was, and prejudice. But they proceeded, not from any revengeful desire to subjugate and penalize our late enemies, but from a fervent aspiration to create and fortify the new nations whom we regarded, with maternal instinct, as the justification of our sufferings and of our victory. The Paris Conference will never be properly understood unless this emotional impulse is emphasised at every stage.[23]

The British role in the settlement of eastern Europe had been highly influential. Britain's mediation in the dispute between Poland and Lithuania over Vilnius, its proposals for Poland's frontier in the east during the Polish–Soviet war, its paternalistic and protective stance on the new Baltic republics, its arbitration of frontier disputes in north-eastern Europe, its active interest in the plebiscites on the disputed Polish–German border – all combine against the popular notion that eastern Europe was a far away place about which London knew nothing. Revealingly, a secret memorandum drawn up within the Foreign Office as late as April 1926 placed the Covenant of the League of Nations and the Treaty of Versailles as first and second on a list of Britain's commitments in 'relative order of importance'.[24]

If there was little prospect of British indifference to the settlement in the East, there was even less chance of this in the case of the French. They developed closer relations with the new states to compensate for the loss of their pre-war ally, Tsarist Russia. The Czech army was built up with the aid of French officers and materials in 1919–20, while limited military co-operation developed between Paris and Warsaw, following the political and military agreements of February 1921 and the trade and finance agreement of 14 January 1922. Ties were also strengthened between France, Romania and Yugoslavia. Hopes were entertained of further links between a Polish-led Baltic bloc and the so-called 'Little Entente' of Czechoslovakia, Yugoslavia and Romania. Whether or not the arrangements attained the sort of cohesion justifying their description

23. H. Nicolson, *Peacemaking 1919* (London, 1964), p. 33.
24. W. N. Medlicott, *British Foreign Policy since Versailles, 1919–1963* (London, 1968), p. xvi. See in general, E. Goldstein, *Winning the Peace. British Diplomatic Strategy, Peace Planning and the Paris Peace Conference 1916–1920* (Oxford, 1991).

as a 'system' must be disputed.[25] What was not in doubt was France's desire that the 'barrier' in the East should be directed primarily against Germany as an aid to maintaining the Versailles order. It was a natural complement to France's policy on Germany's western border, where Marshall Foch greatly valued the Allied military control of the Rhineland. Indeed, the French viewed their presence in the Mainz sector less in terms of defence than as an opportunity to control a strategically important access point for an offensive against a recalcitrant Germany.[26]

In sum, in the matter of East–West relations Germany's options were highly circumscribed, although France's alliance policy strengthened Seeckt's argument for advancing German–Soviet military talks. The latter were linked with the first German–Russian joint undertakings in heavy industry in the autumn of 1921. There was also mounting anxiety in Germany about losing business in the East. Russia was exerting pressure for the normalization of relations but preferred bilateral treaties to an international consortium. A draft German–Soviet agreement was soon thrashed out in secret after Wirth's new administration (October 1921) injected new purpose into the hitherto hesitant German–Soviet exchanges. Yet – disappointed as he was with the partitioning of Silesia – Wirth still could not afford to ignore the West, where we have seen that he pleaded on economic grounds for a moratorium on reparations payments in December. He also tried, not unreasonably, to have reparations included in the discussion of European reconstruction scheduled for the forthcoming world economic conference at Genoa. Walther Rathenau, who took over as Foreign Minister early in 1922, continued to advance German policy interests on both fronts. His directorship of the giant electricity concern, the AEG, gave him an enduring economic interest in rapprochement with Russia; on the other hand his support of fulfilment made him resist premature agreements with Moscow. Only in the turmoil of events at the Genoa conference was he persuaded to sign the prepared text of the German–Soviet agreement at the nearby resort of Rapallo.[27]

25. P. Jardin, 'Locarno und Frankreich's Nachkriegskonzeption, in R. Schattkowsky (ed.), *Locarno und Osteuropa. Fragen eines europäischen Sicherheitssystem in den 20er Jahren* (Marburg, 1994), pp. 53–65.

26. J. Bariety, 'Die französisch-polnische 'Allianz' und Locarno,' in ibid., pp. 75–91.

27. For detail, E. Laubach, 'Maltzans Aufzeichnungen über die letzten Vorgänge vor dem Abschluss des Rapallo-Vertrages', *Jahrbücher für Geschichte Osteuropas*, 22 (1975): 572–3. See generally, D. Felix, *Walther Rathenau and the Weimar Republic. The Politics of Reparations* (Baltimore, 1971); D. G. Williamson, 'Walther Rathenau. Patron Saint of the German liberal establishment' in *Leo Baeck Institute Year Book* (London, 1975), pp. 207–22.

One factor among many leading to this final step was French premier Raymond Poincaré's refusal to consider reparations at Genoa. His action fuelled mischievous rumours in Berlin, before and during the conference, of Russia preparing to add its own claims for reparations against Germany, under the terms of Article 116 of the Versailles treaty. Instead, the Reich secured with the Rapallo agreement the principle of mutual German–Soviet denunciation of war debts, which promised to be a useful precedent in Germany's wider reparations strategy. In any case it was clear that the conference was manifestly not going to fulfil Lloyd George's vision of a 'European understanding with a view to the reconstruction of that battered and shattered old continent'.[28] It became all the more expedient for the German government to secure what fitful advances it had made with the Russians during 1921. When Rapallo restored normal diplomatic relations between Berlin and Moscow and stipulated the principle of most-favoured-nation treatment in economic relations, Germany placed itself at the front of the European trade drive eastwards. Lloyd George, who had been hoping to do the same for Britain, was not unnaturally upset. The French, who saw in the treaty evidence of a renewed German threat to the East European states, were incandescent. Their resentment was an important factor preventing Wirth from having reparations reconsidered and contributed to his resignation on 14 November 1922.

In judging Wirth it is important to remember that, like his contemporary leaders, he was facing an unprecedented challenge in coming to terms with the new order in Russia. His difficulty in reconciling *Ostpolitik* and *Westpolitik* was very much a reflection of the times but the case for the restoration of bilateral German–Soviet relations in 1922 remains a strong one. Both the limits and the potential of the Rapallo 'partnership' were seen in 1923, when Allied–German relations deteriorated to the point where France invaded the Ruhr. Rapallo helped to dissuade Polish and other East European governments from complementing France's action in the West. More decisive for their caution, however, was their belief that the expansion of German–Soviet trade offered them the best hope of prosperity following the collapse of the Genoa conference. It was the growing *economic* weight of Germany in the Baltic and other eastern countries by 1922–3 which promised to undermine France's alliance policy in the long run, rather than any military 'threat' against eastern Europe

28. Minutes of the First (Political) Commission, Volume II of the Genoa Conference Proceedings, 16 May 1922, PRO FO 371/C 6977/458/62.

arising from the Rapallo treaty. Neither Germany nor the USSR could produce such a threat in the 1920s, even if they had wanted to. What was less obvious at the time, but which became abundantly clear after the negotiation of the Dawes plan in 1924, was that Germany's economic attraction for eastern Europe would be maximized not simply through Weimar–Soviet commerce, but rather through Germany's re-integration with the West.

STRESEMANN AND THE PRIMACY OF *WESTPOLITIK*

The crowded years between 1923 and 1929 are invariably termed the 'Stresemann era' by historians of Germany. Like most if not all major personalities, however, Stresemann's successes and indeed his failures were also a reflection of his time. The shocking events of 1923 were by common agreement a formative experience for him. His defence of the Reich under pressure during his brief chancellorship completed the transformation he underwent from ardent annexationist in 1914 to 'republican by conviction' (*Vernünftrepublikaner*). The pursuit of Germany's interests naturally remained his prime goal. The plain fact was that, first as Chancellor and then as Foreign Minister, he could only make progress by working with the Allied powers to restore Germany's international position. The policy had been sketched by Wirth and others; key socio-economic and political groups in Germany were prepared to sustain it. What Stresemann brought to the task was an exceptional clarity of thought and overall purpose, impressive negotiating skills and the remarkable application which would ruin his health and eventually claim his life. Last but by no means least, Stresemann was able to broaden the domestic base for *Verständigung* through his commanding leadership of the German People's Party (*Deutsche Volkspartei* – DVP). Since the overall composition of Weimar governments from 1923 was broadly conservative, his influence was all the more pervasive.

Stresemann was the first Foreign Minister in the Weimar Republic who enjoyed enough party political clout to shield the conduct of foreign policy from the worst excesses in the Reichstag. His peaceful and statesmanlike *methods* have long been acknowledged but by no means all historians have been dissuaded from arguing that his 'peaceful' revisionism prepared the ground for Hitler's diplomacy. Was not the 'nationalistic' pursuit of restoring full German power in

Europe common to both?[29] It is worth reiterating the point already made, that the urge to promote national interests was shared by all European leaders. The question of what policy methods were employed is therefore neither instrumental nor secondary, but of fundamental importance. Methods, in affecting the conduct of Weimar foreign policy, influenced its nature and ultimately its ends. In personal terms, could Stresemann not be a good German as well as a perfectly good European?

The centrepiece of Stresemann's foreign policy was the series of agreements signed by Germany, Britain, France, Italy, Poland and Czechoslovakia at Locarno in October 1925. They followed soundings in Britain and a formal German memorandum to the French government on 9 February of that year. In guaranteeing Germany's western borders Stresemann aimed to reduce French insecurity, thereby shortening the Rhineland occupation and advancing the recovery of full sovereignty for the Reich. The auspices were quite favourable, in so far as the brief juxtaposition of socialist governments in both France and Britain during 1924 had itself encouraged fresh initiatives in international relations. The events of 1923–4, by increasing Britain's influence, also forced the French to accept comparatively modest reparations payments and thereby improved immediate prospects for a greater degree of integration in Europe.[30] Bruised, financially damaged through their Ruhr action and with little tangible gain from their eastern alliance policy, France's leaders were more inclined from 1924 to make the transition from 'execution' to 'negotiation',[31] although they remained troubled about the danger of indirect aggression in the East. The French would dearly have loved a British guarantee 'against a Polish Sadowa, which, for Germany, would be the best preparation for another Sedan'.[32] In this they were virtually certain to be disappointed. Britain, once more under a conservative government, was about to reject the Geneva Protocol of 1924, precisely because of its open-ended commitment to applying sanctions against states resorting to war.

In considering the Geneva Protocol early in 1925, the British cabinet asked itself how it might defend its vital interests in the West while safeguarding itself 'against being drawn into a quarrel over Lithuania or Bessarabia.'[33] Out of sympathy for France, Britain did

29. Cf. K. Hildebrand, *The Foreign Policy of the Third Reich* (London, 1973), p. 9.

30. Cf. the stimulating arguments of J. Jacobson, 'Is there a new international history', *Journal of Modern History* 55 (1983): 78–95.

31. Krüger, *Aussenpolitik*, p. 240.

32. Cited Medlicott, *British Foreign Policy*, p. 12.

33. Sybil Eyre Crowe, 'Sir Eyre Crowe and the Locarno Pact', *English Historical Review*, 87 (1972): 149–74.

agree to postponing the evacuation of the Cologne zone in December 1924, pending satisfactory reports on the progress of German disarmament. British Foreign Minister Austen Chamberlain also worried that if the French continued to feel insecure they might try to maintain an indefinite military occupation of the Rhineland. Stresemann's offer of a new pact guaranteeing Germany's borders with France and Belgium thus came at a particularly favourable moment for the troubled British leadership. Far from seeking to prevent any renewed Anglo-French entente, Stresemann's initiative recognized that Germany's best interests were served by continuing co-operation between London and Paris. His thinking was encouraged by the influential British ambassador in Berlin, Lord D'Abernon, whose views counted with Lord Curzon and who enjoyed good contacts within the AA. D'Abernon warmly supported the concept of a reciprocal guarantee to supplant the unsuccessful French policy of subordinating Germany.[34] Moreover since the conservative imperialists Churchill, Amery, Curzon, Balfour and Birkenhead were opposed to continental commitments as restrictive to Britain's role as a mediator, the proposed Rhineland pact was virtually the only form in which the British cabinet would accept a British guarantee of French security.[35] Britain's readiness to join a security pact covering the Rhine area was crucial in removing French objections.

Significantly, the Treaty of Mutual Guarantee (or Rhineland Pact) signed at Locarno gave Britain military obligations in western Europe more precise than any it had had in 1914, even though British strategists did not plan accordingly and British options in Europe were heavily circumscribed in practice by imperial commitments.[36] It was therefore fortunate for Britain that, at Locarno and after, the emphasis in Europe shifted decisively towards finding common solutions. Admittedly, Stresemann and his French counterpart, Aristide Briand, still found these difficult to reach, as witness their abortive meeting at Thoiry in December 1926. On the other hand, Stresemann's skilful diplomacy finally secured the withdrawal of the IMCC (Inter-Allied Military Control Commission) in January 1927, eventually won Allied agreement to an early end to the Rhineland occupation (30 June 1930) and convinced the Western powers of the need to re-examine

---

34. In general, A. Kaiser, *Lord D'Abernon und die englische Deutschlandpolitik 1920–6* (Frankfurt, 1989).

35. J. Jacobson, *Locarno Diplomacy: Germany and the West 1925–1929* (Princeton, 1972), pp. 16–21.

36. M. Howard, *The Continental Commitment. The Dilemma of British Defence Policy Between Two Wars*, Penguin edn (London, 1974), p. 94.

reparations fundamentally (Young Plan – passed by the Reichstag in 1930). Both landmarks came after Stresemann's death, but he could justly remark some eighteen hours before that sad event: 'We are again masters in our house.'

In contrast to the guarantees in the west, Stresemann would accept only treaties of arbitration with Poland and Czechoslovakia – duly signed at Locarno. These left open the possibility of future peaceful frontier changes and did not expressly rule out the use of force. Neither were the arbitration treaties associated with the Treaty of Mutual Guarantee. The French alliances with Poland and Czechoslovakia – revised at the time of the Locarno agreements – appeared to be weakened. Under the new, post-Locarno conditions, Poland and Czechoslovakia had to appeal first to the League of Nations in the event of being attacked. However, even Marshall Foch had contemplated subordinating the French eastern alliances to the League of Nations as early as 1924. Briand's own recognition of the shortcomings of France's eastern alliance system had in any case been a critical factor in his personal acceptance of the Locarno treaties.[37]

The latter preserved the Anglo-French entente, the 'cardinal objective' of British policy.[38] Britain could scarcely be concerned about both Germany and France and at one and the same time be unconcerned by developments in eastern Europe. As before, British policy continued to foster social, political and economic stability (rather than actively supporting regional alliances), both in Poland and the Baltic states, as well as in south-eastern Europe. What is more, Germany was gradually implicated in this process, as Berlin's mediation in the Italian–Yugoslav conflict in 1927 amply demonstrated. Even in the case of the Polish–Lithuanian dispute, which British diplomacy was repeatedly at pains to settle during the 1920s, the German government felt obliged to help reduce sources of conflict, provided the outcome was not Polish hegemony over Lithuania.[39] This is fragmentary but important evidence that the Locarno process at the very least encouraged the forging of new relations between the different power groupings. The pursuit of European understanding could not be neatly contained once Germany had been locked into its dialogue with the West on equal terms and in that sense '*Westpolitik*', as practised by Stresemann, was the essence of *Weimar* foreign policy.

37. P. Jardin, 'Locarno und Frankreich's Nachkriegskonzeption' in R. Schattkowsky (ed.), *Locarno und Osteuropa*, pp. 53–65.
38. J. Jacobson, *Locarno Diplomacy*, p. 35. See also, A. Kaiser, *Lord D'Abernon*, p. xx.
39. Cf. Krüger, *Aussenpolitik*, pp. 320–1; more generally, H. Olbrich, 'Britische Sicherheitspolitik und Sicherheitsinteressen in Ost- und Südosteuropa während der Locarno-Ära' in R. Schattkowsky (ed.), *Locarno und Osteuropa*, p. 105–6.

STRESEMANN AND RUSSIA

Inside the Eastern Department of the *Auswärtiges Amt* less time was devoted to the USSR after Locarno and more to German minorities and border issues.[40] The Locarno treaties, according to the memoir of Gustav Hilger, convinced the Russians that they had lost their game.[41] Stresemann and his State Secretary, von Schubert, were also personally antipathetic to Russia. The latter once confessed: 'I heartily distrust the gang in Moscow.'[42] However, both recognized the absolute necessity for continuing relations with the USSR. Stresemann certainly took pains to assure the Russians during 1925 that his initiative was emphatically not directed against Soviet interests. In April 1926 he re-affirmed the Rapallo relationship through the Treaty of Berlin. On joining the League of Nations in 1926, Germany secured exemption in the case of Russia from the obligations of League members to impose sanctions against aggressors. A note exchange accompanying the Berlin treaty gave further assurances of German neutrality. However, the German Foreign Office regarded the new German–Soviet agreements as 'only conceivable on the basis created by Locarno and (Germany's) entry to the League'.[43] Whether the Locarno arrangements brought about Germany's re-integration into the West without threatening Soviet security probably depends on the point of view.[44] In any case, most of the powers had by then recognized the USSR, further diluting the 'special relationship' between Berlin and Moscow. The year 1927 found Germany mediating in the crises afflicting both British–Soviet and Sino–Soviet relations. From 1927 the Soviet Commissar for Foreign Affairs, Chicherin – a key architect of Rapallo, along with fellow insomniac Count Brockdorff-Rantzau, German ambassador to Russia – was overshadowed by the Soviet League of Nations expert, Maxim Litvinov. The latter eventually took over foreign affairs in 1930.

In neither the military nor the economic field did the German–Russian relationship ever reach the heights expected in 1922.

40. H. von Dirksen, *Moskau, Tokyo, London. Erinnerungen und Betrachtungen zu 20 Jahren deutscher Aussenpolitik 1919–1939* (Stuttgart, 1949), p. 76.

41. Hilger and Meyer, *Incompatible Allies*, p. 146.

42. Cited in Krüger, *Aussenpolitik*, p. 268.

43. *Akten zur deutschen Auswärtigen Politik 1918–1945*, Series B, 1925–1933, Vol. 1 (Göttingen, 1966–), p. 162. Hereafter *ADAP*.

44. F. A. Krummacher and H. Lange, *Krieg und Frieden. Geschichte der deutsch–soujetische Beziehungen von Brest–Litovsk bis zum Unternehmen Barbarossa* (Munich, 1970), p. 176.

Secret Weimar–Soviet military collaboration – no secret any more after the SPD revelations in 1926 – ultimately provided for little more than joint training and experimentation in aircraft, tanks and the use of gas.[45] The mixed German–Soviet companies founded after 1921 had a patchy record in exploiting Russian concessions, thanks to Soviet obstructiveness towards foreign economic activity, combined with capital shortages in Germany. Eventually a credit fund of some 100 million marks was raised by German banks and in 1925, following guarantees from the Reich government and the *Länder*, there was additional credit of 300 million marks for purchases from Germany. These arrangements also helped to sweeten the pill of Stresemann's political initiative in the West. In 1928 a German counterpart to the Soviet trade monopoly appeared, in the guise of the 'Russian Committee of German Business'. At the same time a German section was formed in the Soviet Chamber of Commerce in Moscow to breathe life into trade between the powers. Ironically, these measures bore fruit after the death of Stresemann and the onset of the Great Depression. For most of the 1920s, however, 'German business had tended to regard trade with Soviet Russia as a risky undertaking made difficult by petty formalism, tiresome bargaining, and an annoying fear of responsibility on the part of the Soviet negotiators. Hence, as German exports rose to the value of 14 billion reich marks annually, no more than three per cent of the total exports went to the Soviet Union.'[46]

For all practical purposes the 'Rapallo relationship' was still less likely after Locarno than before to produce co-ordinated German–Russian initiatives against Poland. Naturally, in order to sell the Locarno package to his domestic critics Stresemann placed considerable public emphasis on frontier revision, on the expansion of German economic influence in the East European realm and on the need to support German minorities in Poland and elsewhere. Fitful exchanges with Moscow helped to counter Poland's diplomacy and to prevent an 'Eastern Locarno', as well as to preserve German interests. Thus the AA was able to insist on any reference to Memel being omitted from the text of the non-aggression treaty between the USSR and Lithuania in 1926. For its part the Bolshevik regime hoped to hinder any growth of British influence in the Baltic states to prevent them becoming an 'outpost of imperialism'.[47] Talk of 'pushing Poland back' never

45. F. L. Carsten, *Reichswehr*, pp. 401ff.
46. Hilger and Meyer, *Incompatible Allies*, p. 236.
47. G. Rosenfeld, *Sowjetunion und Deutschland 1922–1933* (Cologne, 1984), pp. 44ff.

entirely disappeared from the dialogue between Berlin and Moscow but a significant point was reached in 1925, when the *Auswärtiges Amt* considered the prospects of a joint German–Soviet guarantee of the Baltic states to frustrate Polish plans once and for all. Ultimately, the scheme was rejected in Berlin because it threatened to make Germany dependent on the USSR.[48] The failure of Germany and Russia to make common cause in north-eastern Europe thus removed 'the only possibility of any active joint anti-Polish policy as a binding force' between the two big powers.[49]

Independently of Moscow, and with a need to focus efforts on securing Western support, the AA began to concentrate instead on defining more concretely Germany's historic, cultural and linguistic objectives in relation to Poland. A memorandum of 16 November 1925 formally set out the Weimar Republic's claims to the Corridor, Danzig, East Upper Silesia and some parts of Lower Silesia. There was a readiness to abandon Posen, under certain conditions, whilst Poland was to have a free port at Danzig and rights analogous to those accorded Germany in the corridor; that is to say, guaranteed rail and river traffic rights and tariff exemptions, as well as adequate provisions for transit across German territory to the Baltic.[50] By exploiting Germany's growing influence with the West Stresemann was able to prevent Poland from taking a permanent seat in the League of Nations when Germany joined in 1926. The Reich's diplomatic containment of Poland was to be accompanied by the use of German economic weight to make the Poles more amenable to the idea of frontier revision but that strategy was an inherently long-term one. It was just as well, for in 1926 Marshall Pilsudski's seizure of power ultimately led to a strengthening of Poland.

TRADE AND *OSTPOLITIK*

Stresemann thus shifted the emphasis decisively towards winning British and French support for frontier changes, explaining to those prepared to listen that his Polish policy grew from his Western

---

48. Cf. J. Hiden, *The Baltic States and Weimar Ostpolitik* (Cambridge, 1987), pp. 171ff.
49. Krüger, *Aussenpolitik*, p. 282.
50. Cited C. M. Kimmich, 'The Weimar Republic and the German-Polish borders' in T. V. Gromada (ed.), *Essays on Poland's Foreign Policy 1918–1939* (New York, 1970), p. 39.

policy.[51] The strategy had major implications for the role of trade in Weimar foreign policy. An earlier German foreign minister, Friedrich Rosen, had argued that for post-Versailles Germany 'economics alone were decisive and foreign policy as such pointless.'[52] Stresemann's emphasis was somewhat different. In his view Germany had only two sources of power 'now that we no longer have our army . . . One is our united national sentiment. The second is the German economy.'[53] The clear implication of the foreign minister's remarks was that Germany's trade policy *was* 'foreign policy' in these conditions.

Although the Versailles terms placed restrictions on Germany's full freedom to trade until 1925, its cheaper goods, its long-standing network of trade contacts in the East, its demand for raw materials and its quest for markets for its industrial products equipped it well to penetrate the eastern European states after 1918. The latter were in desperate need of foreign capital and expertise to diversify their predominantly agrarian economies and to underpin their independence through industrialization. Although the power of economic facts promised to counter anti-German fears in eastern Europe it by no means removed them altogether. By negotiating trade treaties on a most-favoured-nation basis, German governments therefore also tried to settle outstanding differences arising from the war, including reparations claims, the fate of German property and the position of German minorities left outside the Reich. Trade agreements were expected to help offset the bitter memory of German occupation and to prepare the ground for German economic activity, only now on the basis of sincere, active and friendly collaboration between Germany and the individual states.

In the Baltic, Poland was bound to be a major factor, given the indifference of Scandinavia towards any involvement in the region's security, as well as the loss of much of Germany's Baltic coastline following the peace settlement.[54] Thus in pursuing friendship through trade in the East the AA hoped to reduce the potential client states of Poland, thereby discouraging alliance systems directed against Germany. The dominating German economic position in the Baltic states helped to undermine Polish aspirations to lead a Baltic bloc, as

51. Cf. H. von Riekhoff, *German–Polish Relations 1918–1933* (Baltimore–London, 1971), p. 131.
52. H. Müller-Werth, *Friedrich Rosen. Aus einem diplomatischen Wanderleben* (Wiesbaden, 1959), p. 288.
53. G. Stresemann, *Vermächtnis*, vol. 1 (Berlin, 1932), p. 64.
54. Cf. the interesting overview by O. Hoetsch, 'The Baltic states, Germany and Russia', *Foreign Affairs* 10 (1931): 120–33.

did the German–Polish customs war of 1925. There were other political factors at work here, not least the Polish–Lithuanian dispute over Vilnius from October 1920, but the bloc made little sense economically, since its members had very similar structures and products. Equally, in south-eastern Europe, Germany profited from the fact that Czechoslovakian and Austrian industries needed German aid. The states also had greater spending power following more intensive agricultural development and the exploitation of still unused natural resources. Although both Poland and Czechoslovakia had been conceived as the corner stones of two blocs making up the 'barrier' which France tried to build after 1919, German economic policy helped to create a climate where by 1924 President Beneš justified his call for Franco-German *rapprochement* 'in order to reconcile our [Czechoslovakia's] political and economic interests'.[55]

Beneš's words indicate that Weimar trade policy generated in the East European states a potential conflict between their political loyalty to the Allied powers and their need for economic ties with Germany. Locarno promised to resolve the clash by bringing Germany into closer conjunction with the Allies. In the second part of the 1920s the Weimar Republic settled a wide range of outstanding issues with the East European states and concluded a series of influential most-favoured-nation trade treaties. Before the great depression in 1929 Weimar trade policy appeared, moreover, to be drawing the countries of East Europe into the West European system. The Baltic region again offers an interesting example. Britain, the chief purchaser of Baltic exports, largely agricultural, effectively provided much of the foreign currency used by Estonia, Latvia and Lithuania to buy from Germany, who dominated Baltic imports.[56] The trend was accelerated by the restriction of trade flows between the USSR and the West through the policy of the former. Stalin's pursuit of 'socialism in one country' forced the East European countries to reorient their trade to the West and to their own region.

In this context the re-capitalization of Germany through the Dawes plan, together with Germany's recovery of its unrestricted right to make trade treaties in 1925, opened vistas of a more integrated European free trade system, where Germany's economic might in the East would be harnessed with that of the West. The Franco-German trade agreement in August 1927 reinforced this process and the

---

55. Cited in M. Alexander, *Der Deutsch–Tschechoslowakische Schiedsvertrag im Rahmen der Locarno Verträge* (Munich–Vienna, 1970), p. 27.
56. J. Hiden and P. Salmon, *The Baltic Nations and Europe* (London, 1994), p. 86.

German small tariff, introduced in 1925 to please the Reich's farmers, did not significantly affect the free trade system being constructed by Stresemann. Ironically then, German economic influence in eastern Europe increased not, as originally expected in 1919, through an expansion of economic links between the West and the USSR, but through Germany's *rapprochement* with the Allied powers. The contrast between the Weimar Republic's standing in East Europe and that of the USSR could not have been greater by the mid-1920s. Here, as in the political arena, the differing priorities of Germany and its 'Rapallo partner' prevented a common policy line from evolving. Stability in East Europe assumed growing importance for German trade (as it did for that of Britain, Germany's major economic rival) at a time when the USSR sought rather to divide the capitalist states on its borders.

What Germany's growing economic influence in the East during the second half of the 1920s owed to its re-integration with the West might be seen from the fact that for every US dollar invested in Poland from 1925, eight dollars were invested in Germany.[57] In spite of its political differences with Berlin, Warsaw found it difficult to resist the Weimar Republic's economic weight. Thus between 1926 and 1929, the volume of German–Polish trade 'only' rose by 164 per cent in comparison with an overall surge in Poland's foreign trade of 193 per cent. The Poles were fully justified in fearing that the integrative forces at work in western Europe after Locarno would lead to German hegemony in the East.[58] The *nature* of that hegemony was, however, bound to be affected by the degree to which Germany valued its relationship with the West. In 1926 the *Auswärtiges Amt* resisted deliberately exploiting Poland's financial problems, demonstrating that the pursuit of German interests within the framework of European understanding necessarily extended to eastern Europe. In the interests of its overall strategy, 'Weimar' foreign policy postponed frontier revision in the East. Similarly, Stresemann insisted that *Anschluss* was 'simply a nightmare for the other powers' and appears to have agreed with Schubert in thinking it preferable for Austria to remain independent.[59]

In sum, Weimar *Ostpolitik* could still be extremely uncomfortable to those on the receiving end and the potential for abusing German

57. In general, N. Pease, *Poland, the United States and the stabilization of Europe 1919–1933* (New York–Oxford, 1986).

58. K. Blahut, *Polsko-niemieckie stosuuki gospodarcze w latach 1919–1939* (Warsaw 1974).

59. *ADAP*, Series B, vol. VII, p. 250. Cf. Schubert-Stresemann conversation on 16.7.1927, ibid., vol. VI, p. 84.

economic power to pressurize Poland was considerable. However, it could not be fully realized without endangering relations with the West. Under Stresemann's management, therefore, Weimar policy in eastern Europe had a bark which was worse than its bite. Peaceful methods ostensibly designed to retain the possibility of territorial revision delayed its actuality. In addition, the practical effect of Weimar trade policy was to make large areas of eastern Europe more stable. This process is as worthy of attention as its professed aim to isolate Poland. It is highly doubtful that Stresemann expected or even wished to bring Poland to its knees economically. Stresemann's tactics, here as elsewhere, encouraged a more realistic and long-term view of treaty revision, where a *modus vivendi* could not be ruled out indefinitely. Who could say where such moderation – anathema to extremists – would take Weimar policy? The forces of the extreme right in Germany dimly perceived this because they remained duly incensed.

THE ROLE OF THE *AUSLANDSDEUTSCHE*

Minority questions after 1918 were central to the cause of peace and Stresemann's response to the fate of Germans outside the Reich (*Auslandsdeutsche*) provides another litmus test for the overall integrity of his foreign policy. The issue was bedevilled firstly by the linkage between the survival of German minorities abroad and the maintenance of German claims in disputed territories; secondly by the complex relationship between official bodies in the field – above all the AA – and the many private organizations, mainly of a nationalist–rightist complexion, springing up during and after the war to support the *Auslandsdeutsche*. Some of the more important of these were linked to the radical nationalist 'June Club' (the reference being to the month when the Versailles treaty was signed).[60] However, the organization which best exemplified the murky relationship between official and private bodies was also the most powerful, the government-funded *Deutsche Stiftung*.

It had its origins in the defence of the German minorities in Poland. Before the war these had been deliberately boosted by Prussian settlement policies but that was obviously no longer possible with the

---

60. B. Schot, *Nation oder Staat? Deutschland und der Minderheitenschutz* (Marburg an der Lahn, 1988), pp. 90ff.

defeat of Germany and the birth of an independent Poland. More covert support was required, which is where the *Deutsche Stiftung* entered the picture. Set up in November 1920, it derived in its turn from the so-called 'Eastern Committee', formed in 1919 to prevent the threatened areas in the East from falling to the new Poland. Ostensibly a private body, the *Deutsche Stiftung* functioned as a semi-official organization. Its parliamentary advisory committee, embracing all parties (with the exception of the KPD, the USPD and the NSDAP) became in effect a device for shielding the *Deutsche Stiftung* from detailed parliamentary scrutiny. Through an elaborate and secretive network the *Deutsche Stiftung* distributed money from the *Auswärtiges Amt* via the offices of the Prussian Central Co-operative offices to 'private' individuals in Holland. The various sums received by this route were then paid into the Hollandsche Buitenland Bank, finally reaching the German minorities through co-operative banks in Posen, Upper Silesia and elsewhere. The *Deutsche Stiftung* increasingly concerned itself with the *Auslandsdeutsche* as a whole and was re-organized when Stresemann made available the first really substantial funding of 30 million marks for credit to settled German groups abroad.[61]

This network is the very stuff of intrigue and of itself tended to reinforce arguments depicting the *Auslandsdeutsche* as yet another extension of the long arm of Weimar revisionism. 'What was begun in the Weimar Republic,' it has been said of the work of the *Deutsche Stiftung*, 'the Third Reich continued.'[62] There is in fact little to substantiate such bald assertions of continuity. Not that the AA was unaware of the fact that German settlements were necessary for preserving territorial claims. However, general humanitarian, cultural and economic considerations were of overriding importance to the German government. How, one might well ask, could Germany's leaders *not* have supported their hard pressed minorities abroad after the War? The trouble was that any official support for Germans abroad was a politically sensitive issue and much of the secrecy surrounding the work of the *Deutsche Stiftung* reflected this. Moreover the extent of this support was very limited. The 30 million marks allocated to

61. Stresemann's 'Memorandum concerning the availability of 30 million RM for granting credit to settled groups abroad in Europe' is in *ADAP*, Series B, vol. I, pp. 430–3.
62. N. Krekeler, 'Die deutsche Minderheit in Polen und die Revisionspolitik' in W. Benz (ed.), *Die Vertreibung der Deutschen aus dem Osten* (Frankfurt am Main, 1985), p. 27. See also N. Krekeler, *Revisionsanspruch und geheime Ostpolitik. Die Subventionierung der deutschen Minderheit in Polen 1919–1933* (Stuttgart, 1973).

support settlement in 1926 had to be stretched to apply to German minorities throughout eastern Europe. Although the funding subsequently increased it could only be a contribution to self-help in view of the Weimar Republic's straitened economic circumstances. The idea of self-help ran like a red thread throughout the extensive literature published on the *Auslandsdeutsche* during the 1920s. Since German minorities were seen as vital to the development of commerce between their 'home' and the Reich, they could best maximize their contribution to German wealth through integrating themselves into the economic fabric of the host state. Even though revisionism was nurtured in the *Auslandsdeutsche* movement, practical opportunities for it were therefore severely curtailed. Furthermore, a major consideration of the AA in trying to co-ordinate the work of the private organizations was precisely to prevent the *Auslandsdeutsche* from being regarded as a 'fifth column'.

It remained a high-risk strategy for Stresemann to engage more publicly from 1925 with the thorny minority issues in Europe. On a basic political level he was continuing to make the noises demanded of the electorate over German territorial claims, but we have seen that policy *practice* contradicted his more strident public utterances. In this instance Stresemann headed off opposition to his Locarno strategy by offering more financial support to the *Auslandsdeutsche* organizations and by publicly endorsing their attempt to secure cultural autonomy for German minorities. That promised to increase his supporters among the young and influential conservatives associated with the 'June Club'. By thus making inroads into the clientele of the German Nationalist People's Party (*Deutsch-nationale Volkspartei* – DNVP) Stresemann improved his chances of assuring the process of *Verständigung*. The strategy nonetheless then committed him to the very difficult task of trying to reconcile the minority ideals enshrined in the practice of the League of Nations with the concept of 'cultural autonomy'. The former clearly looked towards the full assimilation of minorities into their home states, whereas the latter emphasized German identity. Thus Baltic German, Werner von Hasselblatt, insisted: 'Europe had to accustom itself to thinking in terms not only of "states" but of "peoples".'[63]

In fact Stresemann's thinking in this matter was far closer to that of another Baltic German, Paul Schiemann, who edited the influential *Rigasche Rundschau* and was highly prominent in the European minorities movement after the war. Although he also stressed the

---

63. B. Schot, *Stresemann, der deutsche Osten und der Völkerbund* (Stuttgart, 1984), pp. 118–23.

importance of preserving different cultures and peoples, in keeping with the *Auslandsdeutsche* movement, Schiemann more explicitly recognized the common awareness and shared fate which arose from different nationality groups sharing a common space. For Schiemann the most effective way to preserve cultural identity was through complete loyalty to the state in which the 'minority' found itself. He insisted, more generally: 'The solution of the struggle between belonging to a state and belonging to a people is the task and aim of the minorities movement, is the essential nature of the minority problem.'[64] To argue convincingly for cultural autonomy for German minorities abroad, the Reich had to be prepared to offer the same for non-German minorities on its own territory and here Stresemann was finally frustrated by the opposition of the Prussian authorities to any private school system. School laws concerning minorities were passed in Prussia in 1928 under some pressure from the *Auswärtiges Amt* but the state, not the minority, remained the supreme arbiter of schooling.[65] The *Länder* were primarily interested in integrating non-Germans residing within their borders.

In the last resort Stresemann's record on minority issues was far from flawless but what can be said in his favour is that he kept alive the European discussion of the problem and at least managed the pressure emanating from the conservative *Auslandsdeutsche* forces in Germany. In his approaches to the League of Nations he could expose the illusions in the camp of the *Auslandsdeutsche* about what they could expect from the international community. He personally also made increasingly positive public statements on minority issues favouring those, such as the Sudeten Germans, who actively worked in and for their new states. The secrecy surrounding the Reich's funding for Germans abroad made it difficult to control, yet their dependence on it conditioned them to recognize the overall priorities of German policy. The principle of international arbitration – invariably dismissed as a German device to prevent Poland from obtaining territorial guarantees – actually had an important role to play in regulating minority disputes. It was also consistent with Stresemann's growing emphasis on the solution of specific day-to-day problems at the day-to-day level of policy making. He could not afford to alienate East European governments by taking the *Auslandsdeutsche*'s cause to extremes, whilst the influence of German minorities might have been

---

64. P. Schiemann, *Ein europäisches Problem. Unabhängige Betrachtungen zur Minderheitenfrage* (Vienna-Leipzig, 1937); also J. Hiden, 'The Baltic Germans and German policy towards Latvia after 1918', *The Historical Journal* 13 (1970): 309 ff.
65. Schot, *Stresemann*, p. 62ff.

further reduced had the League of Nations improved its own system for minority protection.

Central to Stresemann's policy on the *Auslandsdeutsche*, as in his foreign policy generally, was the determination not to risk *Verständigung*, on which the continuing flow of funds and investment from the United States depended. In many important respects, therefore, Weimar policy came to signify the attempt to reconcile treaty revision – demanded by the German domestic situation – with the need to secure European peace over a longer time scale. Not that everything in the garden was rosy. The respective national interests of France and Germany were still some way apart after Locarno; the security issues were as yet unresolved; much dissatisfaction remained over the Rhineland question and over reparations; economic crisis loomed.[66] Yet these difficulties were not caused by the Locarno treaties. The famous settlement of 1925 was not evidence, as often assumed, of the impotence of the League of Nations, so much as of the European states system adjusting to the changing conditions of peace and the necessary re-integration of Germany into the European order. Naturally, Stresemann knew and accepted that the process would inevitably give the Reich the dominant role.

At the same time, in the interests of European collaboration he was prepared to strengthen the procedures of the League of Nations, even if this meant setbacks to Germany's proclaimed goal of revising the peace settlement. Officials who found this approach difficult to handle, like von Bülow, the League expert in the AA, were sidelined, notably during the negotiations for the Kellogg–Briand pact in 1928.[67] Stresemann, together with key officials in the *Auswärtiges Amt* – notably Carl Schubert, the State Secretary – brought the foreign service back to the centre of policy making. These and other key personalities must be credited with (as Hitler must be blamed for not) helping Germany rise above the forces of geography, as well as for defining the Reich's great-power status in a more realistic and pacific fashion. Rejected by powerful sectors of German society, Stresemann's policy yet had support from the SPD, the Democrats, the Centre Party, substantial sections of the DVP and even some of the DNVP. It was wholly credible for the Weimar Republic on 27 August 1928 to join the Kellogg–Briand Pact to outlaw war. Clearly, understanding *could* be pursued beneath the rhetoric of national interests.

66. In general, L. Knipping, *Deutschland, Frankreich und das Ende der Locarno-Ära. Studien zur internationalen Politik in der Anfangsphase der Weltwirtschaftskrise* (Munich, 1987).
67. Cf. P. Krüger, 'Friedenssicherung und deutsche Revisionspolitik. Die deutsche Aussenpolitik und die Verhandlungen über den Kellogg-Pakt', *Vierteljahrshefte für Zeitgeschichte*, 22 (1974): 241.

CHAPTER TWO

Democratic Prospects

Shortly after the National Assembly convened at Weimar on 6 February 1919, even a prominent architect of the new political order, Hugo Preuss, felt jaundiced:

> I have often listened to debates with real concern, glancing rather timidly to the gentlemen of the Right, fearful lest they say to me: 'Do you hope to give a parliamentary system to a nation like this, one that resists it with every sinew of its body? Our people do not comprehend at all what such a system implies.' One finds suspicion everywhere; Germans cannot shake off their old political timidity and their deference to the authoritarian state. They do not understand that the new government must be blood of their blood, flesh of their flesh, that their trusted representatives will have to be an integral part of it. Their constant worry is only: how can we best keep our constituted representatives so shackled that they will be unable to do anything?'[1]

The gloomy note struck by Preuss was echoed in most accounts of the Weimar Republic written in the first decades after the ending of the Second World War. It was not surprising. Non-German scholars, who immediately after 1945 monopolized the field of modern German history, looked unkindly on the political system which had nourished National Socialism. Anglo-Saxon historians in particular barely concealed their contempt for the politics of coalition which characterized Weimar parliamentary democracy. When – particularly from the 1960s – German historians ventured in greater numbers to tackle their painful recent past, they were strongly influenced by the judgements of foreign historians.

1. Hugo Preuss, *Staat, Recht und Freiheit; aus 40 Jahren deutscher Politik und Geschichte* (Tübingen, 1926).

The immediate post-war debate was infected by the legacy of Allied wartime propaganda. Sir Robert Vansittart's *Black Record. Germans past and present* (1941) deliberately set out to encourage virulent anti-German sentiments. The 'findings' of Vansittart, a man once described as pathologically hostile to Germany, continued to colour perceptions of the Weimar Republic long after the war ended. Best-selling paperbacks on Weimar and the rise of Hitler kept alive the habit of scouring the remote past of the German peoples for clues to Hitlerism. In 1955 the world was informed, in a chapter entitled 'The beginnings of megalomania', that 'the danger inherent in German political development was matched by the danger implicit in German thought'.[2] The quest for the 'German mind' made more intimidating the task of German historians trying to analyse the relationship of Hitler to Germany, and therefore to the political system of the Weimar Republic. The historians of what came to be West Germany (FDR) were, it must be said, more preoccupied with self-understanding than those of the German Democratic Republic (DDR). The latter depicted National Socialism as the product of the crisis of monopoly capitalism in the late 1920s. Thus eastern bloc historians were relieved of the need to examine the workings of the Weimar political system because East Germany's abandonment of capitalism in 1945 signified a break from the tainted past of 'Germany'. Such reasoning came to legitimize East Germany as a 'state'.

Nor were West German historians able to divorce historical research entirely from the need to legitimize their own post-war order. The study of the Weimar Republic and the rise of Hitler became an intensely political activity as well as a quest for understanding. The search had strong moral undertones, evident in the *cri de cœur* of the liberal historian, Friedrich Meinecke, who asked: 'Will one ever understand the monstrous experience which fell to our lot in the twelve years of the Third Reich? We have lived through these but up to now, everyone of us without exception, have understood them only incompletely.'[3] Compelled with the onset of Hitler's regime to resign the editorship of the great periodical *Historische Zeitschrift*, Meinecke was well qualified to wander the mean streets of Germany's recent past. He avoided the temptation of portraying Hitler as an Austrian *deus ex machina* inflicted on the German nation. Meinecke's eloquent work focused on the *German* catastrophe and on his own

---

2. T. L. Jarman, *The Rise and Fall of Nazi Germany* (New York, 1956), p. 46.
3. F. Meinecke, *The German Catastrophe. The Social and Historical Influences which led to the Rise and Ruin of Hitler and Germany* (Boston, 1950), p.xi.

nation's problems and structural flaws. A later German historian, Hans Mommsen, described *The German Catastrophe* as of 'fundamental importance' for the examination of German self-assessment after 1945.[4]

Meinecke's achievement is all the more impressive in the context of the jaundiced Allied treatment of German history in the immediate post-war period. A notable contrast to Meinecke's work was that of the conservative historian, Gerhard Ritter, who in *Europe and the German Question* reacted sharply against the Allied images of Germany and analysed National Socialism as part of a *European* disorder.[5] For Ritter, the Third Reich was less the outcome of German history than of the German tradition being violated. Such reasoning, in less scrupulous hands than those of Ritter, who had been associated with Carl Goerdeler of the German resistance, threatened to become a conservative apologia for the German past. Barely concealed beneath the surface of the work of both Ritter and Meinecke was the shock that the German state had succumbed. Their reaction is more intelligible within the then dominant German historiographical tradition of political history. Political factors dominated the proceedings of a symposium of eminent West German historians in 1961, where the note of moral obligation struck by Meinecke was also marked. A major purpose of the symposium was to 'contribute to the permanent establishment of parliamentary government in Germany'. However, the book's blurb focused deliberately on the Weimar Republic, rather than on Germany's entire past. 'There are those who assert that Hitlerism was due to ineradicable faults in the character of the German people. In these ten essays . . . leading German historians . . . set themselves the more constructive task of analysing from an entirely practical point of view, why the Weimar Republic and the tender plant of German parliamentarianism proved so vulnerable and by what methods Hitler destroyed them.'[6]

Perceptions of the German constitutional order after 1919 were influenced from the early 1960s by the revitalized argument about 'continuity' in German history following the publication of Fritz Fischer's monumental study of Germany's aims during the First World War.[7] Unlike the Allied wartime view of continuity the Mark II, West

4. H. Mommsen, 'National socialism: continuity and change' in W. Laqueur, (ed.), *Fascism. A Reader's Guide* (London, 1979), p.185.

5. G. Ritter, *Europa und die deutsche Frage. Betrachtungen über die geschichtliche Eigenart des deutschen Staatsdenkens* (Munich, 1948).

6. *The Road to Dictatorship. Germany 1918 to 1933. A Symposium by German Historians* (London, 1970), p. 27.

7. F. Fischer, *Griff nach der Weltmacht. Die Kriegszielpolitik des kaiserlichen Deutschlands, 1914–1918* (Düsseldorf, 1961).

German version concentrated on the life-span of the united German state, 1871–1945. Fischer sought to document Germany's 'grasp for world power' as a primary cause of the First World War. As well as reaffirming German war guilt in 1914, Fischer's conclusion was that the second bid for hegemony was made by Hitler and that things had gone badly wrong with the German state even before the Weimar Republic came into being. In short, Fischer insisted that Germany's deviant behaviour in the international system was directly related to the flaws in the domestic structures of the German Empire created in 1871. Fischer inevitably affronted the conservative historical guild in the FDR but its younger historians were coming of age and the 1960s witnessed a number of methodological and ideological new departures. There was a renewed challenge to the undue emphasis on political history and more attention was directed towards Germany's long-term social and economic structures.

West German historians engaged more extensively in discussions with non-German historians and, indeed, soon dominated the debate on Germany's past. Under the commodious umbrella of 'continuity', the catalogue of the Reich's shortcomings between 1871 and 1945 grew longer and longer. Vansittart himself would have approved such self-flagellation on the part of so many German historians 'coming to terms with their past'. By the 1970s the chief effect of this activity was to infuse the study of the Weimar political system with profound gloom. It was as if the political parties were locked into a scenario of doom and defeat after 1919 leading inexorably to the triumph of Adolf Hitler. Weimar parliamentary practice was portrayed as flawed by nasty habits picked up in the Reichstag during the Wilhelmine Empire;[8] parties in the new Republic appeared as natural heirs to their Imperial precursors, being merely interest groups, capable of little more than self-seeking bargaining. Under the weight of the accumulated 'top heavy state' (*Obrigkeitsstaat*) which the Bismarckian and Wilhelmine Reich bequeathed to the hapless Republic, Weimar politicians were shown labouring under a new constitution which brought out the worst in them. Its emergency powers encouraged them to side-step their own responsibilities by relying on the President; the number of small parties which the electoral arrangements permitted compounded problems by allowing still more interest groups to clutter up the parliamentary arena. Weimar parliaments were, it seems, predestined for lives that were nasty, brutish and short.

Some of the misery was dispelled by changing perceptions about the

8. Note, for example, M. Stürmer, *Koalition und Opposition in der Weimarer Republik 1924–1928* (Düsseldorf, 1967).

nature of the legacy of the Wilhelmine Empire and by scepticism about Germany's *Sonderweg*. Because Wilhelmine governments were not directly responsible to the Reichstag its elections were not as important as those in France or Great Britain. Yet electoral behaviour provides a vital clue to the general state of health of Wilhelmine politics and here evidence has now accumulated of a ferment of political activity in Germany during the last decade of the nineteenth century. 'Higher election turn-outs, more intensive electioneering and a much greater element of competition in rural elections at every level had changed the fabric of rural politics.'[9] The fact that there were high turn-outs, particularly when big issues were involved, makes it difficult to continue regarding Wilhelmine politics as the mere expression of narrow self-interest. It remained important to affirm loyalty to the party, but links were also being forged between the parties and constructive contacts were made between Reichstag and government. Principled voting was thus far from unknown in the German Empire.[10] The outlines have slowly emerged of a late Imperial German society which was actually highly politicized, peopled by electors who were not by any means all lacking a positive concept of citizenship.

The evidence that the Wilhelmine legacy was not wholly negative further undermines the entrenched idea that the Weimar Republic was doomed from birth. Parentage was of course one important deter-minant of the Republic's health, but emphasis must also be given to the sheer scale, nature and novelty of the crises assaulting it during its lifetime, beginning with the impact of the First World War. The National Socialists had to wage a sustained campaign on many fronts before the Weimar Republic, crisis-ridden as it was, fell to Hitler. In other words, Weimar democracy was more resilient than has often been acknowledged. When Hitler recognized the need to take his cohorts into the Reichstag after the failed 'putsch' of 1923, he chose, in his own words, to hold his nose. What was this, if not an unintended testimonial that parliamentary development was still taking place?

THE WEIMAR CONSTITUTION

Parliamentary practice evolved within the framework of the constitution drafted by Preuss. This had then been subjected to the

9. D. Blackbourn, *Populists and Patricians. Essays in Modern German History* (London, 1987), p. 133.
10. In general, S. Suval, *Electoral policy in Imperial Germany* (1985).

attentions of a twenty-eight strong, all-party committee of the National Assembly, as well as the spokesmen for the different German *Länder*. Why has the constitution frequently been regarded as a cause of the demise of the Weimar Republic? Not, surely, because sovereignty at last resided with the Reichstag, elected under normal circumstances every four years by voters over the age of 21. Was it then because the system of proportional representation, as critics invariably cried, encouraged a proliferation of small parties? It seems inappropriate to criticize a democracy on such grounds, particularly in the atmosphere of expectation of enlightened political reforms generated by the revolutionary councils in Germany. It is also odd to imply that Weimar democracy would have been healthier if the smaller interest groups had been able to continue to work through the ministerial bureaucracies, that is to say, to bypass the Reichstag.[11] Even an observer writing in 1933, a bad year for parliaments, reaffirmed that proportional representation was unavoidable in a heterogeneous country like Germany.[12]

Undoubtedly, making an executive dependent on a Reichstag majority – no matter how it was put together – made particular coalitions fragile and placed extra strains on the head of a government. Minimum electoral requirements could have been imposed on parties to deter the proliferation of smaller groups, but where would the line have been drawn in the troubled post-war and post-revolutionary atmosphere? An examination of Weimar elections shows, for example, that to have insisted on parties gaining at least 5 per cent of the vote (the rule which was applied in the FDR) would have excluded the German Democratic Party (*Deutsche Demokratische Partei* – DDP) from the Reichstag by 1928 and the German People's Party (DVP) by 1930. By contrast, pronouncedly anti-parliamentary forces like the German Communist Party (KPD) and the National Socialists (NSDAP) only ever fell below 5 per cent, respectively in 1920 and in 1924, 1928. The plea to eliminate the issue of proportional representation from the list of factors leading to the collapse of the Weimar parliamentary system has much in its favour.

What of the much maligned emergency powers reserved to the Reich President under the terms of Article 48 of the constitution? After considerable argument, the political parties agreed that the Reich

11. L. E. Jones, 'The dissolution of the bourgeois party system in the Weimar Republic' in R. Bessel and E. J. Feuchtwanger (eds), *Social Change and Political Development in Weimar Germany* (London, 1981), pp. 268–88.
12. C. J. Friedrich, 'The development of the executive power in Germany', *American Political Science Review*, xxvii (1933): 185–203.

President should be elected by a separate popular vote, normally every seven years. The SPD had reservations but the other parties insisted. In any case the Republic's first President was the veteran SPD leader, Friedrich Ebert. Nor did the seven-year rule apply in his case. The Reich Chancellor, formally appointed by the President, depended in normal times on the support of the Reichstag. As head of the government, he was called on to countersign orders issued under presidential emergency action. Parliament had the power to reject measures proposed under emergency procedures. In situations dire enough to cause the dissolution of the Reichstag, fresh elections had to be held within sixty days. A motion supported by two-thirds of the Reichstag could lead to the President's replacement. There were therefore checks and balances which could be operated to curtail ambitious presidents. The constitution sought a judicious balance between plebiscitary and representative elements, rather than any 'dualism' of power between President and Reichstag.

It is almost certainly advisable therefore to regard Article 48 as 'neutral'. It could be exploited for constructive action as much as for sinister ends. The crisis of 1923 demonstrated this. Moreover, since it was applied after the breakdown of parliamentary procedures it is not the ideal scapegoat for the downfall of the Republic. Even the power of the Reich President temporarily to re-appoint as acting head of government a Chancellor who had lost the Reichstag's vote of confidence, could be useful in frustrating any political combination formed with the deliberate aim of bringing down a government. The personality of the President was bound to be of critical importance to the exercise of the office, but this reservation can be made of the executive of virtually any form of government. It was not Hindenburg, who replaced Ebert on the latter's death in 1925 and whose strong political preferences were one factor among many in the Republic's last days, but Hitler who first extensively and systematically abused the powers of the presidential office. The argument that many Germans regarded the President as an Emperor-substitute and that German political parties depended on presidential rule because it was a more 'comfortable' option than parliament is an important one, but very difficult to substantiate.

That is also true of the view that the presidential system of government in Germany from 1930 was the outcome not so much of preference but of drift.[13] Such judgements are really less about the

---

13. E. Friesenhahn, 'Zur Legitimation und zum Scheitern der Weimarer Verfassung' in K. D. Erdmann and H. Schulze (eds), *Weimar: Selbstpreisgabe einer Demokratie. Eine Bilanz Heute* (Düsseldorf, 1980), pp. 81–108.

constitution than about voter habits and preferences. It might be too harsh to insist that the Weimar Republic's *voters* were at fault for electing the wrong sort of politicians, but electoral preferences did play a major part in circumscribing the options of political parties. To the most important of those parties we now turn, beginning with the forces who contributed most to the development of parliamentary practice after 1918.

CHAPTER THREE

The Parties

THE GERMAN SOCIALIST PARTY
(*SOZIALISTISCHE PARTEI DEUTSCHLANDS* – *SPD*)

German social democracy had a long tradition of hostility towards the German Empire. Yet it achieved continuous growth in spite of, or because of, the bursts of anti-socialist legislation and the enduring hostility of the authorities before 1914. At the time of the elections to the National Assembly in 1919, the SPD had the support of more than eleven million voters (some thirty-eight per cent of the electorate) and a million fee-paying members. It maintained a huge electoral machinery with a network of organizations and associations. These covered occupational and other categories of the population and even reached down to the six-year-old, who at that age could enrol in one of the young 'Falcon' groups. The scale of the party's activity may be gauged from the 188 daily newspapers it was pushing onto the streets by 1927. Two years later the SPD's publishers, Dietz-Verlag, had printed 60 million items of literature for the party. Behind the SPD stood the massed ranks of the Free Trade Unions, professedly neutral towards political parties but in reality closely aligned with the SPD and influential in the party's affairs at all levels. One of the organizations, the General Federation of German Trade Unions (*Allgemeiner Deutscher Gewerkschaftsbund* – ADGB) had more members than there were SPD voters in 1920.[1]

Even today, the tone of historical writing on the SPD is predominantly one of regret, mingled with varying degrees of reproach. This is true even of accounts which are sympathetic towards

1. R. N. Hunt, *German Social Democracy 1918–1933* (Chicago, 1970), pp. 168ff.

German social democracy. Thus discussion of the SPD's impressive electoral and organizational network is accompanied by scathing criticism about the top-heavy bureaucracy which drove the machinery along. The SPD leaders have been portrayed as a complacent and ageing clique, distanced from the rank and file by the wonders of the party apparatus and guarding the apex of influence from the young and energetic. To get on in the party required age and contacts, not youth and initiative. The bare recital of statistics does little to improve this image. The national executive of the party was small in number (twelve in 1919, twenty in 1933) and only thirty-one individuals in all served on it throughout the Weimar Republic's life. The party chairmanship was challenged only twice between 1905 and 1933.

In truth all of the German parties found it hard to produce leaders who could steer between the demands of narrow interests and the need for consensus. However, many of the very faults which were attributed to the SPD after 1918 in fact helped the party to grow and to survive before the First World War as a party of opposition to the status quo. Habits were not easily abandoned after the war. In addition the splintering of the socialist movement, which produced the USPD and KPD, reduced pressure for reform of the party organization from within. That same split proved to be a precondition of the growth of electoral support for the SPD in 1919. It could then justly represent itself as the guardian of the national interest and lead the first governments of the Weimar Republic. The Marxist element in the party programme of 1891 had in any event been increasingly marginalized in favour of concentrating on the practical reforms – also endorsed by the Erfurt Party Congress. A more logical outcome of reformism than the assumption of government, after rejecting violent revolution, is difficult to imagine. On the other hand, German social democracy before 1918 developed in an atmosphere deeply hostile to its values, even after the formal ending of the anti-socialist legislation in 1890.

Whatever happened at the apex of the movement, 'the massive organizational growth of the SPD did not produce a uniformly reformist party'.[2] Even if we accept that the pre-war SPD underwent a process of 'negative integration' in Wilhelmine society, this provided absolutely no guarantee of quiescence after 1918. Working-class radicalism persisted and with it a robust aversion in the ranks to the assumption of government in a bourgeois state. The anti-capitalist origins of the SPD made it unique among the parties supporting the

---

2. D. Geary, *European Labour Protest 1848–1939* (London, 1984), p. 119.

Weimar Republic, which in itself explains many of the pressures on the parliamentary leaders of German social democracy during the 1920s.[3] Given these factors, it is not in the least surprising that SPD leaders spent much of their time looking over their shoulders, nor that at critical moments in the Weimar Republic's history they abandoned government coalitions.

Friedrich Ebert and other leading German socialists continue to be charged with failing to maximize opportunities during the German revolution to overhaul the entire socio-economic system. The implication is that the preconditions of Hitler's rise would have been thereby removed. In reality, radical reform on that scale and at that speed has never been achieved in any industrially advanced society.[4] Nevertheless, it is a small step from arguing that the SPD leaders bungled 1918–19 to blaming them for not opposing National Socialism more actively, and for allowing differences within the labour movement fatally to delay the creation of a united front against Hitler. It is as if the SPD leaders could do no right, while their followers could do no wrong. In defence of the former it is important to stress two points. The first concerns the undoubted commitment of the SPD leadership and parliamentary members to the defence of the Weimar Republic. The second relates to broader demographic and electoral trends.

The SPD's allegiance to the cause of democracy can hardly be doubted. For all the difficulties mentioned so far, the party shared power in government for five of the republic's 14 years. Admittedly, the SPD inadvertently demonstrated how much more it could have done at the national level by dominating the administration of Prussia, the largest *Land*, and preserving there the coalition of forces known as the Weimar coalition between 1920 and 1932. On the party political level at least the republic did not 'fail' in Prussia.[5] Nor did the party leaders neglect direct defences. In February 1924, not many months after Hitler's abortive putsch, the SPD leader Friedrich Otto Hoersing, took the initiative to found a para-military organization 'for defence against possible attacks by political enemies on the Constitution or on the Republic'.[6] The *Reichsbanner Schwartz-Rot-Gold*, envisaged as an

---

3. R. Breitman, *German Socialism and Weimar Democracy* (Chapel Hill, 1981), p. 190.

4. H. A. Winkler, 'Spielräume der Sozialdemokratie. Zur Rolle der SPD in Staat und Gesellschaft der Weimarer Republik' in V. Rittberger (ed.), *1933. Wie die Republik der Diktatur erlag* (Berlin–Cologne–Mainz, 1983), p. 64.

5. Cf. D. Orlow, *Weimar Prussia 1918–25. The Unlikely Rock of Democracy* (1988).

6. B. Harms (ed.), *Volk und Reich der Deutschen*, 2 (Berlin, 1929), p. 182; R. Chickering, 'The Reichsbanner and the Weimar Republic 1924–6', *Journal of Modern History*, 40 (1968): 524–34.

organization for all pro-republican parties, was largely staffed and financed by the SPD and the Free Trade Unions. The *Reichsbanner* was not armed but, contrary to the impression gained from studying the growth of the NSDAP in the countryside, the SPD was extremely energetic in opposing Nazi violence in the towns. Part of the problem related to the difficulties the SPD leaders had in interpreting state action in terms of a direct assault on workers.[7] Even after Chancellor von Papen's coup against the Prussian government in 1932 the SPD resorted to the law courts to counter it.

When considering the role of the SPD in the Weimar Republic it is important to take account of demographic trends too. The party represented above all the aristocracy of German labour, that is to say the highly unionized and skilled working classes. The fact that the SPD did less well at the polls in the crises of the 1920s indicates that the disadvantaged and unemployed were looking elsewhere for help, towards the communists and indeed from 1928 towards the National Socialists. There were charges that the SPD was not doing enough to extend its message beyond the proletariat. The parliamentary leadership showed some sensitivity to this argument by trying to broaden the party's appeal and belatedly seeking to capture more votes from women and youth. Other critics felt that the SPD was becoming too bourgeois, which meant among other things that the SPD supporter tended to be older, employed and likely to own a house. Yet most electors would hope for two out of three on this list and the SPD was bound to try to win their support. This was not so much a lapse from ideological purity as a matter of survival.

Nonetheless, the party remained a working-class party, with over four-fifths of its members categorized as workers. Less than a fifth came from the ranks of employees, bureaucrats and small self-employed. The stark truth was that, apart from a small spurt in 1928, the entire vote for the left in Germany declined from 45.5 per cent in 1919 to 30.6 per cent in 1930. The SPD's voting figures were stagnant following its peak of electoral support in 1919. This makes it all the more impressive that, on the whole, the organized (unionized) working class put up considerable resistance to the charms of National Socialism prior to 1933. The inability of the SPD to break through the one-third voting barrier was partly due to some worker support going to the Centre Party. Whether the SPD's shortcomings arose from

---

7. E. Rosenhaft, 'Working class life and working class politics. Communists, Nazis and the state in the battle for the streets' in R. Bessel and L. Feuchtwanger (eds), *Social Change and Political Development in Weimar Germany* (London, 1981), pp. 207ff.

misguided leadership or whether the party was the victim of demographic limits and changes, is a question with which modern readers are all too familiar. Overturned as the largest party in the Reichstag only in 1932, the socialists closed their parliamentary account for the time being by voting against Hitler's infamous Enabling Bill in March 1933. The act was one of considerable although, by then, futile defiance.

THE CENTRE PARTY (*DEUTSCHE ZENTRUMS PARTEI*)

The Centre Party had successfully defended the Catholic Church during the *Kulturkampf* waged by Bismarck in the 1870s. The outcome of this costly and zealous pursuit of what the Iron Chancellor called 'enemies of the Reich' (*Reichsfeinde*) was the growth of the Centre Party's share of the vote. When the *Kulturkampf* was abandoned during the 1880s the experience proved to have been formative for the Centre Party. Thereafter it broadly endorsed the government's economic policies and some of its leaders were even 'assimilated' to the state, notably Georg Graf von Hertling, Martin Spahn and Cardinal Kopp, but the mass of Catholic supporters were never identified as a whole with the imperatives of a Protestant and Prussianized regime. Clear evidence of this came when the Centre Party's left wing, under Matthias Erzberger, attacked the archaic suffrage in Prussia, which effectively blocked parliamentary reform in the Reich as a whole. In proclaiming at the end of the First World War: 'Into the new era under the old flag', the Centre Party capitalized on its dissociation from the defunct German Empire and made its bid to become a focal point in the changed political climate of the Weimar Republic.[8]

The Centre thus became a potential ally of the SPD, an event Bismarck had predicted would occur if the German Empire collapsed. In their different ways both parties had struggled against the inequities of the Imperial administration, so that more than a marriage of convenience was involved after 1918. Co-operation with the socialists also reduced the threat of overt discrimination against

8. R. Morsey, *Die deutsche Zentrumspartei 1917–1923* (Düsseldorf, 1966), pp. 79ff. See also E. L. Evans, *The German Centre Party 1870–1933*, Illinois, 1981.

Catholics. Proof of that was the brief and ignominious career as Prussian Minster of Culture of the USPD member, Adolf Hoffmann, whose anti-clerical postures gained him few friends.[9] Whether or not the Centre and SPD had more in common than they had to divide them after 1918 is a more problematic question. The parties' joint defence of the parliamentary republic at the outset prompted the distinguished German historian, Arthur Rosenberg, to insist later that there was such a phenomenon as 'Catholic democracy', although he used the term to characterize events between 1920 and 1922. Thereafter, at least at Reich level, where it continued to be part of every coalition, the Centre Party put more effort into collaboration with conservatives and nationalists in the Reichstag.

Disillusionment with social democracy's reluctance to shoulder governmental burdens was one factor in causing this shift. The Centre was also anxious not to lose Catholic voters to the nationalist and conservative camp. On the one hand, Centre voters included worker and industrialist, farmer and civil servant, landlord and aristocrat – the sort of mixture which, as it were, predestined the party for the politics of compromise.[10] On the other hand, while anxious to extend its catchment area, the Centre party drew its enduring strength from those actively involved in Church life. What Neumann characterized as an inherently conservative inclination in the Centre affected not only Church, family and marriage matters but also politics. If a party can be said to have an ideal, the Centre wished for a conservative democracy in which strong government was essential. The fact that the Centre contained a cross-section of German society as a whole reinforced its belief in its virtues as a model for an essentially authoritarian political order. Further analysis of the social base of the Centre confirms its inclination to drift towards the right.

The Janus-like quality of the party makes it hard to do full justice to its contribution to political life in Germany after 1918. There are lingering reservations about the extent of the party's positive commitment to the republican cause. The Papal Encyclicals of 1881 and 1885 were to the effect that the concerns of the Church should take priority over the specific state form. Thus, although the Bavarian People's Party (BVP) reacted against the Centre Party's support for centralized government in the Reich by retaining its separate identity, both Catholic parties collaborated on Church issues. There are also doubts about the Centre's leaders, charged with being too

---

9. Morsey, *Zentrumspartei*, pp. 110–17.
10. S. Neumann, *Die Parteien der Weimarer Republik* (Stuttgart, 1965), p. 44.

conservative, too old and uncharismatic. Individuals who did conduct a public and active defence of the republic, notably Joseph Joos, Heinrich Imbusch, Joseph Wirth and of course Matthias Erzberger prior to his assassination, were in a minority. The advancement of their careers was more rather than less likely to cause strains within the Centre Party's ranks. In general, there was a gap between the top of the party hierarchy and the members of the youth organization, *Windthorstbunde*. Thus the political aspirations of the young 'Front' generation were blocked and the party did not achieve renewal from below.

Such criticisms fall far short of proving that the Centre was anti-republican. Even though it modified its political tactics after 1923, it cannot be charged with having turned against the socialists without serious qualifications. The party continued to co-operate with the SPD in the Prussian government until 1932. The fact that almost twenty per cent of the Centre's support came from industrial labour generated a degree of rivalry between the two parties but it meant that they could also share common ground in social policy. It should not be forgotten that the *Rerum Novarum* of 1891 welcomed a rise in the material standards of workers as well as urging their spiritual welfare. The Centre and SPD moreover achieved a working compromise over education policy in a number of *Land* administrations, notably those of Bavaria, Baden and Prussia. In making this concordat at a regional level the Centre succeeded in modifying the aim expressed in the Weimar constitution, namely, of founding Common (non-denominational) Schools throughout the Reich.[11]

Thus the Centre formed coalitions with nationalists and conservatives in the Reich government whilst continuing to rule with the SPD in Prussian administrations. Manifestly, the Centre's propensity to criticize 'Godless Marxists' during election campaigns did not prevent fraternization with social democrats between the hustings. It may be argued that the Centre's exceptional capacity for coalition was not only a reflection of its social composition, but also a precondition of maintaining its diverse following. That would make it easier to forgive the party for exploiting the school issue from time to time to weld together its supporters. It is too harsh to suggest that the party's very existence distracted Catholic voters from joining the overtly pro-republican SPD; or that because there was no threat of a new *Kulturkampf* in the Weimar Republic the Centre should not have

11. G. Gruenthal, *Reichsschulgesetz und Zentrumspartei in der Weimarer Republik* (Düsseldorf, 1968).

wasted its energies in defending denominational schools. Had the party *not* acted so, it would certainly have eroded Catholic electoral support. Historical experience and electoral imperatives dictated that the Centre try to prevent this erosion. For similar reasons the Centre, which had the votes of only 60 per cent of German Catholics, tried to become more than just a confessional party by increasing its share of non-Catholic voters. Doubtless with an eye on its historic clashes with the government, the Centre set out with determination to man the offices of the state. In the bureaucracy at least its personnel policy met with little success, the exception in the early 1920s being the Ministry of Justice. In 1922 a mere 5 per cent of higher civil service posts in Prussia fell to the SPD, DDP and Centre combined. The Weimar Republic continued to ring with the frustrated cries of Catholics failing to achieve parity in office. The fact that frustration caused the Centre to undervalue its presence in all Reich coalitions was regrettable but understandable.

A contemporary tract remarked on the great significance for the Centre of the little word 'and'. The party's message was: 'Religion *and* love of the Fatherland, Fatherland *and* humanity, Germany *and* Europe, Centralization *and* Federalism.'[12] The Centre's propensity for compromise has been seized on as evidence not of a hesitant progress towards mature parliamentarism, but of a failure to initiate policies of its own. In fact the Centre Party strength was in its potential for linking, if indirectly, parties which would not normally have co-existed in one government. This achievement was impressive, even if inevitably tainted by continued sullen resentment here and there in the socialist and indeed liberal camps. Unfortunately, the strengths of the Centre as a 'bridging party' could also be its weaknesses; its priorities an irritant in times of crisis, for parties to the left and right. The party became a natural target for groups determined to frustrate parliamentary development of any sort. Yet the Catholic vote held up at around sixteen per cent and provided a fairly effective innoculation against National Socialism. It provided major statesmen in the early years of the Weimar Republic, in Josef Wirth and Matthias Erzberger and during the crises in 1918 and 1923 played a key role in securing political stability. Sadly, the party's right wing grew increasingly influential, culminating in the Centre abandoning the Weimar coalition in Prussia. That fateful step underlined just how important had been the party's participation in Germany's first attempt to build parliamentary democracy.

12. Neumann, *Die Parteien*, p. 47; K. Ruppert, *Im Dienst der Staat von Weimar. Das Zentrum als regierende Partei in der Weimarer Republik* (Düsseldorf, 1992).

THE GERMAN DEMOCRATIC PARTY (*DEUTSCHE DEMOKRATISCHE PARTEI* – DDP)

There was a schism in the ranks of German liberals dating at least from the revolutionary upheavals of 1848. Later, as the National Liberals made their peace with Bismarck inside the new Germany, the Progressive faction lived up to its name by pursuing a more overtly reformist policy in the Reichstag. On the other hand, a sufficiently broad commitment to advancing parliamentary government slowly developed within German liberalism as a whole before, during and after the First World War. There was some hope for unity in the new Republic, enough at least to inspire the political vision of the group of prominent German liberal intellectuals who launched the initiative to form the Democratic Party in November 1918. Before the month was out plans for remarriage between the Progressives and the National Liberals were dashed. The majority of National Liberals chose to remain apart under the new brand name of the German People's Party (*Deutsche Volkspartei* – DVP).[13] Democrat leaders Hjalmar Schacht, Professor Alfred Weber and the Chief Editor of the *Berliner Tageblatt*, Theodor Wolff, had serious reservations about the DVP's leader, Gustav Stresemann, a man deeply implicated in the German annexationist policies during the War. Democrats also doubted the commitment of the National Liberals to the new Republic. The anxiety was understandable in the 'Professors' party', which played a formative role in the drafting of the new Weimar constitution.[14] The fact that German liberals formed two distinct parties cannot, however, be explained solely in terms of a clash between personalities, however powerful these personalities may have been. Nor were their antics to be dismissed as evidence of political immaturity. On the contrary, they were an indication that strong party lines *had* developed in the Wilhelmine era; the political parties had their constituencies and leaders could not ignore them.

Although largely starved of high public office in Wilhelmine Germany, the Progressives had captured influence in local government. Their political clientele ranged from the Hirsch–Dunker unions to the Hansa–Bund. They enjoyed in addition a broad wedge of support from the Mittelstand. This state of affairs gave some sustenance to the

13. Cf. the memoir of G. W. Heinemann, *Wir müssen Demokraten sein. Tagebuch der Studienjahre 1919–1922* (Munich, 1980).

14. See A. Chanady, 'The dissolution of the German Democratic Party in 1930', *American Historical Review*, 73 (1967): 1433–57.

vision of acting as a bridge between the German bourgeoisie and the working class, an ideal dear to the Democrat leader, Friedrich Naumann. At the same time the range of economic interests supporting the Democrats, which included handicrafts, banking and export industries, could also generate tensions within the party. It lacked the Centre's advantage of having religion as a 'cement'. The inner conflict of the party, which became more apparent with the socio-economic dislocation of 1923–4, to some extent accounts for the fact that the Democrats' message to the electorate was often muted. By 1928 the gap between the financial/industrial sectors of the party and its more radical social elements yawned wider than ever. A long-standing aversion on the right of the DDP towards closer collaboration with the SPD grew more pronounced. Within the Democratic party there was a general shift towards the right in the later 1920s, a trend mirrored in DDP Chairman Erich Koch-Weser's speech at the Democrat conference in 1929.[15]

The problems confronting the Democratic Party in the later 1920s (emphasized by the resignation of such key figures as Hjalmar Schacht, Otto Gessler and Theodor Wolff in 1927–8) were severe enough briefly to stimulate renewed discussions about fusing the two liberal parties. The electoral defeats suffered by the DDP and DVP in 1928 provided an additional thrust in this direction but it proved no easier in the 1920s than it is today to merge different political parties. The impasse between the DVP and DDP generated a proposal for a new political formation, supported by the Berlin Central office of the DDP. All too soon the scene was set for the dissolution of the Democrats on 8 November 1930 and the short-lived appearance of the State Party. Its failure disposed of what little remained of Friedrich Naumann's ambitious vision but it would be a pity to leave only this impression of vainglorious political wrangling, or to minimize the significance of the DDP's effort as a whole to provide domestic cohesion.[16] More than mere political opportunism in the face of a declining share of the poll underlay the DDP's belated effort to forge a bond with the DVP. Even in 1918 projects for liberal mergers had been largely motivated by the wish to counter the dispersal of forces through a proliferation of

15. On the Democratic Party, W. Stephan, *Aufstieg und Verfall des Linksliberalismus 1918–1933. Geschichte der Deutschen Demokratischen Partei* (Göttingen, 1973); W. Schneider, *Die Deutsche Demokratische Partei in der Weimarer Republik* (Munich, 1978); B. Frye, *Liberal Democrats in the Weimar Republic. The History of the German Democratic Party and the German State Party* (Carbondale, 1985).

16. L. E. Jones, *German Liberalism and the Dissolution of the Weimar Party System 1918–1933* (London, 1988), pp. 476–82.

parties. The growing threat of extremists on the right and left after 1928 reinforced these ambitions to rationalize the German party system. Talks on liberal mergers at the end of the 1920s could be charitably regarded as part of an effort to introduce a fourth block alongside the Centre Party, the SPD and the 'New Right'.

The centre ground of German politics in the 1920s provided all the normal discomforts of that chilly region in other parliamentary systems in Europe, and more besides. In the last resort the DDP was unable to prevent the erosion of its electoral base. Inflation further stimulated the commercial middle classes to found their own parties. Such was the case with German handicraft, which had once cultivated contacts with the DDP, when the *Wirtschaftspartei* was founded.[17] The atrophy of the DDP's social base under the impact of inflation, war and the 'anti-social consequences' of government stabilization programmes provide the real clue to its ultimate decline. It could not be reversed by the sporadic economic recovery of the mid 1920s. It is salutary to recall that the Democrat share of parliamentary seats fell from 75 in the National Assembly to 39 in the following year, 1920, when the Republic's new Reichstag was convened. The figures make all the more admirable the DDP's hard fight to fulfil its difficult role in Weimar politics. It was more than just a collection of prominent names, in itself no mean achievement. Ultimately the DDP's worth can be judged from the verdict of historians that its dissolution was a mortal blow for the Weimar political system. It is ironic that the party's desire for a strong, unitary Reich should have been frustrated during the Weimar Republic and have taken such a different form after 1933.

THE GERMAN PEOPLE'S PARTY (*DIE DEUTSCHE VOLKSPARTEI* – DVP)

Neumann's classic early account of the Weimar Parties treated the DVP's history after 1918 as the history of its leader, Gustav Stresemann and implied that his importance concealed National Liberal traits

17. Cf. Neumann, *Die Parteien*, p. 51; also F. Domurad, 'The politics of corporatism. Hamburg handicraft in the late Weimar Republic' in R. Bessel and L. Feuchtwanger (eds), *Social Change and Political Development in Weimar Germany* (London, 1981). Further detail on the Wirtschaftspartei in M. Schumacher, *Mittelstandsfront und Republik. Die Wirtschaftspartei. Reichspartei des deutschen Mittelstandes 1919–1933* (Düsseldorf, 1972).

present in the party. The idea that the development of the DVP was in contradistinction to Stresemann's own career path is, however, misleading. Stresemann certainly encountered punishing resistance within his party, but this is the lot of many political leaders. Any conflict between the leadership and membership of the DVP must be viewed against an awareness of what both had in common. The majority of the old National Liberal Party rejecting the DDP as a new political home shared Stresemann's nationalist pedigree. They, too, had supported the policy of territorial annexations during the First World War. The emphasis on the word 'people' in the DVP's title testified to the strong current of nationalism still running through liberalism. At the same time, although insisting on its own distinct identity from the DDP, Stresemann's party, by definition, supported liberalism. The attempt to maintain an acceptable balance between nationalism and liberalism had obvious advantages in a state trying to escape from the Wilhelmine legacy.

There were differences between the left and right of the party in 1918 on the subject of collaboration with the SPD. The problem was central to Weimar politics for in the DVP industry and business predominated. No fewer than a third of the party's Reichstag deputies in 1930 were leading businessmen, as indeed Stresemann himself had been. Other prominent industrialists in the DVP included men like Hugo Stinnes, Alfred Vögler and Wilhelm Ferdinand Kalle. These and others could be expected to disagree with the SPD about the distribution of wealth, but both parties had a mutual interest in its creation through economic expansion. Their co-operation also depended therefore on what gross national wealth was available for distribution. On the other hand, it was possible, for example, for two-thirds of the DVP's Reichstag deputies to vote in favour of financial support for the locked-out Ruhr workers later in the 1920s. In addition, in the closely related fields of trade and foreign policy, key elements in both parties acknowledged the link between Germany's future economic well-being and the policy of rapprochement (*Verständigung*) with the Allied Powers. By emphasizing *Verständigung* with Britain, France and America, Stresemann sought to consolidate the often precarious domestic base on which that policy rested. The difficulties could be more evident regionally. In Prussia, for example, the SPD and DVP politicians continued their conflict over social and domestic priorities without the constraints applied at Reich level by the requirements of foreign policy.

Once the DVP assumed the responsibilities of government for a state it had viewed with disfavour in 1918, it inevitably sought to influence the nature of that state. High on the party's agenda was the desire to increase the powers of the Reich President and to introduce other centralizing elements. The tendency was admittedly restrained under Stresemann's leadership but was only too evident in the DVP's rightward swing after his death in 1929. Not without irony, this took place during Müller's 'Great Coalition', a political combination which had launched Stresemann as Chancellor in 1923. The next DVP leader, Paul Scholz, was unequal to the task of reconciling Stresemann's legacy with the rightward movement of his party. Yet the electoral decline which afflicted the DVP, *the* party of the bourgeoisie, makes all the more remarkable its continuing participation in government between 1923 and 1930.

The history of the DVP was also the history of German liberalism and it cannot be comprehended in terms of one personality but because Stresemann's influence was paramount his premature death left many unanswered questions. The DVP offers perhaps the most attractive target of all the Weimar Parties for speculation on the 'might-have-beens' of Weimar democracy. How can the DVP be fairly assessed in the interests of a more balanced view of that democracy? In the first place the existence of two liberal parties *reflected* rather than caused the split in the liberal camp. Something like the German People's Party was thus virtually a precondition of tempting overtly nationalistic liberals towards the new Republic, by providing a more congenial shelter than anything the DDP could offer. Secondly, Stresemann was not alone within the DVP in taking the difficult path towards accepting and making the most of the Weimar Republic, becoming 'republicans by conviction' (*Vernünftrepublikaner*). It is a reflection of the impossible demands made by historians of the Weimar party system that this particular term conveys severely qualified approval, indicating something short of wholehearted commitment to the republican cause. The party was liberal, it was admitted, but not democratic; for constitutionalism but not parliamentary democracy.[18] In the end the judgements do insufficient justice to the developments in which the DVP was involved and which offered tantalizing glimpses, for a while at least, of accommodation between the party and the SPD.

18.   Neumann, *Die Parteien*, p. 57. See also L. E. Jones, 'Gustav Stresemann and the crisis of German liberalism', *European Studies Review*, 4 (1974): 141–63; W Hartenstein, *Die Anfänge der Deutschen Volkspartei 1918–1920* (Düsseldorf, 1962).

THE GERMAN NATIONALIST PEOPLE'S PARTY (*DEUTSCHNATIONALE VOLKSPARTEI* – DNVP)

With the DNVP the transition to extremism begins, for it was sometimes difficult to draw a clear line between the DNVP and the numerous *völkisch*/rightist groups flourishing outside the Reichstag in the 1920s, at least in terms of beliefs and values. The party could hardly be held directly responsible for the acts of political murder and terrorism endemic to the extra-parliamentary right in the first three or four years of the Republic. Yet prominent members of the DNVP played handmaiden to Adolf Hitler and his movement at the close of the 1920s. The backing of the nationalist leader from 1928, Alfred Hugenberg, made a major contribution to Hitler's 'breakthrough' to a wider national audience.

In November 1918 the founding of the DNVP, heir to the two conservative parties of the German Empire, created a parliamentary focal point for illiberal and anti-republican sentiments of the right. Anti-Semitism had been a plank of German conservatism since the early 1890s and therefore Pan-Germans naturally gravitated to the DNVP. The importance of nationalism as a binding force can be seen from the DNVP's characterization as the 'Party of the Fatherland'. It offered a natural home for the opponents of revolution in 1918–19. At the same time its post-war political base was enlarged to embrace industrialists, civil servants, the petite bourgeoisie, craftsmen, unionists and workers. The old conservative parties had represented above all the interests of the large landlords of eastern Germany but in the National Assembly elections almost half of the DNVP's votes came from western electoral districts of the Reich. When in the Reichstag poll of 1920 the DNVP managed to capture fifteen per cent of the vote, it arrested three decades of conservative electoral decline, enabling it to represent itself as the main party of the middle classes. Moreover after 1924 this 'Protestant' party even had some appeal for those Catholics who found distasteful the relationship between the Centre Party and the SPD. In other words the DNVP already had the potential to become considerably more than a coalition of non-liberal, rightist forces.[19]

The importance of channelling the resentment and frustration of the

19. L. Hertzmann, 'The founding of the German National People's Party November 1918–January 1919', *Journal of Modern History*, 30 (1958): 24–36; D. P. Walker, *Alfred Hugenberg and the Deutschnationale Volkspartei* (Cambridge, 1976). There is also much in H. A. Turner Jr, *German Big Business and the Rise of Hitler* (New York, Oxford, 1985).

German right towards more constructive ends can hardly be doubted. Even so, the dominant tone of the DNVP was one of outright hostility towards the Republic until 1924, a year whose two parliamentary elections brought the party to the peak of its voting support (May elections 19.5 per cent, December elections 20.5 per cent). The successes at the polls appeared to indicate growing support for opposition to the Republic. Conversely, the DNVP's voting reverses in 1928 and 1930 are invariably viewed as electoral retribution for the nationalists' participation in government in 1925 and in 1927–8. There is doubtless some truth in this line of reasoning. It is difficult to prove conclusively since other divisive forces were operating on the republican political scene at the end of the 1920s. The DNVP had little alternative than to participate in government at some stage of the republic's life. A closer look at the internal struggles within the party makes the point clearer.

The very factors increasing the DNVP's electoral appeal forced it to define more constructively its actual relationship towards the state it claimed to reject. Voters expect policies, and permanent exclusion from government is not normally the best way to change political and socio-economic realities. The powerful economic interests linked to the DNVP, frequently accused of accelerating the parliamentary decline of the Weimar Republic, in fact also impelled the party towards government and accommodation with the new order (*innere Annäherung*). The *Reichslandbund* – the organization of landowners which incidentally provided over half of the DNVP's Reichstag faction – was anxious to exploit governmental office to influence tariff policy in trade and agriculture. Nor could the industrial sectors of the party ignore the economic prospects inherent in the renegotiation of reparations under the Dawes plan in 1924. Other associations linked with the DNVP added their weight. Pressures on the party to work within the state in order to change it were also increased by the participation of the DVP in government, as well as by Stresemann's successes. Under the leadership of Graf Kuno von Westarp, 'conservative participation' was achieved in first the cabinet of Hans Luther (1925) and subsequently that of Wilhelm Marx (1927–8). Why then did the process come to a stop or, more accurately, why did it slow down? The question cannot be answered without reference to the extreme nature of the socio-economic crisis of the late 1920s but the truth is that the tactic of *innere Annäherung* had always been fiercely contested within the party.

The closeness of the struggle inside the DNVP over the strategy and tactics of opposition can be seen from the party's vote in the

Reichstag on the Dawes Plan. Fifty-two DNVP delegates favoured its acceptance, 48 did not. The split proved to some observers how lasting was the influence of the vested landed interests in eastern Germany. Neumann felt that these created a rift fatal to the Republic. In his words: 'Beyond Berlin the new Germany virtually ceases.'[20] The idea that constructive opposition espoused by such as Hans Delbrueck and Kuno von Westarp merely obscured the rift in German politics is unhelpful, however, because it implies that outright opposition to the Republic was the *natural* course for the DNVP to take. Certainly, the reactionary sections of the party represented by Alfred Hugenberg – who after 1928 dominated the DNVP – believed that the voters deserted his party when it shouldered the burdens of government. At the same time, Hugenberg's elevation to the Party Chairmanship in 1928 and his all-out espousal of 'unity through opposition' itself caused defections from the ranks of the DNVP. The electoral setbacks in 1928 and 1930 were as much a reflection of the DNVP's own disunity as of its participation in government.

The Conservative People's Party – the product of a fusion in June 1930 of the People's Conservatives with the Westarp faction of the DNVP, together with the Christian Social People's Service – helped to swell the growing number of middle parties. These were no more purely selfish than were the offshoots of the German Democrats. Within the Conservative People's Party was preserved the patriarchal but dutiful brand of conservatism. As to the Christian Socialists, deputies like Emil Karl Hartwig, Reinhard Mumm and Gustav Hülser specifically set out to inject a stronger moral note with evangelical undertones. They chose pointedly not to portray their party as bourgeois at a time when ninety per cent of wage-earners were receiving less than 200 marks per month. However, amidst the mounting, economic and social conflicts after 1928, the radicalization of politics favoured not the splinter groups from the DNVP, but Hugenberg's all or nothing bid to weld together the parties of the bourgeoisie.

Ultimately, Hugenberg did bring about such a bloc, although in so doing he narrowed his own political and social base. His quest therefore also helped to shift the point of integration for the bourgeois parties ever further towards the right.[21] His money and his press were put at the disposal of Hitler; his was the policy of extreme nationalism and anti-republicanism, of the anti-Young campaign and the Hitler–

---

20. Neumann, *Die Parteien*, p. 65
21. Cf L. E. Jones, *German Liberalism*, pp. 448ff.

Seldte–Hugenberg 'Front'. Hugenberg profited from the decentralized nature of the DNVP organization, using influence through the regional party associations to mobilize discontent against Westarp. Hugenberg's professed belief 'in government by strong men who have the will power and the strength to carry out national decisions' seems an obvious cue to take up the story of Hitler and the NSDAP.[22] First it is necessary to move across sharply to the political extremism on the left, itself an important factor in Hitler's rise to power.

THE GERMAN COMMUNIST PARTY (*KOMMUNISTISHE PARTEI DEUTSCHLANDS* – KPD)

Historians of the Weimar Republic have only rarely resisted the temptation to write harshly of the German Communist Party, founded between 28 December 1918 and 1 January 1919. The tone ranges from incredulity at the contortions of the communists during the 1920s to the sort of contempt expressed by the SPD organ, *Vorwärts*, shortly before the KPD came into being: 'Bolshevism, the militarism of the loafers.' An obvious clue to the KPD's enduring unpopularity was its close association with Moscow. The quotation also exemplifies the corrosive relationship between the KPD and the SPD. This purportedly weakened working-class resistance to National Socialism and facilitated Hitler's entry to government. On this reasoning the KPD was the extreme left counterpart of the National Socialists – ideologically opposed to them but, like the Hitler movement, polarizing political opinion and working through the Reichstag only to destroy the Republic.[23]

The KPD was in fact a *movement*, although 'at times it acquired the character of a mass movement'.[24] Many of the objections leading to the SPD's loss of its radical wing after 1914 were moral as well as ideological. The 'Spartacists', formed round Karl Liebknecht, Rosa Luxemburg and Franz Mehring in 1914, voiced an anti-war attitude

---

22. See H. Holzbach, *Das System Hugenberg. Die Organisation der bürgerlichen Sammlungspolitik vor dem Aufstieg der NSDAP* (Stuttgart, 1981), p. 254.

23. Cf. K. D. Bracher's influential treatment, *Die Auflösung der Weimarer Republik. Eine Studie zum Problem des Machtverfalls in der Demokratie* (Schwarzwald, 1955), pp. 100ff; H. Weber, *Kommunismus in Deutschland 1918–1945* (Darmstadt, 1983); B. Fowkes, *Communism in Germany under the Weimar Republic* (London, 1984).

24. O. Flechtheim, 'The role of the Communist party' in, T. Eschenburg *et al.*, *The Road to Dictatorship. Germany 1918–1933* (London, 1970), p .96.

far from unique on the European left. The minority of German socialists forming the Independent German Social Democratic Party (USPD) in April 1917, to which the Spartacists loosely attached themselves, also had serious reservations about the conduct of the war. On 10 November 1918, however, when the USPD and SPD jointly formed the Provisional Government, the Spartacists were isolated. Other groups who later helped them to found the KPD were the Left Radicals (centred on Bremen but with offshoots in North Germany, Saxony and the Rhineland) and the revolutionary shop stewards (*Obleute*). The latter functioned as a ginger group in the unions. Also involved were members of the Free Socialist Youth.[25] Youth characterized the party membership as a whole.

The immediate prospects for the KPD were less than rosy. The SPD leadership's determination to restore a parliamentary system was widely supported in the Reich, not least in the interests of securing a better peace settlement with the West. Although the USPD was bitter and sufficiently disillusioned with the SPD to leave the Provisional Government on 29 December 1918, it could not bring itself to join the KPD. Objective realities did not favour the 'Russian model' being applied to Germany. Even Rosa Luxemburg recognized this, in spite of her passionate interest in the Bolshevik cause in Russia. Her logic in urging the founding delegates of the KPD to contest the forthcoming elections for the National Assembly was impeccable.[26] On the other hand, there was considerable frustration within the KPD at that stage. The 'reformism' of pre-1914 had lost its appeal after the combined impact of the war and the revolution in Russia. In addition the decline of communist influence in the workers' and soldiers' councils ended lingering hopes of using them as engines of change, whilst post-war uncertainty continued to give credence to those in the KPD advocating 'putschist' tactics. Thus the majority of the Communist Party delegates rejected Luxemburg's plea to work in the first instance for the political re-education of the Germans. As a result a futile uprising took place, leading to the violent death of Luxemburg early in 1919 and subsequently to factional strife within the new KPD.

25. Cf. G. P. Bassler, 'The Communist movement in the German revolution, 1918–1919. A problem of historical typology', *Central European History*, 6 (1973): 233–77. See also W. T. Angress, *Stillborn Revolution. The Communist Bid for Power in Germany* (Princeton, 1963); J. P. Nettl, *Rosa Luxemburg*, 2 vols (Oxford, 1966).

26. See G. Castellan, 'À propos de Rosa Luxemburg', *Revue d'Histoire Moderne et Contemporaine*, 23 (1976): 573–82. For a much more critical view of Luxemburg, D. Weitz, ' "Rosa Luxemburg belongs to us!" German Communism and the Luxemburg legacy', *Central European History* 27 (1994): 27–64.

A later commentator identified in this action the KPD's 'utopian belief that it was only necessary to advance, raise the revolutionary banner and the masses would follow'.[27] By the close of 1919 conflicting pressures were making themselves felt and the much remarked oscillation of the KPD between 'right' and 'left' was well established. A mere catalogue of the next two years illustrates the point. First, the party congress at Heidelberg opted to fight future elections and to begin work inside the Free (Socialist) Trade Unions. Under the leadership of the 'brilliant but egocentric' Paul Levi the KPD shed its ultra-leftists. The latter formed the German Communist Workers' Party (*Kommunistische Arbeiter Partei Deutschlands* – KAPD), soon destined for oblivion. Following the USPD Party Congress at Halle over half the members finally went over to the KPD, giving it a membership of 400,000. It now had 33 daily newspapers and strong positions in the Trade Unions.[28] Significantly, two-thirds of the Halle delegates opted to join the new Communist International (Comintern) after the intervention of its Soviet president, Georgy Zinoviev. Subsequently Levi's effort to counter Comintern control of the enlarged KPD brought displeasure in Moscow. Encouragement was then given to leftist leaders in the Berlin Central Party office of the KPD (*Zentrale*), Ernst Reuter, Ruth Fischer and Arkadi Maslow. These favoured the 'March action' of 1921, when Berlin was distracted by the Allied occupation of the Rhine ports. There ensued yet another defeat for the KPD and a sharp decline in its popularity. Its membership slumped to 180,000. No sooner had the March failure been analysed at the Third Comintern Congress in Moscow, in mid-summer 1921, than a new 'rightist' policy was launched, on this occasion under Ernst Meyer.

The tactical shifts were very much, although by no means exclusively, a product of the KPD's relationship with Moscow. Just as the March action of 1921 had diverted attention from Soviet domestic and foreign difficulties, so the new KPD line complemented Lenin's New Economic Policy (NEP). In the interests of consolidating the revolution in Russia NEP encouraged improved political and economic relations with western Europe. The extent to which this handicapped the KPD was clearly shown in 1923, when the communists were inhibited from direct intervention for the greater part of the Republic's 'year of crisis'. SPD–KPD collaboration in the

---

27. O. Flechtheim, 'The role of the Communist party', p. 105. Cf. the picture given by R. Levine-Meyer, *Inside German Communism. Memoirs of Party Life in the Weimar Republic* (London, 1977).

28. For the USPD see H. Krause, *USPD* (Frankfurt–Cologne, 1975).

governments of Saxony and Thuringia did, indeed, produce defence organizations to counter the activities of the so-called 'Black Reichswehr'. Only in October, belatedly encouraged by Comintern, did the communists prepare to act. Their isolation in Germany was once more cruelly exposed. With minimal effort the Reichswehr inflicted a relatively bloodless but ultimately most decisive defeat on the KPD and deposed the governments in Saxony and Thuringia.

The pursuit of the 'united front'

After 1923 the KPD gave more attention to the ballot box. Its attempts to form a 'united front' with the SPD were reinforced by Stalin's desire for the unconditional support of foreign communist parties and their collaborators in his domestic struggles, first with Trotsky and then with the Soviet 'left'. From 1925 the KPD pursued its new goal of the 'concentration of forces' under the leadership of Ernst Thälmann. The trouble was that the KPD's erratic course between 1919 and 1925 progressively bureaucratized its leadership cliques, fostering the growth of dedicated functionaries who were seeking a tight control of the party organization from the lowest 'cell' upwards. The KPD's proclaimed policy of the 'united front' with the SPD did not allow it to abandon its pretension to be the sole representative of the industrial work force. In fact it made some small headway in the German labour movement as a whole after 1923.[29] The socialists remained distant and sceptical, if also uneasy about the pressure from the far left on their own position. The SPD's self-righteous aloofness helped to keep the German communists isolated but in 1928 the latter promptly executed another dramatic change of direction, echoing the Comintern's belief that the onset of the depression was ushering in the final crisis of world capitalism. Accordingly, the KPD was enjoined not to lag behind the 'rapidly self-radicalising masses' and the SPD was charged with having drifted far enough towards the right for its followers to be labelled 'social fascists'. The SPD leadership could hardly have wished for a more plausible self-justification for its aversion to collaborating with the KPD.

The rift was a culminating point in the long history of socialist discord and division in Germany. It coincided with a growth in electoral support for the KPD (77 seats in the Reichstag by 1930, 100

29. M. Ruck, *Die Freien Gewerkshaften im Ruhrkampf, 1923* (Cologne, 1986), p. 535. Also, F. Eisner, *Das Verhältnis der KPD zu den Gewerkschaften in der Weimarer Republik* (Cologne, 1977).

by 1932). The KPD following was now substantial enough to make it a genuine bogeyman for the right but its chances of leading the working class as a whole were as remote as ever.[30] Some observers even regard the belated success of the KPD at the polls as a *cause* of the Weimar Republic's decline, arguing that the party's totalitarian traits made the actions of the KPD complement those of the NSDAP. Indeed as early as the Ruhr crisis in 1923 the KPD endorsed the right's newest martyr, Albert Leo Schlageter, as 'a good soldier of the counter-revolution'. Later, in 1931, the KPD supported rightist efforts to unseat the 'Weimar coalition' in Prussia. The justification was that: 'the Braun–Severing government . . . is an executive organ of Brüning's policy' and against the interests of the workers.[31] Such actions deepened SPD cynicism about the 'united front' policy which the KPD claimed to desire against Hitler from 1932. In June of that year an internal KPD memo, acquired and published by *Vorwärts*, still identified the SPD as the main target.[32]

The KPD's role in the Weimar Republic

The KPD's role in the Weimar Republic cannot be assessed simply in terms of a misguided tactical odyssey towards deserved 'self-isolation'. Nor does regarding the German communists as merely creatures in Moscow's image fully account for their party's biting and apposite criticism of Weimar politics and society. Opposition to the 'bourgeois' Republic was precisely what made the KPD the beneficiary of youthful working-class hostility to the cuts and unemployment after 1928. The economic crisis itself, at least as much as KPD tactics, made for divisions within German labour. The KPD supporter was more likely than the SPD follower to be young, unskilled and above all unemployed. Unemployment itself thus further weakened the prospects for united working-class resistance to government policies through strikes. Of course the physical contribution of the KPD to the defence against National Socialism has long been acknowledged. The party had its para-military arm, the *Rote Frontkämpferbund*, formed by Thälmann in 1924, and its associated groups, the *Rote Jungfront* and *Rote Marine*. The KPD's familiar readiness to confront the National

30. See S. Bahne, *Die KPD und das Ende von Weimar. Das Scheitern einer Politik 1932–5* (Frankfurt–M, 1976).

31. R. Tosstorff, ' "Einheitsfront" und–oder "Nichtangriffspakt" mit der KPD' in W. Luthardt (ed.), *Sozialdemokratische Arbeiterbewegung und Weimarer Republik. Materialen zur gesellschaftlichen Entwicklung 1927–1933* (Frankfurt, 1978), p. 222.

32. Ibid, p. 239.

Socialists on the streets, for example, in the communist-controlled district of Hamburg, Altona, on 17 July 1932, also emphasized the profound ideological hostility between the KPD and NSDAP which underlay their respective tactical forays in late Weimar.

As well as attributing to communism the 'source of all evil' in its propaganda, the NSDAP specifically targeted communist-dominated enclaves. Here the KPD had to contend with the infiltration from SA *Sturmlokale*, 'part dormitory, part soup kitchen, part guardhouse'. The National Socialists penetrated workers' pubs too. The process has been graphically characterized as an attempt to push the unemployed, who had by definition lost their workplace, from their public space. In countering this, notably in the industrialized quarter of Wedding in north Berlin, one of the few areas with a communist majority in 1933, the KPD developed its activities at the welfare offices where the unemployed congregated.[33] Undoubtedly, the KPD was more aware of the full meaning of the Nazi threat to the working class than the SPD, with its traditional preoccupation with the centres of home and family. Finally, on the general relationship between SPD and KPD, it must be asked if the two parties could have collaborated closely enough to stop Hitler. Whilst the SPD's commitment to saving the Republic can hardly be doubted, the KPD's determination to end the established order was equally strong.[34] At the same time, because the KPD politicized issues and conflicts when the NSDAP was trying to depoliticize them, the KPD cannot be fairly charged with weakening the working-class movement. That task was accomplished above all by the National Socialists.

THE NATIONAL SOCIALIST GERMAN WORKERS' PARTY (*NATIONALSOZIALISTISCHE ARBEITER PARTEI* – NSDAP)

Hitler has bequeathed to posterity an astonishingly durable image of a demonic dictator leading the German nation towards war and ruination in a Wagnerian climax. To question this impression is to dispute neither Hitler's paramount role in the NSDAP nor his share of the burden for the policies which brought about the Second World

---

33. Rosenhaft, 'Working class life' and Tosstorff, ' "Einheitsfront" ', pp. 207ff.
34. Cf. arguments in T. Kurz, *Blutmai. Sozialdemokraten und Kommunisten im Brennpunkt der Berliner Ereignisse von 1929* (Berlin–Bonn, 1988), p. 96.

War. There was more to the National Socialist Party, however, than the history of Adolf Hitler. Its path to power involved much that was banal, provincial and boring, as well as downright alarming – qualities all much in evidence at the fringe of *völkisch* politics from which the German Workers' Party emerged in January 1919 (rechristened the National Socialist German Workers' Party, or NSDAP, in February 1920).

One of the two co-founders of the party, Karl Harrer, belonged to the Thule Society, the headquarters of the *völkisch* movement in Bavaria. Hitler's memorable pen sketch of the early DAP in its 'pathetic little room in a small pub', with at most 17 marks in the kitty, partly served to highlight his own impact after he joined Harrer and his colleague Anton Drexler in September 1919. It now seems likely that Hitler was prompted to assume more control over the NSDAP only in 1921, when discussions about fusing it with the disparate elements of the *völkisch* movement threatened his party's distinct identity and therefore his own position.[35] Hitler's success in resisting this by exploiting his unique value to the NSDAP as a public speaker and propagandist is well known. From the end of July 1921, Hitler became party chairman with new powers, unshackled by any committee. The headquarters of the NSDAP were decreed as being in Munich. In this capital of anti-republicanism, alive with bitter memories of the short-lived revolutionary Eisner regime in Bavaria, Hitler and his cohorts enjoyed a relatively favoured environment, patronized by local dignitaries in 'the bohemian circles, salons and associations of patriotic Munich'.[36]

The NSDAP soon gained a twenty-five point programme, drafted in 1920 almost certainly by Hitler and Drexler. It contained, on the one hand, a mixture of nationalistic, pan-German, racist, anti-Semitic, anti-Marxist and anti-liberal ideas appealing to a broad swathe of German political opinion. This embraced not only the *völkisch–* nationalist right but also, as we have suggested, sections of the German conservative parliamentary parties. Although rooted in the pre-war period, these values exercised a more potent attraction after the experience of war and defeat. Regeneration of Germandom, the rejection of the Versailles Treaty and the union of all Germans in a 'Greater Germany' figured prominently in the party programme. On

35. A. Tyrell, *Vom 'Trommler' zum 'Führer'. Der Wandel von Hitlers Selbstverständnis zwischen 1919 und 1924 und die Entwicklung der NSDAP* (Munich, 1975).

36. M. Broszat, *The Hitler State. The Foundation and Development of the Internal Structure of the Third Reich* (London, 1981), p. 3.

the other hand, the document demonstrated 'socialist' concerns for the work and welfare of the individual, for sharing the profits of large-scale industry, as well as for nationalization and land reform in the interests of the 'community' as a whole. It presented itself as a 'national' and a 'socialist' manifesto.

Hitler's preference for a more disciplined party structure was not matched by the reality of life in the branches struggling into being in less congenial conditions outside Bavaria. Bruno Wenzel and Gustav Seifert, who established the first tributary of the NSDAP in northern Germany in the summer of 1921, were not untypical of such lesser-known early local Nazi leaders. Surveying their new Hanover organization (the twenty-fourth offshoot of the NSDAP) they counted 13 members. After a massive expenditure of effort, rippling out into Lower Saxony and nearby Brunswick, the Hanover constituents still numbered a mere 324 in November 1922.[37] Similar tales could be told about the other early groups surfacing beyond Bavaria, for example, in Mannheim and Dortmund or in Nuremberg. Here the infamous Julius Streicher first flexed his political muscles as leader of the new branch of the NSDAP founded in October 1922.[38] The history of the NSDAP is also the history of such activists. Some of them came to head the various *Gaue* (regions) into which the NSDAP divided Germany for organizational purposes. From 1928 these numbered 35, and corresponded to the Reichstag electoral districts.

Studies of the *Gauleiter* have given a picture of older men invariably reaching maturity before 1914 (in contrast to the youthful membership of the NSDAP as a whole in the mid-1920s). For most of them enlistment during the First World War either disrupted their further education or prevented them from gaining professional experience before the conflict ended. In spite of, or because of this, a principal category among the early *Gau* leaders was that of former teachers or trainee teachers; another large group comprised clerical workers. But a completed higher education was, unsurprisingly, rare. Notable exceptions included Joseph Goebbels, *Gauleiter* of Berlin from 1926, and Robert Ley, future Labour Front Leader in the Third Reich.

---

37. J. F. Farquharson, 'The NSDAP in Hannover and Lower Saxony', *Journal of Contemporary History*, 8 (1973): 103ff.

38. R. Lenman, 'Julius Streicher and the origins of the NSDAP in Nuremberg 1918–1933' in A. Nicholls and E. Matthias (eds), *German Democracy and the Triumph of Hitler* (London, 1971), pp. 140ff. Other regional studies include G. Paul, *Die NSDAP des Saargebietes, 1920–30* (Saarbrücken, 1987); R. Hambrecht, *Der Aufstieg der NSDAP in Mittel- und Oberfranken* (Nuremberg, 1976); W Boehnke, *Die NSDAP im Ruhrgebiet 1920–1933* (Bonn, 1974).

Many *Gauleiter* had fought in a freikorps or border defence unit after the war had ended and none was from a purely proletarian background. 'In most cases the wrench from the normal middle-class vocational existence caused by the war and post-war formed the background of those who were active as organizers and leaders in the NSDAP.'[39] They were without question a politically tough-minded bunch of individuals.

The strength of the *Gauleiter* rested on their critical role in sustaining the party organization in the mid-1920s, and on their adroitness in managing other party officials below them in the neighbourhood. Differences with headquarters over tactics and ideology were inevitable, particularly during Hitler's imprisonment following his abortive coup in 1923. The developing sections of the movement in northern and western Germany resented Munich's pretensions at the best of times. After Hitler's release and the refounding of the party on 27 February 1925, it required all his skill to paper over the cracks which had appeared in the Munich headquarters and the party as a whole. Inexorably, the *interpretation* of the party programme became an integral part of Munich's control mechanism. In 1926 Hitler successfully blocked the 'socialist' revisions demanded by the 'Working Group of the North and West German *Gaue*', under Gregor Strasser and Joseph Goebbels, by declaring the NSDAP's programme to be immutable.

Policy versus organization?

Hitler's ruling in 1926 is invariably regarded as evidence of his determination to avoid weakening the NSDAP through public wrangling over policy detail. However, the argument that lack of precision in policy was more helpful than harmful to the advance of the movement is misleading, particularly if taken to imply that 'ideology' did not matter. In the first place, the programme *did* have real and immediate significance for the *völkisch* groups. The overlap between their world view and the 1920 Programme remained obvious. This is no mere academic point. The expansion of the NSDAP during the difficult years between 1923 and the breakthrough to a mass electorate came from the assimilation of *völkisch* supporters. Secondly, the refounded party's commitment to following the 'legal' road to power through the electoral process demanded that it stand for *something*. Here the striking feature is how much energy the NSDAP

39. Broszat, *Hitler State*, p. 33.

expended on putting over the message to the electorate that it offered radical policy alternatives, as the re-forming of the SA in the autumn of 1926 underlined.

The *Sturmabteilung* (SA), originally created in August 1921 to maintain order at party meetings and to conduct propaganda, inevitably attracted former military personnel and ex-freikorps leaders to its ranks as well as more youthful party adherents. It became plain that the SA was sufficiently dynamic to engender political aspirations. Personnel changes at the leadership level reflected difficulties in preventing the SA from becoming either an autonomous paramilitary force or a body of revolutionary conspirators. Under the title '*Frontbann*' it survived an interdiction for its part in the 1923 Putsch but its future became the object of dispute between its leader, Röhm, and Hitler in 1925. Thereafter wearing its famous brown uniform, it was led until 1930 by Franz Pfeffer von Salomon.[40] Hitler informed von Pfeffer of his view of the SA's role: 'It must not meet in secret but should march in the open air . . . What we need is not a hundred or two hundred daring conspirators, but a hundred thousand and hundreds of thousands more fanatical fighters for our *Weltanschauung* . . . We have to teach Marxism that National Socialism is the future master of the streets, just as it will one day be master of the state.'[41] The SA was intended to be the handmaiden of the party organization, not the other way round.

Amidst the restrictions imposed on the NSDAP during the Republic's middle life, however, it could only exist as a polycentric organization. Hitler's wish to avoid wasting energy through internal wrangling could not therefore prevent continuing concern for 'ideology' and policy. This obvious point is obscured by emphasizing too much Hitler's charismatic leadership, or by an understandable reluctance to analyse thoroughly the disagreeable ideas system of National Socialism, or even by overlooking the beliefs of Nazis other than Hitler.[42] Ultimately, these would have been of little consequence if the party had remained in obscurity. As it is, discussion of what the NSDAP's ideology was must overlap with the more fundamental

40. Cf. C. Fischer, *Stormtroopers. A Social and Ideological Analysis 1929–1935* (London, 1983), pp. 4–5.

41. Cited in J. Noakes and G. Pridham (eds), *Documents on Nazism 1919–1945* (London, 1974), p. 87.

42. For the importance of ideas, E. Jaeckl, *Hitlers Weltanschauung* (Tübingen, 1969) and *Hitlers Herrschaft. Vollzug einer Weltanschauung* (Stuttgart, 1986). On ideas of other Nazis, B. Miller-Lane and L. J. Rupp (eds), *Nazi Ideology before 1933. A Documentation* (Manchester, 1978).

question about what the NSDAP itself 'was' as it became a mass movement. The party's growth alone, by increasingly demanding priorities of control, policy and direction, exacerbated the tensions outlined above between the 'old fighters' of the NSDAP.

The party's composition

A major problem in estimating the extent of those committed enough to become early members of the NSDAP (as distinct from those who merely voted Nazi) is that personnel fluctuated. For example, the NSDAP had about 3,000 members registered by the date of its first congress in January 1921, but 850,000 by 1933. Yet the figures record only those joining the party, not those subsequently leaving it. The widely used official party statistics of 1935 are problematic to interpret for similar reasons, offering snapshots of total membership at three points, in September 1930, January 1933 and January 1935.[43] Equally, attempts to assess accurately the class basis of party membership have been confounded by the self-perceptions of the members in returning their occupational status. Alternatively, as in the case of the party's Munich parent cell, studies have been flawed by the absence of a comparative yardstick for the Reich as a whole.[44] And of course, after 1933 Germans could and did join the NSDAP for reasons other than total conviction. These so-called 'March violets' and the 7 million members registered by the middle of the War are not, therefore, necessarily informative about the nature of the movement in the 1920s.

Not until it became a mass party could the NSDAP's voting support be meaningfully compared with its membership. Nevertheless, membership lists long played a major part in sustaining the idea that the NSDAP was nourished by predominantly Protestant, lower-middle class elements who had been marginalized and therefore radicalized as a result of Germany's advancing industrialization.[45] The thesis about the 'lower-middle class' nature of the NSDAP proved extraordinarily influential precisely because much of the evidence adduced for it was superficially plausible. Modest, bourgeois, prudent, fixed-income,

43. P. Manstein, *Die Mitglieder und Wähler der NSDAP 1919–1933* (Frankfurt, New York, etc., 1988), p. 152.

44. D. M. Douglas, 'The parent cell. Some computor notes on the composition of the first Nazi Party group in Munich, 1919–1921', *Central European History*, 10 (1977): 55–62.

45. See the English version of an early classic, H. Speier, *German White Collar Workers and the Rise of Hitler* (Yale, 1987).

inflation-damaged employees, savers and investors had already been attracted to the 'brown movement' in the 1923 financial collapse. The second surge in the NSDAP's electoral fortunes during the Great Depression of 1929 confirmed the importance of economic crisis to the advance of Hitlerism.

The breakthrough which the party achieved in the 1930 elections was spectacular. Its share of the vote soared from 2.8 per cent in the 1928 Reichstag elections to 18.3 per cent in 1930. The NSDAP had no fewer than 107 seats in the Reichstag. In the elections of July 1932 the respective figures were 37.4 per cent and 230, and in the November polls of that year, 33 per cent and 196. In general, the results of the 1930s elections showed the NSDAP to be stronger on the north German plain and in the south-east, except for the cities and the great industrial centres, and weaker in the south-west, including Bavaria. The resistance of Catholicism to National Socialist appeals was also apparent in the predominantly Catholic south and west during the polling in July 1932. In the elections held in March 1933, after Hitler had become Chancellor, the NSDAP proved to be strongest in East Prussia, with 50–59 per cent of the vote. In none of the Reichstag electoral districts did it go above 56 per cent of the vote and in the industrial west it was below 40 per cent.[46]

The general limits to the NSDAP's electoral appeal, apparently set by Catholicism and 'workers', appeared then to be broadly consistent with earlier classic accounts, like that by Speier, stressing the role of the lower middle class; artisans and shopkeepers – 'little men' squashed between big capital and organized labour; small businessmen appalled at cartelization and unable to stand the pace of economic change. Apart from such 'old' self-employed middle classes, attention was directed at the 'new' elements – white-collar workers of one sort or another, members of the army of modern state civil servants springing up from the last part of the nineteenth century or other salaried employees. Even some contemporary accounts, however, already questioned the sufficiency of that explanation, by stressing the sheer range and depth of protest behind Hitlerism. Modern historians have returned to the subject with a vengeance. Of course, they are unable to question directly voter preference, a shortcoming for which more sophisticated sampling techniques cannot compensate. Statisticians also like to point out, for example, that a larger sample of voters is not necessarily more representative. Thus Childers's valuable study of the

46. See M. Freeman's useful charts and diagrams, *Atlas of Nazi Germany* (London, 1987), pp. 11ff.

Nazi voter, even though it looks at 200 urban and 300 rural constituencies, leaves out almost 50 per cent of the electorate.[47] Hamilton examines the voting records of 14 of the 23 largest German cities, but concentrates on towns in the west, apart from Berlin.[48]

It was axiomatic for those propounding the thesis about the lower-middle-class nature of the NSDAP that working-class support for Hitlerism was minimal. Once more, though, the issue was partly confused by the self-perception individual voters had of themselves and of their status. This, as well as the actual situation of a voter and the extent of National Socialist electioneering, could influence choice at the polls. An insistence on rigid occupational categories can therefore distort the interpretation of questions about the nature and extent of middle-class support. It is often stressed, to take a notable example already raised earlier, that middle-class voters cherished their hard-won social, educational and other advantages including their monthly salaries, and that they turned towards Hitler to save them from a dreaded loss of status; they feared a decline to the proletarian ranks during economic crisis. Yet while a fifth of the National Socialist membership was indeed from such 'white-collar workers', others in this category flirted with socialism after 1918; a quarter of them continued to support the left-wing Afa–Bund. Marginalized elements of the middle class were likely to vote socialist and to be in trade unions. It is inaccurate to describe workers as gentrified if they have not in fact abandoned their working-class milieu, a point which has been made above all about the so-called 'new' middle classes.

Such arguments find support from a reconsidering of the well-known correlation between the electoral decline of the traditional bourgeois parties and the ascendancy of the NSDAP. The DVP, most notably, represented the wealthy middle classes; the above average National Socialist votes were returned in the wealthy middle-class districts, rather than in mixed neighbourhoods, where old party loyalties persisted to a greater extent. None of these findings, it is true, has fundamentally challenged the idea that the middle classes as a whole were, in comparison with their numerical percentage of the German population, over-represented in the NSDAP. Whether the National Socialists ever got a *majority* of lower-middle-class voters has been questioned.[49] Conversely, the weakening of the thesis about

47. T. Childers, *The Nazi Voter. The Social Foundations of Fascism in Germany 1919–1933* (Chapel Hill, London, 1983).
48. R. Hamilton, *Who Voted for Hitler?* (New Jersey, 1982).
49. Manstein, *Mitglieder und Wähler*, p. 199.

lower-middle-class support for Hitler brought a reaction against confining the label 'worker' to the eight million factory labourers in a total of some sixteen million 'wage-earners', thereby underestimating 'blue-collar' support for National Socialism.

In general the large industrial centres and cities were not particularly fertile recruiting grounds for the NSDAP. Moreover, those overwhelmingly affected by unemployment were manual workers and the NSDAP did best after 1928 in those places where unemployment was lowest. In general, the organized working class *was* more resistant to National Socialist appeals – before 1933 at least. Yet economic crisis and unemployment weakened the solidarity of labour. Conventionally, a large number of those who deserted the labour movement with the onset of unemployment were thought to have joined the SA, which one study even argued was predominantly working-class.[50] There may be legitimate reservations about the representative nature of the districts on which these finding are based. It verges on wishful thinking, however, to contend that all those workers who joined the SA did so for employment rather than out of sympathy for National Socialism.[51] Some workers may have acted so, as some KPD and SPD members seem to have joined the Nazis to fight within the movement. Yet on the whole it is sensible not to lose sight of the fact that people invariably join movements because they support them.

Since newer analyses of Nazi electoral support tend to blur the line between the category of 'worker' and *Angestellte* (employee), it is advisable to qualify the argument that in 1928 Hitler 'abandoned' the pursuit of the urban working-class in favour of a strategy concentrating on winning over the Mittelstand and the rural voter. The party did indeed perceive and stress the importance of the rural vote, for the agricultural sector was divided by crisis and government policy after 1928. Undoubtedly, the NSDAP was a beneficiary of the unrest and dislocation in the countryside which caused party allegiances to dissolve and change rapidly. Farmers voted in huge numbers for Hitler from 1929 onwards. Yet it was not until 1930 that the NSDAP produced a programme for agriculture. It is more likely, therefore, that after 1928 the NSDAP wanted to keep what working-class support it already had, as well as gaining new bases.

The party had after all a long if somewhat inconsistent record of

50. C. Fischer, *Stormtroopers*, pp. 25ff, 67, and 'The SA of the NSDAP. Social background and ideology of the rank and file in the early 1930s', *Journal of Contemporary History*, 17 (1982): 651ff.

51. R. Bessel and M. Jamin, 'Problems of research. Nazis, workers and the uses of quantitative evidence', *Social History*, 4 (1979): 111ff.

cultivating the labour constituency. Between 1919 and 1923, a cadre in the party including Drexler and the Austro-Bohemians espoused workers'˙ interests whilst many of the early *völkisch* groups had working-class members. Although the abortive 1923 putsch weakened the 'left wing' of the party, a number of key Nazis made attempts to woo the working-class voters. Gregor Strasser's unpublished programme of 1925 was one obvious example, as was the activity of Joseph Goebbels. Hitler's Bamberg ruling in 1926 did not mean that the NSDAP's 'left' disappeared. Ultimately, pressure from within the party contributed to the setting up of the National Socialist Factory Cells (*Nationalsozialistische Betriebszellen-Organisation* – NSBO), designed to penetrate the working-class organizations at the shop floor level. There may have been as many as 100,000 NSBO members by mid-1932. Although the National Socialists could not win a majority among working-class voters, it did well in the elections of 1930.[52] Between 1930 and 1932 the party continued to stress the abuses of capitalism. There was much talk about profit-sharing and the Hitler movement demonstrated a deep commitment to heavy public spending as a solution to unemployment. Of course, this has to be set against the background of a continuing and increasingly violent attack on the 'Marxist' left.

The National Socialist constituency

Whilst disagreement persists on the extent of working-class backing for Hitler, and indeed on many of the above issues, the surge in electoral studies and class analyses has underscored the NSDAP's achievement in securing such a wide range of votes in a multi-party system – right across the class spectrum. There is now a better understanding of the slow process of formation of such a Nazi constituency during the 1920s. As the inclination to argue that the NSDAP's success was almost exclusively the product of the 'panic of the middle classes' has waned, so all the more importance has been attached to the organizational dynamism of the NSDAP from the mid-1920s, and to its success in chipping away at the foundations of the Weimar political system. Door-to-door campaigning was constant; there were mail shots, posters and slide shows.[53] Admittedly, specific local economic conditions and the state of the district or regional labour market were

52. It is possible to greatly exaggerate worker support, as M. Kele did, *Nazis and Workers. National Socialist Appeals to German Labour* (Chapel Hill, 1972).

53. T. Childers (ed.), *The Formation of the National Socialist Constituency 1918–1933* (London, Sydney, 1986).

important in determining receptivity to National Socialist appeals. The dynamism of the movement as well as Hitler's own charisma remained important. At another level, the NSDAP devoted effort to working within localities and with the grain of established social structures. Ties were cultivated with local worthies, such as the mayors or the chairmen of the ex-service associations. NSDAP members took part in local sports clubs, student societies, professional associations, even choral societies, thus making a 'patterned network' of social life.

In such apolitical settings a political ideology was slowly nurtured and the NSDAP promised to heal the increasingly worrying splits in society's ranks.[54] The party was thereby creating what has been termed a socio-moral environment. It deliberately tried to attach to itself members of different interests or professions, encouraging the formation of a veritable flood of affiliated associations and organizations after the party's refounding in 1925. Apart from the familiar youth organizations, above all the Hitler Youth, the party's cause progressed rapidly in German universities amongst the student associations. A network of interest organizations emerged after the formation of the party's first professional association, The Association of National Socialist Jurists, in October 1928. It was soon joined by the National Socialist Association of German Physicians, the National Socialist Teachers' Association and many, many more. At the same time, links were forged between the NSDAP and major economic groupings, particularly those embracing white-collar workers and farmers.

By the beginning of the 1930s the NSDAP rested on a highly diverse constituency. In the popular mind it was being perceived as classless, although here we have focused in particular on the issue of support from the middle classes and workers. The backing of the latter was significant, even if an imbalance persisted within the movement in favour of the former. At the same time the NSDAP displayed an impressive ability to transcend all social barriers which far outstripped the performance of other German political parties. To achieve this the party had to stand for something, although many doubtless accepted uncritically the need for a 'strong' leader on emotional and other grounds.[55] At any rate, the more detailed knowledge of the National Socialist constituency, of the party's electioneering techniques and its

---

54. R. Koshar, 'Two "Nazisms". The social context of Nazi mobilisation in Marburg and Tübingen', *Social History*, 7 (1982): 27–42; R. Koshar, *Social Life, Local Politics and Nazism. Marburg 1880–1935* (Chapel Hill, 1986).

55. For an interesting view of the pulp literature on Teutonic virtues and a 'redeemer'-like figure, see J. Hermand, *Der alte Traum vom neuen Reich. Völkische Utopien und Nationalsozialismus* (Frankfurt, 1988).

mobilization of support at community level, have enabled the historian to give more differentiated answers to the question, 'who voted for Hitler?' Disagreements persist but an additional gain from examining the slow, complex formation of the NSDAP constituency is that it further lessens the temptation to see the Republic as destroyed largely at the whims of conspiratorial cliques.

CHAPTER FOUR
The Practice of Parliament

COALITION PATTERNS

The moderate parties profiled in the first part of the previous chapter ultimately failed to forge a permanent relationship in the divisive twenties. They were, however, more than mere 'interest' parties, particularly when compared with the irresponsible and dangerous factions which came to litter the republican political scene like confetti. It was precisely because the DDP, SPD, Centre and DVP began to function as 'bridges' between different political persuasions that they became targets for anti-parliamentary extremists. Two promising combinations of political parties were the so-called 'Weimar Coalition' and the 'Great Coalition'. The first embraced the SPD, DDP and Centre and the second included in addition the DVP. The Weimar coalition formed the basis of five out of the six governments between February 1919 and August 1923. The tasks confronting these early cabinets were formidable and a stark reality clouded the horizon. The three parties of the Weimar coalition – who had combined forces in 1917 to pass the famous peace resolution, who formed the first genuine parliamentary government in October 1918 and who enjoyed the support of three-quarters of the German electorate in 1919 – were placed in a minority by the first Reichstag elections in 1920. It was against this background that governments coped with threats from right and left, political assassinations, the acceptance and initial execution of peace terms which were loathed inside the Reich, and a mounting fiscal and economic crisis that overwhelmed Germany in 1923.

Although the government resorted to Article 48 of the constitution, the head of the Reichswehr, General Hans von Seeckt, obediently if reluctantly stood by the head of state. The traumatic emergency of 1923 was resolved by the formation of the Great Coalition and Gustav Stresemann courageously committed his party to the now well-known stabilization process. Economic reconstruction and an improved basis for the conduct of foreign policy duly followed. This alone refutes the facile interpretation of the 1920 elections as an expression of a 'Republic without republicans', as does the view from the regions, where the continuing forces of parliamentarianism sustained democratic administrations, for example in Hesse, Württemberg and Darmstadt. In the case of Prussia, a 'region' occupying three-quarters of the territory of the German Reich, threats such as that from the rightist Kapp putsch in 1920 acted as a catalyst to weld together the Prussian wings of the DVP, Centre and SPD. Prussia also demonstrated that changing administrations (four Minister Presidents in Prussia in the first seven years of the Republic) did not necessarily cause political instability. A well-governed, stable Prussia, where 'pragmatists rather than ideologues dominated the state's political scene', played a major part in the survival of the Weimar Republic as a whole in the first half of the 1920s.[1] The Prussian experience was still more of an obstacle to anti-parliamentary interests during the second half of the Republic's life. Its example casts doubt on the entrenched argument that the mere survival of the socio-economic system of Wilhelmine Germany was a *cause* of parliamentary failure. The survival of old elites, particularly in the eastern provinces of Prussia, did not prevent constitutional progress in the *Land* as such.

In Prussia, unlike in the Reich, the parliamentary body (*Landtag*) was alone responsible for choosing the Minister President and for resolving party disputes. The long tradition of separatism in Germany was expressed in the Weimar constitution and Prussia could, like the other *Länder*, influence the central government for the better. The *Reichsrat* represented the regions and with the exception of Thuringia the *Länder* had been able to resist plans to change their boundaries. Of course, their federal association with the Reich after 1919 demoted them from the sovereign states they had been in the German Empire. The process naturally curtailed the powers of the *Reichsrat* as a second house. Reich laws continued to take precedence over those of the *Land* administrations. Nonetheless, powers of direct legislation

---

1. D. Orlow, *Weimar Prussia 1918–25. The Unlikely Rock of Democracy* (London, 1986). Cf. A. Glees, 'Albert C. Grzesinski and the politics of Prussia, 1926–30', *English Historical Review*, 353 (1974): 814–34.

accorded to the central government after 1919 left important sources of influence with the regional governments, notably in the realms of education, the judiciary and – of critical importance in view of later events – the police. The *Reichsrat*'s power of veto over the Reichstag's measures could be disabled by a two-thirds majority in the lower chamber, but it was a potentially useful restraint.

None of this is to deny the seriousness of problems persisting in the central parliamentary arena during the middle years of the Republic. Difficulties included the alienation of voters from the responsible parties, the increasing fragmentation of political life and the obscure, erratic but none the less continuing advance of National Socialism at the grass-roots level of political life. After 1923, as before, governments changed as often as the seasons. There were twenty-one admin-istrations between June 1920 and March 1930. Of these only four enjoyed an express vote of confidence from the Reichstag. They were the first and second governments headed by Gustav Stresemann (1923), Luther's second cabinet (1926) and Marx's fourth (January 1927–June 1928). Still more remarkable, of the 21 governments only three had a majority in the Reichstag, those of Stresemann in 1923 and the second cabinet headed by Müller during the 20 months prior to March 1930. Such chilling statistics partly explain why historians have suggested confining the term 'parliamentary government' to the years between 1924 and 1930.[2]

Statistics alone give an inadequate picture of the way in which coalition experience developed in the troubled post-war period, or of how parties rose to the occasion at times of crisis. In this respect Stresemann was one of several major politicians who worked for the Republic's survival in the early years. Others included Joseph Wirth, Walther Rathenau and Matthias Erzberger – all men whose careers disprove the later charges of Hitler that the Republic produced only weak politicians. Stresemann's influence was, however, paramount. His two cabinets between August and the end of November 1923 brought about the all-important partnership in the Great Coalition of the SPD and DVP, 'spokesmen' respectively for labour and industry. A wide recognition in Germany of the need for economic recovery and stable finances partly explains why the fierce opposition of the nationalists (DNVP) did less harm than it might otherwise have done to these early coalitions of moderate parties. The effects of inflation were too capricious and uneven to conclude that the 1923 crisis induced an immediate turn against the Republic.

2 Cf. M. Stürmer, *Koalition und Opposition in der Weimarer Republik 1924–1928* (Düsseldorf, 1967).

INTERLUDE – THE ELECTION OF PRESIDENT HINDENBURG

Two years later, the death of Friedrich Ebert precipitated new elections for Reich President. When the socialist hero and co-founder of the Republic was succeeded, in the second round of presidential elections, by Paul von Hindenburg, the military leader who had resisted parliamentary government in Wilhelmine Germany, the Republic's obituarists sharpened their pencils. Yet the die was not cast against the Republic, and the episode repays a more detailed examination before returning to the broader picture of Weimar politics.

Otto Gessler, the Minister of Defence, came very near in the early days of the proceedings to being endorsed by the moderate parties as a whole. A Catholic as well as a member of the DDP, he could count on the support of the Centre Party and of republicans in general. Moreover, since he had defended the interests of the Reichswehr he enjoyed some sympathy in rightist circles too. Ultimately, Gessler's candidature was blocked by Stresemann's justified objections about the adverse affect of the Defence Minister's election on Franco-German relations. In the absence of an agreed bourgeois candidate the various parties proceeded to nominate their own choices, thus presenting the German people with no fewer than seven aspirants on 29 March 1925. Karl Jarres, the candidate of the DVP and DNVP, received 10.7 million votes; Otto Braun, SPD, 7.8 million; Wilhelm Marx, Centre, 3.9 million; Willy Hugo Hellpach, DDP, 1.5 million. The BVP candidate, Heinrich Held, had 1 million votes; the KPD picked up 1.8 million. The party most devoted to the ending of parliamentary democracy in Germany, the NSDAP, could muster only a risible 200,000 votes for their man, Erich Ludendorff. By contrast, support for the three 'Weimar' parties totalled 13.3 million. Ideally, this combination should have defeated the right in the second ballot, when numerical superiority was required for victory.

Hindenburg's late entry to the presidential stakes prevented this. The DNVP, needless to say, supported Hindenburg. Since he was at least as likely to upset French sensitivities as would Gessler, Stresemann's reluctant endorsement of Hindenburg must be seen in the context of his attempts to implicate the nationalists in government. Ranged against this so-called *Reichsbloc* was the *Volksbloc*, comprising the SPD, Centre and DDP, whose candidate was Wilhelm Marx. Again – and why should German politicians be different from those of other nations? – short-sightedness, vanity and downright hostility were in evidence. Many Protestant liberal voters could not bring themselves to vote for the Catholic Marx. Conversely, the BVP, while with the Centre on Church policy in general, voted for Protestant Hindenburg because they could not abide Marx's working relationship with social democracy. Within the SPD ranks, particularly in Thuringia and Saxony, residual antagonism to the confessional nature of Centre Party politics caused the switch of some socialist votes to either Hindenburg or Ernst Thaelmann (KPD). Right-wing, monarchist elements in the Centre Party opted for Hindenburg rather than for Marx, a tendency aggravated by a grumbling concern of Catholics about the SPD's education policy. Finally, the KPD's insistence on maintaining their own candidate tipped the balance against Marx. Hindenburg was elected on 26 April 1925, securing 14.6 million votes against the 13.7 million cast for his opponent.

There were, however, positive aspects of the presidential elections. The SPD and DDP had abandoned their individual candidates when it became vital to do so. In the face of the barrage of anti-Catholic propaganda against Marx from the Protestant establishment behind the DNVP, key liberal evangelical theologians, like Ernst Troeltsch, Adolf von Harnack, Otto Baumgarten, Friedrich Naumann and Martin Rade were moved to develop a spirited plea for the Republic. Baumgarten's article in the *Frankfurter Zeitung*, 'For Marx, come what may', was noteworthy by any standard. Interpreting the final vote, which was close in itself, is more problematic than many have admitted. First, Hindenburg's commitment to the *office* of president has hardly been questioned. His preference was for a government of the right but this still depended in the first instance on parliamentary realities. Secondly, precisely Hindenburg's popular fame as an ageing war hero makes it unwise automatically to interpret support for him as manifestly anti-Republican. Erich Eyck's older but classic study of the Weimar Republic is simply misleading when at this point it argues: 'No matter how Hindenburg might comport himself in the immediate future, his election as president for Germany was a triumph of nationalism and militarism and a heavy defeat for the Republic and parliamentary government.'

On the contrary, the presidential election is interesting because it shows how finely balanced was the tussle between party and state interests during the Republic's mid-life; it perfectly illustrates that tantalizing see-saw between promise and failure so characteristic of Weimar Germany until almost the very end.

SECTIONAL INTERESTS IN POLITICS

Reverting to the general sweep of Weimar politics, it is clear that the crisis of 1923 did boost the efforts of sectional interests to penetrate the political system, not least because of the disputes about how best to bear the burden of the new reparations settlement of 1924, the Dawes plan. Large and powerful organizations already existed, like the National Association of German Industry (*Reichsverband der deutschen Industrie* – RDI) or the Agrarian League (*Landbund*), which had close ties respectively with the DVP and the DNVP. There were also such influential pressure groups as the German National Union of Commercial Employees, the German Civil Service Union (*Deutscher Beamtenbund*). In addition, the second half of the 1920s brought a surge in middle-class political formations. The Reichstag elections of 1924 indicated the electorate's impatience with not only the DDP and DVP but also the DNVP. New bourgeois parties such as the Business Party (*Wirtschaftspartei*), the Reich Party for People's Right and Evaluation (1926), as well as other splinter parties, comprised twelve per cent of the vote by the time of the 1928 Reichstag elections. Mention could be made too of the German Peasant's Party, the Christian National Peasants' and Farmers' Party, the Christian Social People's Service, the Conservative People's Party – and more besides.

It is helpful to set this array of parties against the broader, traditional pattern of German politics. In general, the long-term cleavage in the German Empire between, on the one hand, socialists and, on the other, liberals and conservatives, persisted after 1918, although competition between the latter increased for the vote of the urban middle classes. The electoral map also continued to reflect broad religious differences. As to the smaller interest groups, these too had been prominent earlier, appealing to occupational or shared economic interests. Purporting to be non-political, they could in fact be rabidly anti-socialist and nationalistic. Lurking at the fringes of the main blocs of voters, they confirmed the fragmentation of the German political system as a result of Germany's transformation into one of the world's leading industrial powers. Although not statistically significant in the 1919 and 1920 elections, making up respectively only two per cent and three per cent of the vote, it was from this fringe that the NSDAP would mount its challenge. However, none of the broad cleavages indicated here predetermined the day-to-day political round. The interest groups and hyperactive coalition building do not themselves justify analysing the political life of the Weimar Republic as a whole in terms of 'dissolution'.[3] It was surely preferable to have vociferous opposition within the Reichstag rather than outside waging the politics of violence; better to heckle a political leader than to shoot him; preferable for powerful interests in agriculture and industry to have to try to work through the parties. Behind the uneasy fragmentation of political life there was some continuity of administration provided by the civil service – often wrongly seen as automatically bad for parliament. In addition the same parties were invariably involved in the different governments. Five of the seven cabinets between 1923 and 1928 included the DVP, Centre and Democrats. The remaining two briefly involved the DNVP (in 1926 and 1928).

The general pattern of government in the mid- to late 1920s was profoundly affected by the SPD's reversion to opposition until it helped to form the Great Coalition again in 1928, under its own leader, Herman Müller. Between 1923 and 1928, therefore, moderate governments were in a minority and had to conduct business by making concessions either to the right (DNVP) or to the left (SPD). On the other hand, although the right could muster a numerical majority in the Reichstag, it contained many divergent and conflicting elements within it. In practice, therefore, government was based on achieving different majorities for different problems. This was less disruptive than it could have been, in that during the Weimar Republic's entire life only two governments were forced to leave office as a result of a vote of non-confidence. Two factors among many were important here. The first concerned the nature of the SPD's opposition. The second related to at least a workable degree of consensus between the major parties and interest groups on several important policy matters.

The class conflict within Germany was a major determinant of political instability in the long run and it was given a new dimension after 1923. The impact of the economic crisis made it imperative that the parliamentary parties most obviously representing two sides of the conflict, namely the SPD and DVP, should preserve a working political relationship beyond the demise of the first Great Coalition in 1923. Stresemann sought to capitalize on this politically in proclaiming his duty: 'to do all I can to unite the German people . . . and not to force upon them the question bourgeois or socialist'.[4] Foreign policy helped in this respect. The goal of *Verständigung* pursued by

3. See L. E. Jones, *German Liberalism and the Dissolution of the Weimar Party System* (Chapel Hill, 1988).
4. See H. A. Turner Jr, *Stresemann and the politics of the Weimar Republic* (Princeton, 1963), p. 164.

Stresemann with the Western powers had the solid backing not only of the Centre and DDP but of the SPD. In the words of the socialist journal, *Vorwärts*, commenting on the Locarno negotiations in 1925: 'The question of European security is of such overriding importance that it must be separated from domestic issues.'[5] In effect, the SPD postponed final confrontation with the right over such important disputes as taxation and customs, in the national interest. Irrespective of formal political arrangements made in the Reichstag, SPD collaboration with the middle groups over foreign policy remained a remarkable and valuable constant of Weimar politics.

The premise on which this rested, however, was that undue concessions were not made to the right, although some collaboration with the DNVP was essential for economic recovery to take place. In this instance Stresemann derived some benefit from the obvious importance of the policy of *Verständigung* for Germany's economic renewal. Although the DNVP as a whole favoured resisting the Allied peace terms, a minority within the party urged tactical collaboration with Stresemann over foreign policy in order to secure the general economic rewards of expanded trade following the Dawes plan, as well as to wrest concessions from the government over tariffs. Graf Cuno Westarp, the DNVP leader, developed the concept of 'conservative participation'. In 1925 and again in 1927 he all too briefly modified his party's refusal actually to govern under a Republic. The SPD tried to expose the DNVP's basic anti-republicanism, even by tactically abstaining at one stage of voting over Locarno. The aim in this instance was to manoeuvre the DNVP into direct responsibility for Stresemann's policy. The conservatives were to be prevented from exploiting their presence in the cabinet simply to secure higher protective tariffs for agriculture and then, once these were agreed, sabotaging the Locarno initiatives.

Ultimately, the compromise agreed between industry and agriculture on trade treaties and tariffs in 1925 continued to provide damage limitation in parliamentary politics. In the interests of German foreign policy the SPD did not engage in the 'ruthless struggle against the DNVP' for which *Vorwärts* called in 1925. The charge that the SPD's 'toleration' of the bourgeois governments of the mid-1920s was minimal should be considered in the light of the economic difficulties during the later 1920s. The SPD's claim for a 30 per cent rise in unemployment benefits in 1926 stood as a reminder of the strains of

5. K. E. Rieseberg, 'Die SPD in der Locarnokrise Oct–Nov 1925', *Vierteljahrshefte für Zeitgeschichte*, 30 (1982): 134–5.

SPD–DVP collaboration in the economic arena. Nevertheless, socialists as well as businessmen stood to gain from Germany's recovery. Thus the most dangerous party-political dimensions of the class conflict fully re-emerged only after 1928. As well as supporting Stresemann's foreign and trade policy prior to that, the SPD found a measure of agreement with the DDP and Centre on social policy. Hermann Müller himself argued in the spring of 1926 that the formation of a government based on the Great Coalition 'under the pressure of the growing burdens of the Dawes (plan) and perhaps after new elections . . . might once more be the irresistible demand of the hour'.[6]

Within the more responsible parties self-interest was therefore tempered by a perception, however dim at times, of the need for a combined defence of the nation's health. Undoubtedly the shifting tactical alliances between the middle parties on the one hand and, on the other, the two 'wings', the DNVP and SPD, did not always endear politicians and parliaments to the German public. The Reichstag was an easy object of political satirists even at the best of times and particularly during the mounting economic crisis at the close of the 1920s. However, on a broader comparative basis, which would include other European parliamentary systems during the interwar years, a number of the devices for parliamentary management under the Weimar system could be reviewed more sympathetically in the interests of a balanced verdict. Thus some tactics were devised to circumvent problems impeding the evolution of collective cabinet responsibility. One such obstacle was the way in which individual ministers could be withdrawn from the government at the whim of the parliamentary faction during inter-party clashes in the Reichstag. This problem was compounded by the practice of allowing the strength of the respective parliamentary parties to determine the final composition of a coalition. Stresemann opposed this doctrine with energy.[7] An obvious way round it was to form an above-party cabinet of 'experts'. That could not substitute for collective cabinet responsibility, admittedly, but it fell within the bounds of parliamentary conventions. Similarly, evidence that the relationship between the legislative and executive bodies was not functioning smoothly generated schemes to redefine the role of the 'party' in the political process. Not all such schemes were sinister, any more than

---

6. Rieseberg, 'Die SPD in der Locarnokrise', p. 149.
7. Cf. Stresemann's speech of 26 February 1928, cited in H. Michaelis (ed.), *Ursachen und Folgen. Vom deutschen Zusammenbruch 1918 und 1945 bis zur staatlichen Neuordnung Deutschlands in der Gegenwart* (Berlin, 1958), vol. 7, pp. 236–7.

were the various attempts at party mergers and re-formations at the close of the 1920s.

Setting aside for the moment the machinations of the extreme right, it is notable that moderate liberal and conservative merger plans unfolding between 1928 and 1930 were partly intended to counter the disintegration of political life. Of course the new formations were also a response to the dismal election results of the moderate parties in 1928. Both considerations influenced the revived plans for liberal unity. They were backed initially by key political figures such as Wilhelm Groener, Otto Gessler and Friedrich Meinecke, as well as by regional sections of the DVP and DDP. All shared the desire to counter the growth of extremism on the right and left. Ultimately, efforts to build a 'fourth bloc', to stand alongside socialism, the Centre Party and the 'New Right', produced a whimper rather than a bang, in the form of the State Party. It was launched on 9 November 1930, following the formal dissolution of the DDP on the previous day. Backed by the DDP leader, Erich Koch-Weser, it remained an uneasy fusion between DDP elements and the newish Young German Order. Ultimately, it had no significant or durable appeal to the voters of the late Weimar Republic.

The failure of attempts to integrate the voters of the middle ground can be explained to some extent by the longer-term demographic trends underlying the electoral performance of the moderate Weimar parties. Yet those trends did not preordain the final outcome. The severity of the economic crisis after 1928–29 was the critical factor in making more difficult the already hard task of holding cabinets together. The reappearance of the Great Coalition in 1928 was hopeful, but at its centre lurked unresolved differences between the DVP and SPD over economic policy. The disagreements have been succinctly summarized as those between *Produktionspolitik* and *Verteilungspolitik*; that is to say, the difficulty of reconciling the priorities of wealth *creation* with those of its *redistribution*. The mounting economic crisis – with its ripple effects on trade and fiscal policies, unemployment and financial relations with the Allied powers – tested to the limit the relationship between socialism and industry. The class conflict was worsened by the tremendous pressure from both extremes of the political spectrum, which narrowed the freedom of movement for Stresemann and Hermann Müller. An inclination long present in the DVP to distrust socialism became more pronounced. It was symbolized by the late Weimar election slogan of the 'people's party': '*Von roten Ketten macht Euch Frei allein die Deutsche Volkspartei*' (Only the German People's Party can free you from the Marxist yoke).

After Stresemann's death, these virulent sentiments became more marked than ever. Such ill will goes some way to explain the SPD's tactical ineptness in allowing the coalition to fall as a result, ostensibly, of a minute difference between its figure for unemployment benefits and that of the DVP. In reality, as we have argued, the conflict was about basic principles rather than details.

The break up of the Great Coalition in March 1930 has been dubbed an act of self-exclusion, bringing the chronic structural crisis of the party state into the open.[8] For the time being a greater burden than ever was imposed on the Centre Party to maintain parliamentary procedures. Here, too, the balance of leadership had tipped to the right when Monsignor Ludwig Kaas took over from Wilhelm Marx in December 1928. The event was a disappointment to those members of the Centre Party who had maintained good relations with the SPD, notably Joseph Joos and Adam Stegerwald. Both politicians had stood for the party leadership and both were close to the Catholic labour movement. At the same time, some damage had been done to the nationalist cause through the virulent attacks on the Müller government by the self-styled 'National Opposition' of the right and its tactics over the new reparations scheme, the Young Plan.

The SPD proposed an immediate and ultimately abortive no-confidence motion in Brüning's government but there were soon signs of remorse within the party's Reichstag faction. It should have been feasible, therefore, for Brüning to have secured socialist support for a compromise on fiscal policy in June 1930. Instead the Chancellor's 'benevolent authoritarianism' expressed itself in a preference for a broad-based cabinet of the right. The tactical rationale was the need to undermine the NSDAP and the more extreme elements of the DNVP. Brüning was also well aware that Hindenburg would make available emergency powers under Article 48 to push through financial reforms if negotiations for a coalition were deadlocked. Hermann Müller had been granted no such luxury. Brüning thus accepted the further extension of Article 48 into the realm of economic policy, albeit it with Hindenburg's protestations about observing the spirit of the constitution. These were the realities which underlay Brüning's ostensibly 'above-party' cabinet.[9] 1930 was a significant year indeed but did the Republic 'end' there?

8. E. Matthias, 'Social Democracy and the power in the state' in T. Eschenburg *et al.*, *The road to dictatorship. Germany 1918–1933* (London, 1970), p. 62.

9. H. Brüning, *Memoiren. 1918–1934* (Stuttgart, 1972), vol. I, p. 170.

AN INDECENT BURIAL – 1930–33

The fashionable contention that the Weimar Republic was afflicted by a 'permanent structural crisis' appears on the face of it to deny that any one year was more significant than another. This cannot be. Even if it were possible to prove beyond doubt that the Republic was so afflicted, it could never be a sufficient explanation for its final collapse. The severe nature of the actual crisis visited on Germany from 1930 onwards weakens the 'structuralist' argument that there *was* no decisive 'turning point' for a permanently sick Weimar Republic. Looking back dispassionately to the train of events following Brüning's appointment as Reich Chancellor, the astonishing thing is the Weimar Republic's capacity to absorb so much punishment before keeling over like an exhausted but ill-matched contender for a heavyweight boxing championship. Political damage was inflicted beyond doubt by economic collapse. This ultimately nurtured both extremes of the Weimar party system. National Socialism profited above all from the rapid electoral decline afflicting the bourgeois middle parties. These failed as we saw to overcome the 'party crisis' by providing a new rallying point to integrate the fragmented middle classes. Instead, the 'point of integration' had moved increasingly towards the right.[10] There alas Hitler still stood, with his relatively fresh and dynamic message. Middle-class Germans, like those in Marburg, who were upset by the growing asymmetry between their social status and their political impotence, increasingly looked towards Hitler's party to square the circle.[11]

Those who disagree that the political parties played the determining role in the National Socialist *Machtergreifung*, imply instead that the individual actors in the final drama were more important. Key personalities, including Hindenburg, favoured reforms to dismantle the 'party state'. The Reich President promoted the idea of a rightist, authoritarian government *before* the Great Coalition actually fell. In refusing to grant SPD Chancellor Müller the sort of emergency powers he allowed Brüning to wield, his actions became as much a cause as a consequence of the failure of the moderates in politics. However, a note of caution must be sounded about exaggerating the role of

---

10. L. E. Jones, ' "The dying middle." Weimar Germany and the failure of Bourgeois politics', *Central European History*, 5 (1972): 23–54.
11. See R. Koshar, *Social Life, Local Politics and Nazism. Marburg 1880–1935* (Chapel Hill, 1986).

individuals, even powerful ones. The Reichstag could still repeal statutes after 1930 and ideally the Chancellor continued to need the confidence of the legislature. Presidential powers could override these requirements if need be but Hindenburg was reluctant to move too openly against constitutional conventions.

This was restraint of a sort. In spite of the growing contempt being shown for parliament by large sections of the electorate, matters were not so clear-cut that the party system was decisively rejected in 1930. It would be more accurate to say that the dualism of power enshrined in the constitution became much more evident after the fall of Müller. The defeatism and self-doubt of Weimar parliamentarians, so apparent by 1932 when they failed even to field an alternative candidate to contest Hindenburg's re-election as Reich President, was not so noticeable when Brüning first became Chancellor at the end of March 1930. The fact that this 46-year-old headed a minority cabinet was hardly novel for the Weimar Republic as we have seen. However, against the background of a soaring budget deficit, reaching 1.1 billion marks by the end of May 1932, it proved impossible to bridge fundamental differences between the social democrat and DVP components in Brüning's Cabinet. That was one factor prompting the Chancellor to call new elections for September 1930. The gamble was felt worthwhile in order to extend the basis of his parliamentary support in the camp of the conservative–nationalist right. It is all too well known that the 'right' targeted by Brüning and Hindenburg fared disastrously during the September poll. Instead the NSDAP vote soared and furnished Hitler's followers with 107 seats in the Reichstag. Unpalatable as it was to the President and his Chancellor, the question of the National Socialists being included in government was placed firmly on the political agenda.

At the same time, the electoral dose of icy water stimulated the residual survival mechanisms of Weimar politicians, notably those of the SPD. Its new policy of 'tolerating' Brüning's administration in effect postponed a social and economic reckoning, giving the Chancellor at least a chance of deflecting extremist attacks on the floor of the Reichstag. The violence of Communist and National Socialist clashes, after the opening of parliament in October 1930, produced a majority for limiting the misuse of parliamentary immunity. Brüning was able to suspend parliamentary proceedings until October 1931. The vote was facilitated by the tactical ineptness of the KPD, NSDAP and DNVP in making their protest by temporarily absenting themselves from the Reichstag. Paradoxically, the suspension of parliament itself indicated that the 'presidential government' could stabilize state power against extremism on both sides of the political spectrum.[12]

Arguably, this could be most clearly seen in Prussia, where the Weimar coalition survived the September 1930 elections and remained under Otto Braun until 1932. He continued to defend the constitutional order in Prussia, where the decree against political violence of 17 July 1931 was applied to both left and right. Prussian minister of the interior, Carl Severing, together with his under-secretary of state, Otto Abegg, resolutely maintained that membership of the civil service or the holding of public office was incompatible with membership of either the NSDAP or the KPD. Later, Braun even offered to resign in favour of Brüning, providing the latter combined the Chancellorship of the Reich with the Minister Presidency of Prussia. Hindenburg's rebuttal of this interesting device to prop up the republic speaks volumes and tension persisted between the two sides of Berlin's Wilhelmstrasse, the street housing the offices of both the Reich and Prussia.

In the elections to the Prussian Diet on 24 April 1932 the Weimar Coalition lost its majority. To Hindenburg's chagrin, Braun, with Brüning's agreement, remained as head of a caretaker administration. At that stage the Prussian Centre Party was still opposed to entering a coalition with the nationalist right in Prussia. Hindenburg's distaste for the socialists and the Centre Party might have been deepened by the knowledge that he had been dependent on their support to win the second round of voting during the bruising presidential election against Hitler in March 1932. The mere suggestion of dependence on the combined forces of Marxism and the Papacy was enough to make Hindenburg shudder. This was emphatically not what Brüning had been hired to bring about and the removal of any future Prussian obstacle to the Reich government thus became a priority for Hindenburg. Brüning's own fate was inexorably linked with this.

The Chancellor's unpopularity was growing because of his social and economic policy, which in turn was integral to his foreign policy. While the considerable external pressures on late Weimar Germany certainly constrained Brüning's options, his unpopular, 'uncharismatic inflexibility' evidenced his unexpected development of conviction politics, even to the extent of further upsetting Hindenburg. The latter was notoriously offended over proposals for land reform in eastern Germany. The President was equally annoyed at Brüning's insistence

---

12. M. Broszat, *Hitler and the Collapse of Weimar Germany* (Leamington Spa, New York, 1987), p. 93.

on banning the SA under a decree introduced after much provocation on 13 April 1932. These brief glimpses of purpose argue against the view that Brüning took the first steps in the destruction of democracy. The Chancellor in fact rejected any resort to dictatorship either through dissolving the Reichstag or by means of all-embracing emergency decrees enabling the cabinet to justify any measures in terms of an 'administrative ordinance'.[13] There is thus some evidence that Brüning's administration offered the last chance to salvage something from the Weimar political system and only after his fall on 30 May 1932 was decisive action taken against Prussia by his successor, Franz von Papen.

Von Papen's scheme, hatched with his mentor, General Kurt von Schleicher, Minister for Defence in the new cabinet, was directed at bringing the National Socialists into a governing coalition. The price for extending the popular base of the government in this way was paid in instalments. The first came in the shape of new elections in July, where the NSDAP's share of the vote rose to 13.7 million (37.4 per cent of the poll), making it the largest party in the Reichstag, with 230 seats. Its case for becoming part of the government was now overwhelming in electoral terms, even after its drop to 33.1 per cent of the vote in the elections of 6 November 1932. The proof of the NSDAP's huge popular support also reinforced the determination of von Papen and Schleicher to lift the SA ban and to deal with Prussia. These were, so to speak, the other components of a package deal to tempt Hitler into a coalition. When von Papen's government finally moved against Braun's caretaker administration it was dealing with a worn and damaged body of men, resignedly aware that they were no longer fully supported even inside Prussia. The surge in NSDAP street fighting with the KPD following the lifting of the ban on Hitler's paramilitary forces on 4 June 1932 reached a peak in the Altona district of Hamburg on 17 July. Public authority was taxed to the limit. It was also, constitutionally, virtually impossible for Severing to resist the appointment on 20 July of a Reich Commissioner for Prussia, executing a decree signed by Hindenburg eight days earlier. The attempt made by the SPD on 25 July to reverse the decree in the Supervisory Committee of the dissolved Reichstag was blocked by the Centre Party, by now itself cruelly exposed.

The existence of Von Papen's conservative, nationalist coalition,

---

13. In general, G. Schulz, *Von Brüning zu Hitler. Der Wandel des politischen Systems in Deutschland 1930–1933, vol. 3. Zwischen Demokratie und Diktatur. Verfassungspolitik und Reichsreform in der Weimarer Republik* (Berlin, 1992).

together with the fall of a vital bastion of federalism when the Reich took over Prussia, convinced Otto Braun that the time of republican ministers was now over.[14] Instead, von Papen and Hindenburg were anxious to secure NSDAP support for their own authoritarian plans to reform the constitution. Neither von Papen nor Hindenburg wanted the National Socialists to control government. Indeed, the President made plain to Hitler, on 13 August 1932, that he would not allow him to head a cabinet with presidential powers. The ensuing harassment of von Papen in the Reichstag by the disappointed Nazis was a factor in the calling for yet another round of elections. The ad hoc collaboration between the NSDSP and the KPD during the Berlin transport workers strike prior to the polls did not help Hitler's cause. Superficially, the outcome of the voting on 6 November 1932 appeared to vindicate von Papen, in so far as the German nationalists gained votes whilst for the first time since 1928 the NSDAP share declined, showing a drop of more than 4 per cent.

In this sense at least the judgement of Germany's finance minister, Schäfer, that von Papen's government was the 'first stage of the Third Reich', must also be qualified.[15] Von Papen was, ultimately, directly involved in the final movements bringing Hitler to power, but the machinations of his erstwhile ally, Schleicher, provided the critical link. The 'political general' claimed after the November 1932 elections to fear civil war. As spokesman for the Reichswehr he managed to overcome Hindenburg's reluctance to letting von Papen depart from office in December 1932, on the grounds that the Chancellor had no prospect of gaining widespread popular support. In the event Schleicher could neither control the Reichstag nor manoeuvre the NSDAP into a government coalition under his leadership. His plan to outflank Hitler by negotiating with Gregor Strasser revealed a poor grasp of the reality of power inside the NSDAP. Moreover, Schleicher's policy proposals ultimately alarmed Germany's economic leaders. Von Papen therefore continued to be influential behind the scenes throughout the short-lived Schleicher government. He was actually allowed to remain in the official Chancellor's residence after

---

14. O. Braun, *Von Weimar zu Hitler*, 3rd edn (Hamburg, 1948), p. 395. Cf. H. Schulze, 'Rückblick auf Weimar. Ein Briefwechsel zwischen Otto Braun und Joseph Wirth im Exil', *Vierteljahrsheft für Zeitsgeschichte* (1978): 144–85. See also H. Schulze, *Otto Braun oder Preussens demokratische Sendung. Eine Biographie* (Frankfurt, 1977).

15. Cited in Broszat, *Hitler and the Collapse of Weimar*, p. 115. On Papen's political ideas cf. W. Braatz, 'Franz von Papen and the Preussenschlag', *European Studies Review*, 3 (1973): 157–80. See also U. Hoerster-Philipps (ed.), *Konservative Politik in der Endphase der Weimarer Republik. Die Regierung Franz von Papen* (Cologne, 1982) and G. O. Kent, 'Problems and pitfalls of a Papen biography', *Central European History*, 20 (1987): 191–7.

his own fall from office. Working within the conservative establishment, von Papen was able to nourish the growing readiness in both industrial and agricultural power groups to contemplate Hitler's chancellorship. Armed with this knowledge and with the support of Hindenburg's own son, Oscar, von Papen finally overcame the President's resistance to a government headed by Adolf Hitler. He insisted of course on the nationalists retaining a comfortable majority in such an administration. The outcome of this final rash of intrigues is only too well known. Hitler became Chancellor on 30 January 1933.

Our understanding of the Hitler phenomenon is not advanced by regarding National Socialism as an irresistible force moving inexorably towards government. The time lag between the NSDAP's electoral breakthrough in 1930 and its final assumption of office is significant, confirming that the road to the Chancellor's office was littered with obstacles to the very end. The eventual success Hitler and his fellow leaders had during this period in overcoming some of the resistance within the elites in the armed forces, the civil service and in the economy was hard won. Here it is relevant to stress that the SA input into street violence generated precisely the sort of disorder which Hitler claimed his movement could end. It may have helped to condition the political climate to welcome a 'strong' leader to end unrest, but it was always a potential threat to Hitler's bid for establishment backing. Nonetheless, key elements in that establishment continued to keep Hitler's sometimes shaky political chances alive between 1930 and 1933, notwithstanding the clear evidence of criminality in his actions and in the movement.

A graphic example of this was provided by Hitler's open telegram of support to the so-called Potempa murderers. Such instances make it exceedingly difficult to accept the rationale of some of the German elites that they sought to 'contain' Hitler's movement by bringing it into government. The keynote of the establishment figures flirting with Hitler was one of desperation and/or wishful thinking on a grand scale, or something rather worse. The sheer disorganization of the conservative Right was obviously as big a factor in the demise of Weimar as the divisions of the left or the collapse of the middle classes. Hugenberg and his supporters appear to have had little idea *how* the crisis they had helped to provoke could or would be resolved and the President was deeply troubled by the negotiations with Hitler.[16]

16 H. Weiss and P. Hoser (eds), *Die Deutschnationalen und die Zerstörung der Weimarer Republik. Aus dem Tagebuch von Reinhold Quaatz, 1928–33* (Munich, 1989); L. E. Jones, 'Die Tage vor Hitlers Machtübernahme. Aufzeichnungen des Deutsch-nationalen Reinhold Quaatz', *Vierteljahrsheft für Zeitgeschichte*, 37 (1989): 759–74.

However, Hindenburg's predicament arose from a wilful exclusion of other forms of democratic government as a remedy for the ills of the late Weimar Republic, from an aversion to left-wing solutions bordering on the murderous and from the absence of any broad-based rightist political party other than the NSDAP. It remains profoundly misleading to argue that Hitler's appointment 'was wholly unnecessary'.[17] The intrigues which historians have delineated were informed by the brute fact of the movement's massive popular support.

17. As in A. J. Nicholls, *Weimar and the Rise of Hitler* (Macmillan; London–Melbourne–Toronto, 1968), p. 166.

CHAPTER FIVE

Governmental Plurality in the 'Single-Party State'

The manner in which the National Socialist movement had grown in the 1920s and the way in which it came to power helped to form the party's practice in the political arena after 1933. Nothing illustrated this more clearly than the initial process of *Gleichschaltung* (co-ordination of state and Party offices) during 1933 and 1934 which began to shift the prevailing balance between the party and the traditional elites who had eased Hitler's path to high office. After January 1933 only the conservative elements in Hitler's cabinet stood in the way of a full National Socialist government. They were unlikely in the extreme to offer outright resistance in spite of holding powerful state posts. These included the Ministry of Defence under Werner von Blomberg. Alfred Hugenberg, who certainly entertained doubts about Hitler, now acquired a vested interest in the success of the new cabinet by becoming virtually an 'economic dictator'. As well as being Minister for Economics and Agriculture, Hugenberg exercised provisional control of the Prussian Departments of Economics, Agriculture and Labour from 4 February 1933. Vice Chancellor von Papen was consoled with the position of Reich Commissioner for Prussia, making him Goering's superior, on paper at least. Unsurprisingly, neither von Papen nor Hugenberg argued effectively against Hitler's request to the cabinet, on 31 January 1933, for new elections to boost the authority of his 'National Government'.

At the same cabinet session Hitler deftly side-stepped Hugenberg's suggestion that the government secure its majority by simply banning the KPD forthwith. The new Chancellor justified his refusal to take the proffered route on the grounds that it would force the Reichswehr to deal with a likely communist uprising. Nor would Hitler entertain von Papen's idea of simply proceeding with the planned Enabling Law to secure increased governmental powers under emergency rule. Any such proposal would at that stage have needed the support of the Centre in the Reichstag and the price tag would doubtless have included constitutional restraints on the government. New elections offered Hitler the best prospect of increasing his authority, both in the country at large and inside the ruling coalition. There was also the chance of lessening the cabinet's dependence on the Reich President. The non-National Socialist members of the government therefore accepted the case for fresh elections for 5 March largely on the strength of Hitler's promises and reassurances.

As the elections approached resistance was anticipated from the communists, who had appealed for a general strike on 31 January. The government already had powers to curb press activities and public meetings considered threatening to the Reich, but greater resolution was displayed after the Reichstag fire on 27 February, for which the communists were blamed. The decree passed on the following day, for *The Protection Of People And State*, set aside the basic rights of the Weimar constitution. Opposition could thereafter be harassed under cover of a more or less permanent state of emergency. The Reich government now also had the right to exercise the powers of the *Land* authorities if these failed to implement any necessary emergency measures. This was not unconnected with the extension of National Socialist control in Prussia, where the Reich government simply prolonged the 'provisional' control it exercised following von Papen's coup. The Braun–Severing administration, still technically in control of Prussia, watched its residual rights being transferred to Hitler's cabinet following the presidential decree of 6 February, *For The Restoration Of Orderly Government In Prussia*. On the previous day Prussian provincial diets, district assemblies, parish councils and other electoral bodies had been dissolved and new elections fixed for 12 March. That particular manoeuvre was geared up to changing the composition of the Prussian Privy Council (where the NSDAP and the DNVP had no majority) *before* there was time for an appeal to be heard in the Reich Supreme Court. The immediate impact of central government encroachments on *Land* authority was felt precisely where it was intended, in the realm of policing. The importance of this at a time of heightened political excitement and unrest in the run up to the elections hardly needs underlining.

The process also perfectly illustrates the personal aggrandizement characteristic of the top National Socialist leaders after 1933. In this instance Goering was the beneficiary. Already Reich Commissioner for the Prussian Ministry of the Interior as well as Reich Commissioner for Air Transport, Goering now assumed responsibility for the Prussian police. Frick, as Minister of the Interior, supported Goering. Action was taken against a number of uncooperative Prussian police chiefs and officials, while Commissioners for Special Duty were appointed. A noted example was Berlin SS *Gruppenführer* Kurt Daluege, who took over the Prussian Police Department from Grauert. Even before the Reichstag fire Goering had ordered the reinforcement of police by the enlistment of voluntary 'auxiliaries'. In practice these further extended the National Socialist power base. As in the other Nazi controlled *Länder* (Thuringia, Braunschweig, Oldenburg), so in Prussia, there was now a relatively secure foundation from which to enforce draconian bans against the left. It made little difference that the Supreme Court found many of these actions illegal. Inevitably, violent action against the KPD was extended to those who 'helped' the communists. Significantly, when the SA and SS auxiliary police units were disbanded in the second half of 1933, they retained control of the concentration camps which had sprung up for detaining political prisoners. From 30 June 1934 the camps were run by the SS alone.

The election turnout of 5 March was high at 80 per cent. Even allowing for intimidation, the National Socialist share of the vote (at some 43 per cent) was large. The party managed to increase its support in parts of Germany where previously it had fallen behind the Reich average, notably in Bavaria and Württemberg. There were substantial gains in the agrarian areas of northern and eastern Germany. On the other hand, there was not overwhelming support in any district. In eleven constituencies, especially the urban-industrial regions of central Germany and the Catholic west, the National Socialist share of the poll was between 30 and 40 per cent. Hitler welcomed the results as a National Socialist victory and as a mandate for revolutionary change, although the support of the Battle Front Black- White-Red of Alfred Hugenberg, Franz Seldte and Franz von Papen was required to bring the government's majority to 51.8 per cent. In spite of this the fate of the other parties in the elections gave credence to Hitler's triumphant claims. Whilst the DNVP and Centre gained something like 200,000 votes each and the SDP and State Party held on with relatively small losses, the DVP, the Middle Class Party and the Farmers' Party all suffered a further decline in voting support. The dramatic loss to the KPD of more than a million votes underlined just how effectively the National Socialists had crusaded against the left. Outside the Reichstag Hitler could draw on the reserves of the party organization as well as that of the SA and the SS. What could be more predictable than the extension of the party's control in the non-National Socialist *Länder*,

helped by the spread of auxiliary police forces and the institution of
Reich Commissioners to 'govern' them? The KPD deputies were soon
locked up; the Centre Party's doubts were soothed by promises
concerning the Church and its role in the state; the parties of the
moderate right were in fragments. The Enabling Bill could not be
prevented by the one group voting against it, the socialists. It became
law on 23 March 1933. Thereafter it was a matter of time before the
parties were persuaded to wind themselves up or, in the case of the
KPD and SPD, compelled to by another wave of arrests and seizures
of property.

THE DEBATE ON POLYCRACY

The bare recital of 'co-ordination' appears at first glance to support the
durable popular image of a meticulously organized drive for office by
the National Socialists. In reality it offers further evidence of the
prolonged and erratic nature of Hitler's progress towards dictatorship.
Established constitutional landmarks were not so much obliterated by a
juggernaut as circumvented. Hitler did indeed wield immense personal
power and it is clearly unwise to take literally the private remark he
is purported to have made to Herman Rauschning, that he was no
dictator and that there was no such thing as dictatorship in the
accepted sense. This is more likely to have been an expression of
the constraints on political leaders in advanced industrial states in the
conduct of government. The view of Hitler's regime as a monolithic
dictatorship guaranteed to ensure that the trains always ran on time
has, however, long been out of favour among historians of Germany.
Doubts had already been expressed by early observers before the cold
war generated its vast literature on 'totalitarianism', lumping Hitler and
Stalin together and obscuring the complex and differing realities of
administration and of policy rationale under 'dictatorships'. Even in
1947, Trevor-Roper's classic investigation of the last days of the Third
Reich argued that the National Socialist state was not 'in any
significant use of the word' totalitarian; that its leaders were 'a court';
that far from being monolithic the Third Reich was 'a confusion of
private empires, private armies and private intelligence services'. Under
these conditions, 'only policy, not administration, was controlled at the
centre'.[1]

1. H. R. Trevor-Roper, *The Last Days of Hitler* (London, 1952), pp. 53–4.

When during the course of the 1960s the rigid explanatory concepts of the cold war began to break up and the results of historical research in the archives were gradually published, the picture sketched by Trevor-Roper was elaborated in immense detail. The cold war orthodoxy was replaced by a newer one, still holding sway, where the Third Reich was indeed perceived as a system of competing institutions and personalities, comprising different centres of power. In such a 'polycracy' only the fittest survived. The processes of government, it was felt, could best be characterized by the description 'institutional Darwinism'. The model accorded perfectly with the extraordinarily fitful and eventful progress of the NSDAP towards power in its *Kampfzeit*. A movement which had relied so much on the capacity of its leaders to use their elbows could be expected to produce a particularly virulent bunch of office-seekers when it moved into government. Hitler himself reflected: 'When you have a group of powerful personalities, it is inevitable that occasionally friction is produced.'[2] This is a massive understatement of the realities of administration after 1933.

In theory the party and state were one according to Hitler's declaration in 1934. In practice there were inevitably clashes between party and state, between the traditional forces of government and the newcomers. These were added to the inevitable sordid struggles within the party itself over the spoils of office. Even then the opportunities for political intrigue were far from exhausted. Quarrels took place within and between departments of state. Nor was the cleavage between party and state as clear cut as some have assumed. Most obviously, the state administrative apparatus had already been penetrated by National Socialist ideas and personnel, as the case of the civil service showed. The tolerance of, if not adherence to, National Socialist values by key elites helped to blur the edges still more, at least until 1937–8 when the regime asserted itself far more aggressively against its one-time nationalist and conservative helpmates. In this general context it was not impossible to find instances where co-operation occurred across the party–state divide *against* leading party figures, such as Robert Ley, the head of the German Labour Front. Many such conflicts, as well as those within the economic sphere, were still far from resolved when war broke out, but this in turn brought with it new opportunities to create even more powerful fiefdoms in occupied Europe.

2. N. H. Baynes, *Hitler's Speeches*, vol. 1 (London, 1941), p. 209.

THE PRACTICE OF POLYCRACY

In this polycratic system the party's *Gauleiter* played a major role. If the transition to government resulted in a demotion for the central Political Organization (PO) of the National Socialist Party, many *Gauleiter* became even more powerful figures by gaining state positions. Frequently they took up the newly created posts of Reich Governors of the *Länder*. Others became *Oberpräsidenten* in the provinces of Prussia. In the latter case, however, party *Gauleiter* were more numerous than the provinces, so that frustrated office-hunters were thicker on the ground. Those *Gauleiter* fortunate enough to secure a post of *Oberpräsident* in one of Prussia's 12 provinces could, if able and energetic, even create a new provincial counterweight to the central Prussian government. Conflicts over competence were thus virtually built into the newly 'centralized' administration of Germany. Not surprisingly, the *Reichsgau* was seen as a model for provincial administration, both within the Reich and, later, in the annexed or satellite states of the Third Reich.

It was naturally not just the better known National Socialists who availed themselves of the opportunities for advancement. There are now numerous studies dealing with National Socialist leaders outside the very top ranks. One such figure, Hans Schemm, *Gauleiter* of Bayreuth, was of a type eulogized in the annals of his party, not least perhaps because of his premature death by accident. A power-hungry and energetic man, responsible for the organization of the National Socialist organization in Upper Franconia, Schemm subsequently built up the Reich Teachers' Association on a nationwide basis and became Bavarian Minister of Culture.[3] *Gauleiter* of such robustness were likely to resist efforts to subordinate them to local and regional government officials. Some lay awake pondering the question of whether they were responsible to Hitler personally, or to the Ministry of the Interior under Frick. Other *Gauleiter* worried about the definition of their authority in relation to the *Regierungspräsidenten* in Prussia, or to the Minister Presidents in the other *Länder*. Hitler compounded the struggles by encouraging the *Gauleiter* to get on with the job and make of it what they could. In permitting, if not embracing, rivalry as an instrument of government, significantly enhancing his own personal capacity as an arbiter if not as an efficient ruler, Hitler thus virtually

3. F. Kühnl, *Hans Schemm. Gauleiter und Kultusminister, 1891–1935* (Nuremberg, 1985).

ensured feverish conflicts for and within office. Even Goebbels wryly observed of a conflict concerning the Ministry of Labour in 1943: 'Here we have another case of a ministry being hollowed out bit by bit without the head being removed.'[4]

The territorial sectioning of Germany for administrative purposes itself increased the difficulties of the National Socialist aspirants and office-holders scattered throughout the Reich. Notwithstanding the centralization of government the Finance Ministry, for example, divided Germany into 28 districts for its purposes. The Ministry of Propaganda required 38 districts whilst the Ministry of Post could not manage with fewer than 46. Needless to say, these subdivisions were not coterminous with the party *Gaue*. In addition to the territorial divisions favoured by the different Reich ministries, the civil service and the army all had their own units of administration. Finally, the Supreme Reich Agencies, which were set up in the course of the 1930s to deal with particular tasks, cut across several areas of competence. Opportunities for confusion, conflict and the use of elbows were many and glorious. Such authorities extended the power base of individuals who were already important within the party. This was obviously also the case with the Office of the Four Year Plan, created under Goering's leadership in 1936 to prepare the economy more efficiently for the eventuality of a war. His organization could cut across the patterns of administration and generate a momentum of its own. It was in turn rivalled in key areas of its activity by the Reich Labour Service or by Fritz Todt's General Inspectorate of the German Road System. The latter indeed provided a perfect example of the dynamism which could be generated under polycracy. In tackling autobahn servicing and military construction in general, Todt – who also became Minister for Armaments and Munitions in March 1940 – could conscript both workers and firms and even influence prices. Pretensions to control these and other economic factors also developed in the organization with which the National Socialists replaced the detested trade unions, the German Labour Front.

Schematic illustrations of administration after 1933 have never been able to do full justice to the bewildering inter-linking of persons and offices underpinning Germany in the 1930s. A powerful personality could transcend his authority in a way impossible to illustrate on any chart. Heinrich Himmler, for example, originally called to head the SS in 1929, was said to have acquired so many duties and offices that he

---

4. Cited in E. Homze, *Foreign Labour in Nazi Germany* (Princeton, New Jersey, 1967), p. 213.

himself was unsure of their full extent. Martin Bormann, on the other hand, concentrated the threads of routine administration increasingly in his own hands as the Cabinet became largely redundant, in keeping with Hitler's style of government. Bormann attracted Hitler's attention in the 1930s as Chief of Staff of the Führer's Deputy (Hess). At the outset of the war Bormann was asked to attend on Hitler personally. Hess's office, after his flight to Britain, was re-designated as Party Chancellery and placed under Bormann. Finally, on 12 April 1943, Bormann became Secretary to the Führer. His actual power eventually far exceeded his formal duties, not least because he controlled access to Hitler, who became particularly preoccupied with the war as it unfolded. The late Martin Broszat felt that the situation reached a point from 1941, where 'the secretary (i.e. Bormann) had taken over the government'.[5] In reality, Hitler never entirely absented himself from the general machinery of government. In addition, Bormann had to share power – in domestic affairs at least – with people like Himmler, Albert Speer, later Minister for Armaments, and even the head of the Reich Chancellery, Hans Lammers.

A precondition of serious political power, in the old Reich at least, was the occupation of a strong position both in the party apparatus and in the machinery of state. Bormann had both. Conversely, a figure like Alfred Rosenberg, notwithstanding his ideological influence in the party, was wholly unable to translate his expertise in foreign affairs to the level of government policy. Ultimately he suffered from an ineffectual personality, a lack of administrative skill and money and, fatally, he was all too often out of tune with Hitler's own ideas on foreign policy.[6] Even when in charge of the Reich Ministry for the East (*Ostministerium*) during the war he found it impossible to gain support for his attempts to win over the minority nationalities in the USSR, which did not accord at all with the top Nazi leadership's racialist approach. Richard Darré provides another example of failure to transform an initially influential position, this time in agriculture, into a centre of real authority. Thus if loyalty to Hitler was vital to wielding real power, it was still not enough in itself.

---

5. M. Broszat, *The Hitler State. The Foundation and Development of the Internal Structure of the Third Reich* (London, 1981), p. 318. For fuller treatment, P. Longerich, *Hitlers Stellvertreter. Führung der Partei und Kontrolle des Staatsapparates durch den Stab Hess und die Partei-Kanzlei* (Munich, 1992); H. Peuschel, *Die Männer um Hitler. Braune Biographien: Martin Bormann, Joseph Goebbels* (Düsseldorf, 1982).

6. S. Kuusisto, *Alfred Rosenberg in der nationalsozialistischen Aussenpolitik 1933–1939* (Helsinki, 1984).

A better illustration of this state of affairs is provided by Wilhelm Frick, Hitler's Minister of the Interior. The filling of this particular office for a regime whose top leaders had not considered in any detail how to *govern* presented a challenge to say the least. The National Socialists had failed even to undertake any systematic evaluation of Frick's own pre-1933 governmental experience as Minister of the Interior for Thuringia. There was, admittedly, a rudimentary planning office in the Party's Headquarters (*Reichsleitung*) under Helmut Nicolai from 1931, a man who was curiously gripped by the subject of administration. Ad hoc thought was also given to the processes of governing by well-placed higher civil servants sympathetic to National Socialism, notably Wilhelm Stuckart, Hans Pfundtner and Heinrich Lammers. At the lower administrative levels party State Secretaries were not installed until after March–April 1933. Frick erroneously believed that the law passed in 1933, for *The Restoration Of the Professional Civil Service*, gave him a mandate to overhaul the state bureaucracy. Indeed, a new civil service code was eventually issued in 1937. Frick had some success in restraining excessive interference from the party in the bureaucracy. Yet throughout the 1930s civil servants were assailed on the emotional, ideological and material levels from a variety of party agencies and organizations. The latter included the Reich Association for Civil Servants (*Reichsbund der Deutschen Beamten* – RDB), under Hermann Neef. By 1938, ninety-eight per cent of civil servants had felt the need to join this non-compulsory organization.[7] The Deputy Leader of the NSDAP, Rudolf Hess, retained vague powers to intervene in administrative and civil service issues. In particular he had the 'right of consultation' on promotions and appointments to senior civil service posts. Although Frick was able to reverse salary cuts by 1937, he experienced deep frustration in trying to rationalize and strengthen the civil service. The truth was that the very concept of a streamlined civil service could barely be reconciled with the pretensions of other, still more powerful party leaders.

In any event, when war came the fragmented and conflict-ridden practices within the Old Reich were extended in the newly occupied areas, where the *Wehrmacht* was also a player alongside the SS and the *Gauleiter*. Ambitious *Gauleiter*, such as Arthur Greiser (Warthegau) or Albert Forster (Danzig-West Prussia), were still able to extend party control to all levels. The post of *Gauleiter* was generally strengthened

---

7. J. Caplan, *Government Without Administration. State and Civil Service in Weimar and Nazi Germany* (Oxford, 1988), p. 192.

when from 1942 the *Gau* replaced the army district as the main territorial unit for organizing defence. In addition they were freed from the administrative and legal shell still existing inside the old Reich, although at the same time they had to cope with a more sustained challenge from the SS which was responsible for racial policy in German-occupied Europe. It does not appear that Frick had anything against the *Gauleiter* as such; rather, the practitioners themselves were not disposed to acknowledge the authority of the Minister of the Interior. Hitler himself encouraged this attitude in the *Gauleiter* outside the old Reich. Frick's hope that the *Gauleiter* would become powerful intermediary bodies in his drive for administrative rationalization and centralization was therefore doomed. The Minister of the Interior failed among other things to gauge the extent of Hitler's aversion to the inherited establishment. Frick finally had to abandon his vision of the civil service with a leading role in *government*, along with his job, when Himmler replaced him as Minister of the Interior in August 1943.

In such an environment administrative developments were not only moulded by struggles at the very top political levels; until relatively recently, however, there have been few extensive studies of specific conflicts and motives at the middle level. One valuable example features a quarrel between Helmut Nicolai and *Gauleiter* Wilhelm Loeper. The former was a bureaucrat with deeply entrenched beliefs in racial superiority and a fervent devotion to National Socialism. Trained as a lawyer, he had joined the Prussian civil service after the war. As one of the few experienced administrators in the Nazi ranks he had worked at the Brown House in Munich, the party's headquarters. He had also published writings on problems of constitutional reform, so his appointment as a *Regierungspräsident* in the spring of 1933 was a logical one. Nicolai was placed in charge of Magdeburg. The latter, however, also fell within the sphere of influence of the *Gauleiter* for Magdeburg and Anhalt, Loeper, who at once showed 'that in his region he would suffer no gods besides himself '. When Loeper also became a Governor he became even more arrogant and the scene was set for a clash with Nicolai. The personality conflict took on wider dimensions when Nicolai was seconded to the Reich Ministry of the Interior by Frick to help work on the proposed reconstruction of Germany's administrative boundaries. One of Nicolai's earlier writings had been entitled, *The Future Foundations of the Constitution and the State in the National Socialist Order*. In Nicolai's conception there was no room for independent provinces like Saxony and Thuringia and, 'as luck would have it', Brunswick and Anhalt. Ultimately, however, it was Nicolai's personal choice to confront Loeper, rather than something conditioned by his office or even necessarily engendered by institutional opposition. His was a 'personal crusade on behalf of professional administrative orderliness in the face of ever encroaching party disorder'. Ultimately, he failed to match the combined weight of *Gauleiter* Loeper and Röver and eventually fell victim to the former's vendetta. After being forced to confess his homosexuality in March 1935, Nicolai was expelled from the party. Ironically, Loeper hardly had time to enjoy his triumph before dying in the autumn of that same year.[8]

More such studies – considering as this one does the question of personal choices – will contribute towards a fuller understanding of how party–state conflicts ultimately moulded the practice of government in the Third Reich. It will almost certainly be confirmed that the administrative chaos which developed after 1933 did not result solely from irrational actions coming from the party. Rational and irrational elements co-existed in both the party and the state machinery. The final outcome was less the result of any systematic and coherent theory of administration than of events, the weight of personal ambition and sheer opportunities for action. At the same time the frustration experienced by Frick in his lone attempts to build a civil service on National Socialist lines suggests that Germany's new rulers knew at least what they did *not* want. Their reaction against the old order and the licence given to the party amounted in itself to a policy. Not without justice the Third Reich has been characterized as 'a period of profound assault on the personnel and principles of the German administration'.[9]

HITLER IN GOVERNMENT

Does this basic reality have clear implications for the now long-standing discussion of the role of Hitler himself in the governmental apparatus of his state? Students sometimes greatly oversimplify the debate to one where those explaining the Third Reich and its policies in terms of Hitler's intentions are opposed to those primarily

---

8. The incident described is from M. Housden's *Helmut Nicolai and Nazi Ideology* (London, 1992), pp. 167ff.
9. Caplan, *Government Without Administration*, p. 323.

concerned with the functioning of the Hitler State, and the way in which dynamism was engendered by its very structures. Although threatening at times to become tedious, the rigorous questioning of the 'intentionalists' by the 'functionalists' has had its historiographical uses. Not the least of these is the way in which it shifted the parameters of study of the Third Reich beyond Hitler-centric concerns. At the same time, Hitler-centricity has always reflected the not unfounded conviction that the Führer was *not* interchangeable; that his personal desires, particularly in the field of foreign policy and ideology but in other spheres too, were paramount. Hitler's values system was surely in the final resort a crucially important mainspring of decision-making.

The evidence is not wholly conclusive but not least because so many National Socialists already fervently embraced ideas akin to Hitler's own. In any case polycracy was perfectly compatible with strong central impulses operating in *some* areas. In a competing system a highly motivated individual could also drive his own determined pathway right through the thicket of competencies. Nowhere was this truer, as we have already implied, than in the areas of Europe which came under German occupation and where flourished some of the more brutal *Gauleiter* such as Erich Koch in the Ukraine or Hinrich Lohse in the Baltic region, both of whom were nominally under Alfred Rosenberg's *Ostministerium*. Their ensuing struggles were heightened by rivalry from both the armed forces and the ever-spreading influence of the SS (an organization demanding more detailed consideration elsewhere). Moreover, the model developed by Koch, Lohse and other rulers in the newly–seized areas eventually influenced the ambitions of *Gauleiter* within the old Reich. In this sense the Second World War might be said to have begun the second phase of the National Socialist revolution, where the new style of government was first implemented in an unrestrained way.[10]

In trying to understand the processes of government under National Socialism it is important to remember that behind the warring centres of power in Germany during the 1930s lay Hitler's dislike of the state as such. He was fully prepared to see the old order disappear in due course, along with the detested old elites. Until that day dualism between party and state and indeed between party and industry was unavoidable. Much of this dualism was, however, increasingly, confined to the levels below the very top leadership. As to the day-to-day tasks of government, Hitler saved his energies for major policy

---

10. D. Rebentisch, *Führerstaat und Verwaltung im Zweiten Weltkrieg. Verfassungsentwicklung und Verwaltungspolitik 1939–1945* (Stuttgart, 1989), for the impact of war on government in general.

priorities. This accorded with his work habits, which involved intense bursts of activity as well as long pauses, particularly once war broke out. He then became physically remote from the government, thanks to the changing location of his 'Führer HQ'. The actual business of government was delegated more to the Ministerial Council for the Defence of the Reich, set up in August 1939. Chaired by Hermann Goering, it failed to develop any serious ambitions to become a proper cabinet. What was in effect a permanent committee of the council, The Board of Three, came to focus primarily on laws and regulations essential to the defence of the Reich. None of this suggests that Hitler shunned decisions. Analysis of his war leadership confirms that he had bold ideas, if execution was sometimes timid, as well as a facility for quickly mastering the terms of any discussion.[11]

Yet it remains difficult to uncover wholly clear chains of command linking Hitler with some of his major policy initiatives. The problem of tracing decision-making arises partly because of Hitler's predilection for bypassing institutional channels. This could obviously generate great inefficiency and might even in extreme cases give the wholly misleading impression that Hitler could not permit the development of any other personality besides his. In fact, the emergence of powerful leaders would have been impossible to prevent, even if Hitler had wished to do this, and huge concentrations of power within the Third Reich were tolerated by him, if managed loyally by personalities close to his own beliefs (witness the SS again). The important point was the overriding desire of the leadership echelons of the Third Reich not to displease Hitler personally, and this was possible on such a comprehensive scale in so far as their own ambitions were, generally, equally destructive of the old order. From this perspective Frick's great failing was his misconceived aim of strengthening the *state* authorities. Hitler did not at all welcome attempts to place institutional or legal restraints on his office or person.

What decisions were made by Hitler could nevertheless certainly benefit from a very considerable information flow. Martin Bormann, Heinrich Lammers, Herbert Backe, Albert Speer and Joseph Goebbels, to name but a few, all provided briefings for Hitler. It is also highly likely that in order to determine the top priorities, which he believed should take up his energy as leader, Hitler was exposed to a far wider range of intelligence about the processes of government than is normally assumed. One interesting piece of evidence suggesting this

11. M. van Creveld, 'War Lord Hitler. Some points reconsidered', *European Studies Review*, 4 (1974): 57–79.

concerned the case of a Berlin provisioner, Nöthling, who was arraigned in 1942 for trafficking in black market goods and luxuries. His proposed defence was that he had in fact been 'illegally' supplying highly prominent state and party officials. A list of these duly arrived with Goebbels. One can only speculate at the glee he might have felt as a major player in the game of polycracy on seeing some of the names. The important point is that the Propaganda Minister eventually brought the affair to Hitler's personal attention in March 1943, on the grounds that such corruption was inadmissible and risked upsetting the population at war. Outraged, Hitler nonetheless ruled out any formal legal action against the culprits on the grounds of high policy. Instead, the offending officials were made to give a full account of the affair to the Minister for Justice, Otto Thierack. The ensuing responses of these men – some blamed either their wives (Darré and Lammers) or the grocer or, in the case of Foreign Minister Ribbentrop, official entertainment duties – are less interesting for their sordid nature than for the insight they give into the information flow passing across Hitler's desk. Indeed, some of the 'accused' successfully insisted on giving their self-serving accounts personally to Hitler rather than to Thierack. Incidentally, in the midst of the shameful recriminations of the officials caught with their hands in the jar over the Nöthling case, the Berlin grocer collapsed from the strain in prison and died.[12]

Hitler may well have despised this sort of detailed exposure to the workings of his administration. It was anything but the sort of thing great leaders should spend their time on, but he could not always avoid it. As to major developments, he obviously kept himself perfectly well-informed enough to ensure that actions taken were at least generally in accordance with his own wishes. It is frankly impossible to see how any major policy choices which were made under his regime could fail to be in keeping with Hitler's own priorities and ideas. In that sense at least, Hans Mommsen's famous reference to Hitler's rule as a 'weak dictatorship' must not be taken literally. The full decision-making processes of Hitler's rule are still not clear, but it was precisely because of the zealous rivalry for favour of Hitler's key followers that they could be nudged into action without a full documentary record surviving, notably in the case of the 'final solution' to the Jewish question and the making of foreign policy. Here were examples of the chilling efficiency and single-mindedness with which policy goals could be pursued in the prevailing 'polycratic incompetence'.

12. L. Gruchmann, 'Korruption im Dritten Reich', *Vierteljahrsheft für Zeitgeschichte*, 42 (1994): 571–93.

CHAPTER SIX

Life at the Top; State Economic Policy and Big Business

The agreement concluded between Hugo Stinnes and Carl Legien on 15 November 1918 offered at least to industrialists the prospect of restoring normal production. The target of an eight-hour working day was agreed, joint unemployment and arbitration groups were established and plants with more than 50 workers had to have workers' committees. The creation of a central joint labour committee on 4 December 1918 completed the package. It was hoped that the state would now abandon the interventionist role it had played during the First World War. This may have been the desire of governments too. The vision of returning to the 'free', liberal economic order haunted politicians and businessmen alike. Yet the 'state' was there to stay. The extent of the economic and fiscal problems after 1918 involved governments ever more in macro-economic policy. Inevitably, the public blamed the state, rather than the devastating and costly war, for the economic problems of the 1920s. There was rough justice in this, in so far as German governments had put the wrong fiscal foot forward in the first place. The war effort was financed not by new taxation but largely by borrowing. A colossal public debt of 150 milliard marks was bequeathed to the Weimar Republic. In abandoning the gold standard on August 1914 and allowing securities other than gold, the government also caused the note supply to accelerate twelvefold in the course of the next four years.

Inflation was well established by the time peace came, bringing with it the demand for reparations for the 'the loss and damage to which the Allied and Associated Governments and their nationals have been subjected as a consequence of the war imposed on them by the aggression of Germany and her allies' (Article 231 of the Treaty of Versailles). Germany was expected to 'make compensation for all damage done to the civilian population of the Allied and Associated Powers and to their property during the period of the belligerency of each as an Allied or Associated Power against Germany by such aggression by land, by sea and from the air'. (Article 232)[1] The peace treaty mentioned no specific sums but it did broadly establish the main areas for claims. They included material destruction (most important for France and Belgium) as well as the provision of war pensions, the latter at Britain's insistence. Under Article 233 an Inter-Allied Reparation Commission was called into being to 'consider the claims and give to the German government a just opportunity to be heard'. It was not until May 1921 that the commission announced the figure of 132,000 million gold marks under the London schedule of payments. At the same time the debt was divided into sections, represented by A, B and C class bonds. The last named were to be held by the commission pending an assessment of Germany's capacity to pay. Effectively, this meant postponing payment of almost two-thirds of the total sum. Nonetheless the reparations burden posed great difficulties for post-war Europe. Quite apart from arranging transfers of payments on such a scale it was not certain that Germany would be able to earn enough to meet its obligations.

The bankers, entrepreneurs and top civil servants determining Germany's early reparations policy wasted time prior to the drawing up of the London schedule by trying to make a case for German payments in kind, or through rebuilding damaged enemy property, rather than in cash. In the process the German public was encouraged to believe that reparations provided *the* key to their economic ills and that the only cure to be found was in their abolition; that this should be the aim of all government policy.[2] Thus attention was diverted from the indicators showing inflation to be a product primarily of domestic rather than external factors. After all, many German industrialists and speculators derived some profit and Germany's currency was eventually stabilized by Stresemann without recourse to outside aid in the autumn of 1923, with the issue of the transitional *Rentenmark*. None of this proved, however, that German governments deliberately engineered hyperinflation in order to escape their international obligations. Here it

1. A useful survey of the text of Versailles is in J. A. S. Grenville, *The Major International Treaties 1914–1973. A History and Guide with Texts* (London, 1974), pp. 59ff.

2. P. Krüger, *Deutschland und die Reparationen 1918–1919. Die Genesis des Reparationsproblem in Deutschland zwischen Waffenstillstand und Versailler Friedenschluss* (Stuttgart, 1973), pp. 210–13.

is vital to stress once more the novelty of the challenge to economic policy facing Europe after 1918.[3]

The traumatic nature of the crisis of 1923 indicated exactly how steep the learning curve was, for it resulted in nothing less than a completely remodelled reparations scheme in the form of the Dawes plan. This meant that from 1 September 1924 the size of reparation instalments was fixed according to a rising scale (a mere 200 million marks in the first year of the scheme) reaching the annual maximum of 2.5 milliard marks only in 1928–9. Payments were guaranteed by assigning the revenues of German railways and of large German industries, as well as some customs and excise duties. A small transport tax was also imposed. All in all, the pressure on the state budget – which later in the 1920s was to cover barely half the total annual outgoings – was reduced. Additional protection for the mark and for Germany's balance of payments was provided by the careful monitoring of the transfer process by the newly appointed Allied Reparations Agent, Parker Gilbert. The Reichsbank was compelled to maintain sufficient reserves of gold and foreign exchange to cover at least forty per cent of the value of its note issue. It also had to preserve the currency's exchange value under a fixed rate system and was forbidden to discount treasury bills.

These and other anti-inflationary measures thus severely curtailed the Reichsbank's capacity to extend liberal domestic credit.[4] However, the Dawes plan was premised on Germany's economic recovery, belatedly acknowledging the link between this and world growth. Still the 'cycle of debt' remained and German payments to the Allies continued to service the latter's war debts to the United States. At the same time the narrowly political view of reparations (locking defeated and victors in mutually frustrating and fruitless combat) gave way to the concept of partnership, although still very weakly developed. The policy of the United States was critically important, in that the 800 million marks in loans arranged for Germany under the plan were to come largely from America. The increased flow of foreign capital was the most obvious indication that Germany had been abruptly tied back into the international economy. However, this brought disadvantages as well as gains. The point can be illustrated by glancing at the larger German economic picture, of which the reparations question was merely one, if highly important, aspect.

3. Cf. remarks of S. Schuker, 'American "reparations" to Germany, 1919–1933' in G. D. Feldman (ed.) *Die Nachwirkungen der Inflation auf die deutsche Geschichte 1924–1933* (Munich, 1985), pp. 335–7.

4. S. A. Schuker, *American 'Reparations' to Germany, 1919–1933. Implications for the Third World Debt Crisis* (Princeton, N J, 1988), p. 24.

SOME ECONOMIC FACTS OF LIFE

Because of its reliance on exports Germany was badly hit by the general contraction of world trade after the war. Its share of international commerce fell by thirty-one per cent between 1913 and 1929.[5] Increased exports were all the more important in that demand was unlikely to grow much in the domestic market either. In the first place the substantial sectors of the population involved in agriculture (thirty-five per cent) and in crafts and retail (thirteen per cent in 1925) had a low purchasing power. Although there was a surge in productivity between 1925 and 1929, as there was later in 1937–9, economic growth in Germany between the wars was generally sluggish. Mining, metal and chemical industries continued to achieve production rises until late 1928 but the output in other sectors peaked in 1927. Even in that year, which witnessed a small investment 'boom', unemployment failed to drop below 1.3 million. In general, investment remained comparatively low throughout the 1920s. The very tight long-term capital market in the 1920s inevitably placed obstacles in the way of restructuring industry. High war losses and the impact of hyperinflation in 1923 had also eliminated much working finance. In this harsh climate German banks tended to back established businesses, such as food and textiles in particular, and were more reluctant to take risks on newer ventures. The rate of technical change and productivity was therefore poor. At the same time there was over-capacity in some branches, further heightening the demand to increase German exports.[6]

Naturally, investment and productivity can hardly be considered in isolation from the foreign funding flowing in to Germany following stabilization and then, alas, out again at the end of the 1920s. Compared with French plans for breaking the political and economic power of the Reich the Dawes scheme was of course very much the lesser evil. Tellingly, though, the plan struck some observers as being a pax Americana imposed on the European nations as the expression of the victory of the dollar over the franc and the pound sterling, let alone the mark.[7] The Reich's passage, through Dawes, into the Anglo-American world economic system had a price tag attached to it

---

5. R. J. Overy, *The Nazi Economic Recovery 1932–1938* (London, 1982), p. 14.
6. H. James, *The German slump. Politics and economics, 1924–1936* (Oxford, 1984), pp. 110ff.
7. See for example H. O. Schötz, *Der Kampf um die Mark 1923–4* (Berlin, 1987), pp. 117–80.

in the form of a growing dependence on foreign, chiefly American, capital. Although most of it was advanced on a short-term basis, much was used by industry for essentially long-term investments. In addition, short-term capital went into 'unproductive' regional and municipal projects such as hospital building. Between 1925 and 1927 German municipal and *Land* authorities attracted over 4 billion marks in foreign loans.[8]

Naturally, external factors cannot be wholly blamed for the uses to which foreign capital was put inside the Weimar Republic, and the underlying weaknesses of the German economy again intrude themselves into any considerations of the late 1920s and the onset of depression. Germany's national income only exceeded 1913 levels in 1927. Productivity was thus unable to cover all the domestic demands and expectations even without reparations payments. The loss of German competitiveness in international terms was still pronounced after the currency was stabilized, and German prices increasingly diverged from international trends in the decade after 1919.[9] When the depression came to Germany it was characterized by a sustained drop in investment, high unemployment, and a dramatic rise in business failures as foreign trade levels plummeted and with them, income. There appears to have been a downturn in investment in Germany *prior* to the onset of the world slump as a result of the depressed domestic demand noted earlier.[10] The situation worsened as foreign capital began to dry up and then to leave Germany. The impact on the credit system as a whole may be imagined from the bare fact that many German banks had a ratio of capital to deposits of as high as 1 : 20. Fifty per cent of those deposits were foreign by the onset of depression.

GOVERNMENTAL STRATEGIES IN THE WEIMAR REPUBLIC

There were limits to what the state could do to offset the defects of Germany's economic structure. Governments faced tremendous problems in balancing budgets and securing adequate revenue

8. E. Eyck, *A History of the Weimar Republic*, vol. 2 (New York, 1963), pp. 119–20.

9. See tables in Schuker *American Reparations*, pp. 24–33.

10. See the controversy summarized in M. E. Falkus, 'The German business cycle in the 1920s', *Economic History Review*, 28 (1975).

throughout the 1920s. Under the reforms of Matthias Erzberger in 1920, income tax and corporation tax became the main sources of revenue for the Reich; the central authorities were also to issue tax guidelines for the *Länder*. Yet rational fiscal policy proved to be barely possible during the years of falling money values and hyperinflation. After stabilization in 1924 the only political consensus on taxation was to reduce it. German business in particular saw the tax rates as unduly burdensome, as indeed they were in comparison with those in Britain and France. In 1929 the Reich Association of Industry (*Reichsverband der deutschen Industrie* – RDI) intensified its resistance to tax rises in a memorandum entitled 'Advance or decline'. The state had also been compelled to finance the surge in public sector employment during the war. The ambitious social welfare policies and the costs of the 1927 unemployment insurance law imposed another and growing burden on the public purse. In general, governments absorbed a rising proportion of national income, particularly to fund public sector salaries and social services. Reparations agent Parker Gilbert's annual survey indicated a rise in transfers from the Reich to the *Länder* and municipalities of 19.1 per cent and a surge in the administrative costs of government by 57.7 per cent. Social expenses 'ballooned' by almost 420 per cent.[11] Communal authorities had obviously spent freely in the name of social order. Government borrowing to fund the budget became increasingly difficult and revenue fell rapidly during the depression. By March 1931 the state budget was showing a 431 million mark deficit.[12]

In this atmosphere, ending reparations remained absolutely central to government policy. The goal moved nearer with the replacement of the Dawes scheme by the Young plan, which at last set a time limit to payments of 59 years, reduced the final sum to between 37 and 40 (as opposed to the original 132) milliard marks and ended foreign controls. Germany was to assume full responsibility for transferring payments but in 1932 the Lausanne conference finally abandoned reparations completely. Overall calculations of reparations flows and foreign loans for the period 1919–31 now indicate that the European allies but above all the Americans actually subsidized Germany during the Weimar era.[13] Although the political impact of reparations cannot be stressed too strongly, it is therefore likely that in economic terms they only marginally worsened Germany's existing problems.

11. Schuker, *American Reparations*, pp. 32–3.
12. James, *The German Slump*, pp. 23ff.
13. S. Schuker, 'The end of Versailles', in G. Martel (ed.) *The Origins of the Second World War Reconsidered: The A. J. P. Taylor debate after twenty-five years* (London, 1986), p. 56.

Ultimately, the combination of expensive social welfare schemes, growing wage burdens and failing productivity, not to mention bad management, brought about a state of affairs where by the late 1920s the Weimar Republic was living beyond its means. Its economy was simply too weak to sustain the enormous rises in public expenditure. More charitably, its governments might be regarded as the victims of a bold but premature attempt (characteristic of Europe after 1945) to maintain both full employment and adequate welfare as the pillars of democratic consensus.[14]

BRÜNING'S ECONOMIC POLICY

Heinrich Brüning undoubtedly exploited the crisis to achieve specific economic objectives when he became Chancellor in 1930. As in the political field, however, it is by no means clear that he can be blamed for the destruction of the Weimar system. In the last resort Brüning could not manage to eliminate the budget deficit which had dogged all Weimar governments. This is partly why critics have attacked his resolution in pursuing a deflationary policy instead of seeking alternatives. The decrees initiating deflation began on 7 July 1930, with a ten per cent reduction in wages, prices, rents and profits, and continued through 1931 and into 1932. During his term in office Brüning made a remarkable cut of thirty-eight per cent in public expenditure. What is more he quite deliberately capitalized on the public fear of inflation and the memory of 1923 to reinforce the idea of fiscal rectitude – stressing balanced budgets, penalizing consumption in favour of investment and reducing social expenditure.[15]

Did Brüning *have* to deflate or could he have resorted to a range of options, including that of deficit financing, to stimulate among other things work creation schemes? In fairness he can only sensibly be criticized for not pursuing such Keynesian strategies by ignoring the obvious point that economic orthodoxy *at the time* favoured Brüning's tactics in dealing with the crisis. Those radical German economists who did advocate new approaches and who have been described as 'Keynesian before Keynes' gained precious little support in the

14. Cf. J. Baron von Kruedener (ed.), *Economic Crisis and Political Collapse. The Weimar Republic 1924–1933* (New York, Oxford, 1990).

15. Cf. P.-C. Witt, 'Die Auswirkungen der Inflation auf die Finanzpolitik des Deutschen Reiches 1924–1935' in Feldman (ed.), *Nachwirkungen der Inflation*, pp. 43–93.

establishment. Their main audience was to be found in the National Socialist movement.[16] Nor is it at all obvious that devaluation would necessarily have increased German exports. As to reducing interest rates, such a step was felt to be damaging to Germany's attempt to sustain its international creditworthiness. Finally, Brüning appears to have had a distinctly jaundiced view of German business performance before and after the banking crisis in 1931, and indeed of the banks themselves. He believed strongly that they did too little for medium and small concerns and did not co-operate properly with each other.[17]

The essence of the problem was that by 1931 the government appeared to be trapped in a network of vicious circles, where even raising taxes would further reduce business profits and worsen the depression. Thus by 1931 at the latest it was impossible even to raise enough domestic credit to finance a work-creation programme. The alternative of foreign loans was not seriously viable owing to external risk assessments of Germany.[18] Trying to balance the conflicting demands of agriculture and industry during the depression presented additional difficulties. Under these circumstances deflation seemed the safest and indeed minimalist option.[19] There is nonetheless a case for arguing that Brüning continued to embrace deflation long after it was needed, in so far as the material distress of the German population facilitated his drive in the foreign policy arena to have reparations abolished.[20] Although industry benefited from Brüning's policies through lower wages, the hoped for surge in German exports failed to appear in the prevailing world climate. Protectionist pressures on Brüning increased. Other measures to tackle unemployment became imperative. The fact remains that when Brüning's successors did get round to introducing major public spending programmes they did so without the outside funding still considered essential by the government in 1931. From September 1932 onwards von Papen allocated 700 million marks for such schemes, including premiums to firms of 400 marks per annum for each individual worker hired. Von

16. Cf. J. W. Hiden and J. Farquharson, *Explaining Hitler's Germany. Historians and the Third Reich* (2nd edn, 1989), p. 134.

17. G. D. Feldman, 'Industrialists, bankers and the problem of unemployment in the Weimar Republic', *Central European History*, 25 (1993): 76–96.

18. K. Borchardt and H. O. Schötz (eds), *Wirtschaftspolitik in der Krise. Die (Geheim-) Konferenz der Friedrich List-Gesellschaft im Sept 1931 über Möglichkeiten und Folgen einer Kreditausweiterung* (Baden-Baden, 1991).

19. Overy, *Nazi Economic Recovery*, p. 23

20. In general, G. Schulz, *Von Brüning zu Hitler. Der Wandel des politischen Systems in Deutschland 1930–1933. Vol 3. Zwischen Demokratie und Diktatur. Verfassungspolitik und Reichsreform in der Weimarer Republik* (Berlin, New York, 1993).

Schleicher subsequently set up a Reichs Commissariat for Work Creation under Dr Gereke. The Schleicher cabinet's *Sofort* programme began to pay concerns engaged in state- funded projects with 'work creation bills'. Since these could be discounted by private banks the effect was to increase the amount of credit in circulation, something Brüning had tried to avoid as far as possible.[21]

THE VIEW FROM THE BOARD ROOM; BIG BUSINESS, THE REPUBLIC AND THE RISE OF HITLER

Germany has been charged with having a non-competitive, highly concentrated, high-priced industrial economy, with a disproportionate influence of a small class of large landowners, a high birth rate until 1914, too many rural smallholders and an influential petite bourgeoisie. Here we focus on German industry. Its structural problems have attracted less attention from historians than have its attitudes towards the Weimar Republic and the Hitler movement.

The difficulty of generalizing about business is clear even from the divisions within the Reich Association of German Industry (RDI). The organization arose as a fusion between the pre-war groups representing respectively light and export industry on the one hand, heavy industry on the other: the League of Industrialists (*Bund der Industriellen* – BDI) and the Central Association of German Industrialists (*Centralverband Deutscher Industrieller*). Until the end of the 1920s big business as a whole – export-oriented branches as well as the heavy industrialists of the Ruhr – in fact acknowledged the vital importance of the German export drive. Thus although protectionist tariffs were reinstated at agriculture's insistence in August 1925 (small tariff revision), they were kept beneath the original high levels of 1902. They were low enough not to seriously impede Stresemann's pursuit of most-favoured-nation trade treaties with Germany's international partners. Too steep a rise in tariffs in any case would have increased demands for wage rises, making it still more difficult than it already was to maintain agreement between employers and unions. The RDI therefore backed the free trade treaties concluded after 1925, the year incidentally when Germany recovered sovereignty over its trade policy in accordance with the Versailles terms.[22]

21. W. Fischer, *Deutsche Wirtschaftspolitik 1918–1945* (Opladen, 1968), pp. 57–8.

22. D. Gessner, 'The dilemma of German agriculture during the Weimar Republic' in R. Bessel and E. Feuchtwanger (eds), *Social Change and Political Development in Weimar Germany* (London, 1981).

After 1929, however, rifts in the RDI ranks became more apparent whilst at the same time the immensely powerful agricultural lobby began to use its considerable political weight more aggressively to pressure governments for greater protection.[23] Few historians would now accept that big business as a whole was against the Weimar Republic as such, although it found extreme difficulty in swallowing the social gains of the revolution. Indeed, the agreement between workers and big business reached during the revolution had already tilted in favour of employers by 1923.[24] The latter exploited the Ruhr crisis to try to breach the eight-hour working day and later responded to the great depression by calling for social welfare to be rolled back. An examination of the chemical industry confirms that the major employers had long aimed to have the maximum independence in regulating conditions in their factories. Increasingly they sought to operate through private agreements with the unions to contain shop floor militants.[25] On the other hand, not all employers were in favour of the Ruhr lockout of labour in 1927. It cannot even be said for certain that newer and older industries were respectively more or less sympathetic to the Republic. The management of an enterprise was the crucial factor. In the event, an uneasy but usually peaceful co-existence between big business and government was practised for most of the 1920s. Backing from industry went overwhelmingly to the main conservative parties, the DNVP and the DVP. The decline of the latter during the final crisis is evidence, if anything, that business could be surprisingly weak in the Weimar Republic when it came to exercising political influence.[26]

In this and other important respects Alfred Hugenberg was an exception amongst German industrialists in dedicating his resources so assiduously to overthrowing the Weimar political order. In November 1925, reacting to the Locarno treaties, the press baron insisted:

Those who follow in Rathenau's track, who spoke of the primacy of the economy in relation to politics, fail to appreciate that our current economic ills have political rather than economic origins: the loss of the

---

23. For documents on this, I. Maurer and U. Wengst (eds), *Politik und Wirtschaft in der Krise 1930–32. Quellen zur Ära Bruening*, 2 vols, (Düsseldorf, 1980). See also M. Gruebler, *Die Spitzenverbände der Wirtschaft und das erste Kabinett Bruening* (Düsseldorf, 1982).

24. Cf. M. Ruck, *Die Freien Gewerkschaften im Ruhrkampf 1923* (Cologne, 1986), pp. 11–12.

25. C. D. Patton, 'The myth of moderation: German chemical employer responses to labour conflict, 1914–1924', *European History* 24 (1994): 31–52.

26. Cf. H. James, *The German Slump*, p. 178.

war, the revolution, the dependence of everything happening in Germany on the ballot box . . . Salvation can only come from within rather than without, above all not with foreign aid.[27]

He applied funds, patronage and influence to achieve his ends and his 'system was based on the highly organized and persistent application of all the traditional means . . . and was amplified by means of a modern press geared up to mass society'.[28] If he differed from most industrialists in putting politics before profit, his disillusionment with Weimar ultimately came to be shared by other business leaders as the 1920s wore on. Moreover, although relatively few German industrialists put much money into the NSDAP, *some* did. In the early post-war years a few minor Bavarian firms gave support, as did the industrialist Ernst von Borsig. Fritz Thyssen is an obvious example of a major backer from 1923 onwards, while the Daimler Motor Company was also one of the select group donating money to the NSDAP in its formative years. Indeed the director of the merged Daimler-Benz group, Jakob Werlin, became a personal friend of Hitler's from 1923.[29] Individual Nazis, notably Hermann Goering, Gregor Strasser, Walther Funk, had subsidies from entrepreneurs. The greater financial backing from industrialists after 1932 may well have been a form of 'insurance', but it represented valuable assistance at a time when party funds were stretched.[30]

On balance, therefore, Germany's major industrialists hardly match up en bloc to the image propagated by Marxist historical writing of German big business as the paymaster of National Socialism. Apart from small businesses and the occasional prominent entrepreneur, most captains of industry reverted to authoritarian conservatism when contemplating the political conflicts in the Reichstag and when responding to what they regarded as the state's pro-labour legislation. In Franz von Papen, many businessmen felt they had the ideal leader, with twenty-one major industrialists prepared to fund parties supporting him. Even the great I. G. Farben combine, *bête noire* of Marxist historiography, turns out on closer examination to have shunned the rabid nationalism of the right during the 1920s. It

27. H. Holzbach, *Das System Hugenberg. Die Organization der bürgerlichen Sammlungspolitik vor dem Aufstieg der NSDAP* (Stuttgart, 1981), p. 189.
28. Ibid., p. 254.
29. B. P. Bellon, *Mercedes in Peace and War. German Automobile Workers 1903–1945* (New York, 1990), pp. 195, 197.
30. H. A. Turner Jr, 'Big business and the rise of Hitler', *American Historical Review*, 75 (1969): 115. Also his major book, *German Big Business and the Rise of Hitler* (New York, Oxford, 1985).

favoured the consolidation of a bourgeois bloc crossing the confessional divide, and provided funds for the DDP, the DVP and the Centre Party. The chemicals giant supported the principles of free trade until 1933, adopted a moderate line on trade unions and had very little direct contact with National Socialists. The latter even attacked the IG Farben cartel as the 'agents of destructive Jewish international finance'.

The fact is, however, that through their widespread indifference to the parliamentary system established after 1918, the German business community must shoulder its due share of the blame for Hitler's eventual success in taking over the state. Far more attention must also be given to the exchange of ideas between the business community and the radical right as a whole, rather than narrowing the discussion to the question of how extensive was the financial backing of industry for the NSDAP. There are disturbing suggestions, for example, that the labour policy of the giant Siemens concern had affinities with National Socialist ideology, in placing emphasis on recruiting and maintaining an elite core of skilled workers.[31] Similar overlaps could be found in the case of the Daimler-Benz group, which the metal-workers' union dubbed 'The German–nationalist swastika company' during the 1920s.[32] In the end the complexity and ambiguity characterizing NSDAP/business relations in the 1920s provide an important key to the uneasy relationship between party and industry during the Third Reich and particularly after 1936.

GOVERNMENTAL STRATEGIES IN THE THIRD REICH

The dominant role played by rearmament in National Socialist economic strategies throughout the 1930s was stressed in virtually all accounts from 1940 onwards, popularizing the notion of the Third Reich as a war economy in peacetime. It was inferred that National Socialism pursued territorial conquest and plunder as a substitute for economic policy, an idea in keeping with the view that Hitler and other National Socialists were ignorant about economics. That was not

---

31. C. Sachse, *Siemens, der Nationalsozialismus und die moderne Familie. Eine Untersuchung zur sozialen Rationalisierung in Deutschland im 20 Jahrhundert* (Hamburg, 1990).

32. Bellon, *Mercedes*, p. 208.

strictly true. Some of the ideas within the National Socialist movement, such as those advanced by Gottfried Feder on the need to distinguish between 'creative' and 'parasitic' capitalism, are indeed odd. Yet they represent part of a wider process of economic thought developing within the NSDAP. The party programme of 1920 had no fewer than ten out of its twenty-five points devoted to general economic issues. Other elements were being fed into the economic *Weltanschauung* of National Socialism by party activists like Otto Wagener and Gregor Strasser. The latter was influenced in turn by the unorthodox ideas of economists such as Friedlander-Prechtl, who advocated greater state intervention to generate economic recovery.[33] The influence of both Strasser and Wagener on economic policy survived their personal falls from grace with Hitler. Strasser's policy proposals in the 'Immediate Programme' of 1932, for example, appear even to have influenced Hjalmar Schacht's better known 'New Plan' of 1934.[34]

Hitler also took part in the economic debate, notably in the confidential economic policy conferences which Wagener conducted at the Führer's request in the Brown House at Munich, during 1931 and 1932. While few would wish to claim Hitler as a master of the dismal science, he was far from being the economic ignoramus portrayed by many of his biographers.[35] His unwillingness to make detailed commitments prior to seizing power barely concealed his acute awareness of the importance of promoting economic recovery. Into the discussions Hitler injected his belief in the fittest individuals and businesses surviving in the coming economic order, as well as the vision of a huge Central European economic bloc, or *Grossraumwirtschaft*, where the German economy could be 'crisis free'. Rearmament was therefore an integral part of a broader autarkic economic strategy, transcending preparations for war alone, central as these undoubtedly always were.

Within this broad context Hjalmar Schacht, President of the Reichsbank from 17 March 1933 and Reich Minister of Economics and Minister for the Prussian Economy from 30 July 1934, no longer appears as the sole economic mastermind of Nazi recovery. In discussing Schacht with Wagener during 1932, Hitler observed that he could afford not to demand the Ministry of Economics for a Nazi in

33. A. Barkai, *Das Wirtschaftssystem des Nationalsozialismus* (Cologne, 1977), pp. 27–8.
34. G. Kroll, *Von der Weltwirtschaftskrise zur Staatskonjunktur* (Berlin, 1958), p. 433.
35. J. Heyl, 'Hitler's economic thought. A reappraisal', *Central European History*, 6 (1973): 83ff.

his future government precisely because the movement would be determining the salient features anyway:

> What is crucial is whether he [Schacht] can agree to finance the jobs-creation programme along our lines. He seems willing. After all, he has no choice. If he refuses, and we put another man in the post who manages to solve the problem – and we have no doubts that the programme will succeed – then the aura of infallibility in which the great men of the banking world have enveloped themselves so far dissolves into thin air. And they will not incur this risk. They prefer to swallow the bitter pill and allow Schacht to perform the magic.[36]

Schacht duly pulled some rabbits out of the hat and overcame credit restrictions to the expansion of the armaments sector through the issue of the so-called 'Mefo' Bills (the name derived from the *Metallurgische Forschungs-GmbH*, set up by the Reichsbank and the Reich Ministry of Defence). Mefo Bills met the needs of the government contractors. The Bills, held by the Reichsbank as well as by private investors, were to be repaid in five years from the increased tax revenues. Not only did this bring back liquidity into the system but it helped to ensure that the expansion of private savings benefited the finances of the Reich rather than the private capital market. The Mefo Bills contributed some 20 per cent of total armaments costs before the outbreak of war in 1939.[37]

Yet no single sector of the economy on its own could generate the sort of growth to explain the remarkable recovery in Germany by the mid-1930s. Laws to reduce unemployment were passed on 1 June and 21 September 1933. Loans and advances, tax concessions – all were made available for relevant projects. These included improvement and maintenance schemes in the private and public sector. Most of the one milliard marks under the first law went to the building industry. On 27 June 1933 came the law initiating the construction of the first autobahn. Car production was up 50 per cent by 1934 (road expenditure had risen by 100 per cent in comparison with the 1920s high point) and money was spent on electrification projects. Other ways of massaging unemployment figures included 'voluntary' labour service (later, from March 1935, compulsory labour service). Unemployed rural workers were put to work for low wages or allocated to poorly rewarded relief works. Propaganda emphasized the value of employing manpower rather than machinery, arguably

---

36. H. A. Turner Jr (ed.) *Hitler. Memoirs of a Confidant* (New Haven, London, 1985), p. 321.
37. Overy, *Nazi Economic Recovery*, pp. 45–6.

exposing the party's fundamental indifference to the questions concerning the long-term modernization of the German economy. Thus the three groups accounting for the largest falls in unemployment were in agriculture, in the building industry and among unskilled labour.[38]

The part played by public expenditure in the recovery process was paramount. The public debt rose from 12.9 milliard on 31 March 1933 to 42.7 milliard by 31 March 1939. The intention was to replace export-led demand (an impossible dream during the conditions of the 1930s) with the demand from the growth of heavy industry. That is to say, construction, rather than consumption, was to be favoured above all. This was reflected in the surge of government investment and state spending in the 1930s. However, private investment was also stimulated by government policy, either through incentives or through direct government intervention. The credit act of September 1934, on which Schacht's 'New Plan' rested, provides an example. As well as seeking to reduce passive foreign trade balances by introducing clearing credits, the New Plan further restricted the mechanisms traditionally determining the flow of credit. Restraints on capital issues and severe levies on dividends above six per cent through the corporation laws of 1934 also helped to control the capital market, diminishing the independent role of the stock exchange and the banks while exerting pressure on firms to plough back their undistributed profits into their business.[39] There were also tax concessions for new machinery purchased from profits. Private investment rose above public investment levels by 1938. Of the pressure exerted on industry to maintain high investment from undistributed profits it has been said: 'The freedom to issue shares for industrial expansion was effectively removed.'[40]

Contemporary economists such as Guillebaud argued in pre-war studies that the German government could if it so chose exploit its control of investment and savings to minimize inflationary risks once full employment returned to the economy by 1935–36.[41] Arguments like this assumed a return to more normal economic intercourse between Germany and the other powers. We are now all too aware that Hitler desired anything but the return of normal trade and

38. Ibid., pp. 49–50.

39. O. Nathan, *The Nazi Economic System. Germany's mobilisation for War* (Durham, North Carolina, 1944), p. 32.

40. Overy, *Nazi Economic Recovery*, p. 35.

41. C. W. Guillebaud, *The Economic Recovery of Germany from 1933 to the Incorporation of Austria* (London, 1939).

consumption patterns. Instead he planned to increase heavy industry's output and to accelerate the pace of rearmament. Hermann Goering, who shared these views, was placed in control of the Office of the Third Year Plan, inaugurated in August 1936. In Hitler's secret memorandum accompanying the Four Year Plan the goal of Lebensraum was used to justify the drive for greater self-sufficiency for Germany. This involved among other measures the production of synthetic fuels and other substitutes to supplement stocks of raw materials. The export offensive in south-eastern Europe and in South America, which Schacht's legislation had initiated, was to be intensified.

Schacht and the National Socialists had been at one in fostering huge increases in public expenditure between 1933 and 1936 to kick-start the economy. Once Hitler had made it clear that rearmament took absolute priority over the pursuit of profits, the Minister for Economics began to play a lesser role, resigning from his post in November 1937. He lingered on ineffectually in his capacity as president of the Reichsbank until January 1939. Walter Funk, Schacht's successor at the economics ministry, in effect deferred increasingly to Goering, in whose hands the real powers of economic decision-making were concentrated.

BIG BUSINESS AND 'FULL FASCISM'

The variations in the degree and rigour of state intervention in the private sector before and after 1936 have often been described in terms of the difference between 'partial' and 'full' fascism. It would have been difficult in fact to find an absolutely clear break. The regime manifestly set great store at first by the collaboration of industry in the wider task of economic recovery. Radicals within the party were muzzled and Schacht's own appointment underpinned the co-operation between Hitler and big business. After the Reich Association of German Industry became the Reich Corporation of German Industry on 19 June 1933, the industrialists continued to dominate it. The general situation remained much the same after the *Law for the Preparation of the Organic Construction of the German Economy* (27.2.1934), and the reorganization of industrial associations in the Reich Chamber of Industry.[42]

42. M. Broszat, *The Hitler State. The Foundation and Development of the Internal Structure of the Third Reich* (London, 1981), pp. 170–1.

Analysts of the left who observed the situation at the time might be forgiven for concluding of the National Socialist economy that 'the single, sole and dominating purpose is necessarily profits' and that German business still called the tune.[43] In reality, the penetration of the Reich associations by National Socialism was in itself deeply significant, as was the extension of controls in the financial and banking sectors already noted. Moreover, the state deliberately favoured different facets of industrial production, with consumer goods falling far behind building and heavy industry. More ominously, examples soon abounded where industrial managers who espoused the National Socialist ideology were favoured. It has been said that economic anti-Semitism was exercised with relative restraint prior to 1937–38, since the regime's priority was to end unemployment. In fact Jewish business leaders were subjected to boycotts long before this. The take-over of Jewish businesses, particularly when measured at village and small town levels, was a cumulative process.[44]

What the changes of 1936 would ultimately mean for German business Goering had no hesitation in spelling out during his speech to industrialists on 17 December of that year. It was another landmark in the regime's progress in breaking free of the traditional elites in economy and society, with whom Hitler had felt obliged to work in 1933:

> The context to which we look forward calls for enormous efficiency. No end to rearmament is in sight. All that matters is victory or defeat. If we conquer, the business world will be fully indemnified. We must not reckon profit and loss according to the book, but only according to political needs. There must be no calculations of cost. I require you to do all you can and to prove that part of the national fortune is in your hands. Whether new investment can be written off in every case is a matter of indifference. We are playing for the highest stakes. What can be more profitable than rearmament orders?[45]

If the private sector had any doubts about what the Four Year Plan implied, these were removed by Goering's confrontation with the Ruhr iron and steel producers in 1937. The producers were unwilling to increase their own costs of production by using the inferior grades of domestic produced ore, which Goering favoured in order to reduce

---

43. R. A. Brady, *The Spirit and Structure of German Fascism* (London, 1937), p. 321.
44. Cf. A. Barkai, *Vom Boykott zur 'Entjudung'. Der wirtschaftliche Existenzkampf der Juden im Dritten Reich 1933–1943* (Frankfurt am Main, 1988), p. 72.
45. Cited in K. Hildebrand, *The Third Reich* (London, 1984), p. 43.

Germany's dependence on foreign supplies in any possible war. The response of the leader of the Office of the Four Year Plan was to set up a state firm, the *Reichswerke Hermann Goering*. The new concern monopolized the nation's ore deposits and forced heavy industry to use the more expensive iron. In August of the same year Goering confronted the opposition of heavy industry to nationalization and self-sufficiency head on, threatening business leaders with charges of sabotage. Another example of the regime's determination to force through its own priorities was the setting up of the Reich Coal Association (*Reichsvereinigung Kohle* – RVK) in 1941. This was a response to the Ruhr mining industry's persistent failure to develop the necessary 'commitment' to the regime, in spite of the incentives given to coal producers in the 1930s – operating autonomy, labour discipline, export subsidies and large public contracts.[46]

Ruhr coal was perhaps 'the "worst case" example of industry–regime relationships during the Nazi years'.[47] On the face of it profits went above all to the industries who were prepared to collaborate actively with the regime. The Daimler–Benz company almost immediately reaped its rewards and its disastrous performance during the slump was soon reversed. Jakob Werlin was deliberately given responsibility for ensuring that the motor car giant kept in the regime's good books. The heavy tax on cars was lifted in 1933 and Daimler–Benz was soon playing a major role in motorizing the armed forces. Business doubled by 1934. The company's plants at Sindelfingen and Untertuerkheim were designated 'armaments factories' and thereby assured of special treatment. Together with the regime the Daimler–Benz concern agreed in 1935 to the building of a mass aircraft motor factory at Genshagen, which was employing some 10,000 workers by 1941. The construction costs of this factory were covered by the air ministry. Between 1932 and 1941, Daimler–Benz production soared by 830 per cent. With some justice it has been argued that: 'The great Mercedes Reich was built with the Hitler regime's massive military build-up.'[48]

However, IG Farben is invariably cited as the prime example of industry profiting from the Third Reich. 'Farben's products became ubiquitous and essential. . . . By 1943, the concern's 334 plants and mines across Germany and occupied Europe were turning out more than three billion marks' worth of goods and earning net profits of

46. J. Gillingham, *Industry and Politics in the Third Reich. Ruhr Coal, Hitler and Europe* (London, 1985), p. 114.
47. Ibid., p. 163.
48. Bellon, *Mercedes*, p. 219.

over half a billion.'[49] This is all the more interesting in view of the conglomerate's cautious response to National Socialism during the 1920s. There is little doubt that the chemicals combine *wanted* to influence policy to favour its own commercial priorities. In co-operating with Goering to build up a new synthetics industry, a member of the IG Farben board, Carl Krauch, also played a major role in the Office of the Four Year Plan by directing its critically important research and development section. Krauch's dual authority was said to exemplify 'the personal union of private and state leadership', giving extra flexibility to economic management under the Four Year Plan.[50] On such evidence was built the all too familiar argument that the Four Year Plan began and ended as the IG Farben plan. Closer examination of the complex structure of the Four Year Plan office reveals that only Carl Krauch's domain and the section concerned with financing, under Kurt Lange, were headed by personnel drawn from the ranks of German big business. While Lange had close links with the NSDAP, Krauch was initially often under attack from the party as well as from the Ministry of Economics and some army leaders because of his links with IG and because of his tendency to select his subordinates from the world of industry.[51]

The reality was that in time 'both Krauch and his subordinates rapidly identified with their new tasks, not their old employers, even when private corporations continued to pay their salaries'.[52] Ultimately, not only were IG Farben managers unable to deflect the ill effects of the Four Year Plan on their firm's foreign trade, but increasingly had to run with government priorities. An obvious example of this concerned the chemical industries before the war in Austria, Czechoslovakia, Poland, Alsace-Lorraine, the Baltic states and Russia. IG had largely ignored concerns in these places because there had been insignificant sales openings and no major competition. However, IG was soon compelled to involve itself with these chemical industries as the states concerned came under the control of the Reich. The overriding priority for IG was to defend its own market position in the Old Reich, but in order to shut down potential intruders into its domestic spheres of interest, the company had to make major concessions to the regime to achieve 'even a portion of its objectives'. IG's imperialism tended if anything to follow the flag.[53] It would be

49. P. Hayes, *Industry and Ideology. I. G. Farben in the Nazi Era* (Cambridge, 1989), pp. xi–xii.
50. Broszat, *Hitler State*, pp. 301–2.
51. Hayes, *Industry and Ideology*, p. 176.
52. Ibid., p. 178.
53. Ibid., pp. 264–5.

going too far to suggest that German enterprise would have preferred to buy eastern Europe rather than to conquer it physically, but the case of IG Farben reveals how the disruption to normal business and foreign trade entailed by the war could also make it unpopular with the private sector.

THE ECONOMY AND WAR PREPARATIONS

The relationship between government economic policy and both the timing and nature of the war for which Germany was preparing is a problematic one. Early accounts of the Third Reich written soon after the battle started did not doubt that Germany's economy had been put on a secure footing for war *before* 1939.[54] Not until the late 1950s, after a study based among other things on the United States's strategic bombing surveys, was the idea more widely accepted that the Third Reich was not properly prepared for the war on which it actually embarked in 1939.[55] This suggested a number of possibilities. One was that Hitler had not really intended a full-scale European war (Taylor); alternatively, that the regime had deliberately calculated a series of limited conflicts (Milward). On the latter assumption, the German leaders could afford to be sanguine about the poor performance indicators of the German economy by 1936–7. These included a shortage of skilled labour following the return to full employment by the mid-1930s, causing competition among employers and exerting pressure on wage and price controls aimed at checking consumer demand. The dread threat of inflation lurked. In addition Germany's foreign currency reserves could not cover the costs of imported foodstuffs as well as the raw materials required to sustain heavy industry's production. Yet those same conditions have been interpreted as forcing the regime to respond by launching war against Poland and, through conquest, sparing the German public the looming economic hardship. Blitzkrieg would then appear as a leap forward to escape domestic problems (Mason).[56]

54. Nathan, *Nazi Economic System*, p. 32.
55. B. H. Klein, *Germany's Economic Preparations for War* (Yale, 1959).
56. A. J. P. Taylor, *The Origins of the Second World War* (London, 1964 edition): see for example pp. 16–17; A. S. Milward, *The German Economy at War* (London, 1965); T. W. Mason, 'Innere Krise und Angriffskrieg 1938–9' in F. Forstmeier and H. E. Volkmann (eds), *Wirtschaft und Rüstung am Vorabend des zweiten Weltkrieges* (Düsseldorf, 1975), pp. 158–88.

Part of the problem with the latter explanation is that economists like Guillebaud, writing before 1939, stressed the options open to the National Socialists in regulating the economy, not least because of the government's extensive control over investment among other things. Moreover it has proved difficult to demonstrate conclusively that there *was* a general and agreed strategy for Blitzkrieg before the unexpectedly rapid German military successes in the west in 1940.[57] On balance, it begins to look more likely that the crisis in Germany's economy in the late 1930s was not the cause of the war's outbreak but rather a manifestation of the regime's adherence to an increasingly risky foreign policy. The economy was subjected to mounting strain because of Hitler's foreign policy agenda and a deep-seated resistance to arguments in favour of returning to something like more normal economic intercourse. The economy then suddenly had to catch up with foreign policy in 1939, when Goering's original remit to prepare the economy for a prolonged conflict was abruptly transformed into a demand to actually produce materials for the battlefield. Not for the first or last time the regime's own actions restricted Germany's freedom of manoeuvre.[58]

The victory over Poland and the subsequent exploitation of that country for labour and materials relieved the Reich of some of its bottlenecks. In addition the 1939 pact with the USSR removed the threat of blockade and allowed vital Russian exports to be concentrated on Germany. Hitler's ensuing and astonishingly rapid military victories in the west in 1940 then offered the prospect of an economic European 'New Order' being constructed. It became clear from an outpouring of internal memoranda that the economic preponderance Germany already enjoyed in the Balkan region would now be enlarged through the incorporation of Holland, Belgium, Luxembourg, Denmark and Norway in the greater economic sphere. This could be augmented in time by a firmer economic integration of Sweden and Finland, along the lines already drawn by Germany's treaties with the three Baltic states in 1939–40.[59] The clear implication of all this was that any European new order would be primarily for

57. Cf. B. R. Kroener, 'Squaring the circle. Blitzkrieg strategy and manpower shortage 1939–1942' in W. Deist (ed.), *The German Military in the Age of Total War* (Leamington Spa, 1985), pp. 284–5.

58. See R. Overy's lucid exposition in his books *Goering. The 'Iron Man'* (London, 1984) and *Nazi Economic Recovery*, cited earlier in this chapter at notes 5, 19, 37, 40.

59. See for example the memorandum of 1 June 1940 by Karl Ritter, 'The Greater Economic Sphere' in Noakes and Pridham, *Nazism 1919–1945. Volume 3. Foreign Policy, War and Racial Extermination* (Exeter, 1988), pp. 886–8.

Germany's benefit in the long run. However, from the autumn of 1940 the German government was forced to concentrate increasingly on extracting as much as possible from the occupied territories in order to prosecute the war. How this would influence the nature of the new order became immediately clear from the treatment of occupied Poland.

The German share of Poland now comprised two new *Gaue* incorporated into the Reich, the Warthegau and Danzig, as well as the General Government 'appended' to the Third Reich under Hans Frank's administration. Hitler left Frank in no doubt that 'this territory in its entirety is booty of the German Reich . . . the territory in its entirety shall be economically used'.[60] This meant among other things massive displacement of persons from occupied Poland to the General Government, which promised to be a vast reservoir of forced labour for the Third Reich. In insisting that Germany was only interested in Polish workers Hitler underlined his utter indifference to the fate of the Polish intelligentsia, clergy, nobility and of course Jews, to which we shall return in the penultimate chapter. The ideological imperatives of the regime were equally clear as Hitler again considered economic prospects shortly after the invasion of Russia had begun. He specifically referred to the way in which the Reich had concealed its long-term motives in the case of Norway, Denmark, Holland and Belgium and stressed the need to do the same in occupied Soviet territory.

> We shall then emphasise again that we are forced to occupy, administer and secure a certain area; it was in the interests of the inhabitants that we should provide order, food, traffic etc., hence our measures. It should not be made obvious that a final settlement is therefore being initiated! We can nonetheless take all necessary measures – shooting, resettling etc. – and we shall take them . . . It must be clear to *us*, however, that we shall never withdraw from these areas.[61]

No detailed economic plans had been prepared for dealing with Soviet-occupied territories, broadly governed by Alfred Rosenberg's *Ostministerium*, but Goering favoured straightforward exploitation. As the Third Reich became enmeshed in the struggle for survival following the reverses in the Russian campaign by late 1941, economic policy in German-occupied Europe became ever more geared to Germany' s own determination to survive at any cost. Doubtless, many

---

60. Cited in E. Homze, *Foreign Labour in Nazi Germany* (Princeton, New Jersey, 1967), p. 28.
61. Document printed in Noakes and Pridham, *Nazism*, volume 3, pp. 898–9.

private German concerns profited from the opportunities for plunder and/or for settling the score with foreign competitors during the war, although we have seen from the example of IG Farben the need for caution in making this the prime explanation of German business behaviour. In reality, German business soon found itself locked into a war effort over which it had little real say. The extensive controls with which the regime had equipped itself in 1939 enabled Goering's economic empire to grow accordingly. The *Reichswerke* eventually became the centre of a vast self-serving enterprise, sprawling throughout Europe and the occupied countries. The bureaucracy spawned by this creation was a radical one. Many of Goering's aides were attracted to the sort of new order where the focus of German industry would shift eastwards, fleshing out the National Socialist vision of hewing out an Empire at the expense of the Soviet Union and the East European states. The importance of the regime's ideological grip is hugely underestimated by describing *Mitteleuropa* during the war as 'little more than a synonym for German economic hegemony'.[62]

True, the frenetic improvisation on which Goering and others embarked under pressure of war brought with it wastefulness and inefficiency and with this a growing pressure to involve the business world more in economic management. Goering's failure to harness the expertise in the private sector properly was an important factor in his inability to provide equipment and supplies on the scale demanded by Hitler to sustain the increasingly costly war effort. Goering's slide from grace during the crisis of 1941 led eventually to the appointment of the architect Albert Speer as Armaments Minister in February 1942 after the accidental death of Fritz Todt. Speer was effectively given powers to bypass the Office of the Four Year Plan, since Hitler said of Goering at this time: 'This man cannot look after armaments within the framework of the Four Year Plan.'[63] The success of what Speer described as his own 'organized improvisation' was remarkable. With his authority secured by the *Order on the Control of the War Economy* (2.9.43), Speer increasingly involved the industrial experts in the war effort and managed to create the conditions for almost a threefold increase in war production from 1941 to 1944. At the same time, there proved to be small comfort here for those foolish enough to believe that Speer's activities heralded the reassertion of business primacy in the management of the economy.

62. A. McElligott, 'Reforging Mitteleuropa in the crucible of war', in P. Stirk (ed.), *Mitteleuropa. History and Prospects* (Edinburgh, 1994), p. 150.
63. A. Speer, *Inside the Third Reich* (London, 1971), p. 285.

The complex interpenetration of private and state economic structures so characteristic of the Third Reich was ultimately at the expense of the former. Whilst having more involvement in production and planning after 1941, German business leaders could not so easily escape the ideological grip of the regime. Nor did Speer, a dedicated National Socialist, suggest that matters should be otherwise. As we have seen, even the hugely powerful IG Farben combine could not actually determine policy objectives. Its influence was strongest where its technical know-how and capability was most in demand. Whenever the group tried to assert its interests in non-technical areas it invariably lost out to the political leadership. In this respect, however, even by continuing to function, IG Farben – like most if not all German business ventures, was thoroughly impregnated by the regime's values system and implicated in its consequences. Apart from making the synthetic rubber for Nazi war vehicles it manufactured the gas that murdered over a million people at Auschwitz, whilst almost 50 per cent of its work force came to consist of conscript or slave labour.[64] Daimler-Benz also benefited from such labour and as total war took over after autumn 1941 the company 'threw tens of thousands of foreign workers and concentration camp inmates into its battle to produce . . . Barracks, camps and "combing out" missions became integral parts of the Mercedes complex. Its facilities had become collections of labour processes and assembly lines which the brutalized men and women deported from their homes could service.'[65]

Depressingly, dependence on the state induced political compliance. The Daimler-Benz directors who mounted no significant opposition to the new economic realities were mirrored countless times over in other concerns, even if they were not regarded as such successful models of what a Nazi factory should be. In the interests of an economic efficiency as dictated by the political system, all too many German business leaders concentrated on doing their job and narrowly defending their own firms or shareholders. In that sense it is not possible to agree with David Schoenbaum that ideology stopped at the door of the boardroom. In the last resort German big business did not escape the dilemma which Goering had described in 1937: 'It comes down to this, whether the interests of the Reich or the crassest economic egoism shall prevail.'[66] The question was purely rhetorical as far as the National Socialist leadership was concerned.

64. Hayes, *Industry and Ideology*, p. xii.
65. Bellon, *Mercedes*, p. 265.
66. Cited by R. Overy, 'Business and the Third Reich', *History Review*, 13 (1992): 12–13.

CHAPTER SEVEN

Drudgery for Germany; The Path from Worker to Soldier of Labour

What the employers gained from their agreement with the trade unions in November–December 1918 was the stabilization of their own position and the prevention of full-blooded socialization. Workers, too, appeared to benefit from this community of intent. In the interests of keeping the factories going they were offered the eight-hour day and a greater voice in social policy and plant management. Within four years the bargain looked distinctly less appealing from the shop floor. Employers became more resistant to the expensive social demands of the unions after 1923 and were positively icy on the subject of parity of management. Yet the erosion of the 'civil truce' of 1918–19 cannot be fully understood without a wider view of the German workers' political organizations.

TRADE UNIONS AND THE LAW

The definition of a 'worker' presents problems for the electoral analysis of National Socialist support as we have seen but here the emphasis is broadly on the organizations of industrial workers. In the late nineteenth century such a worker was distinguished from a salaried employee (*Angestellte*) and a civil servant (*Beamte*) in the division of occupational organizations. When anti-combination laws were repealed from the end of the 1860s only industrial workers (*gewerbliche Arbeiter*) were allowed freedom of association. Their allegiance at that time was divided between the 'Free Unions' associated with the SPD, the Christian unions, formed at the turn of the century, and the liberal Hirsch–Dunker unions. Into this picture intruded the 'yellow' or tame company unions, although the latter were adversely affected by the agreement between Stinnes and Legien. Membership of the Christian trade unions reached a peak of more than one million members in 1920. Nominally inter-confessional, they mobilized mainly Catholics. 'Free' unions grew most of all, having 2 million members by 1914 and 8 million by 1920, and they dominated the General Federation of German Trade Unions (*Allgemeiner Deutscher Gewerkschaftsbund* – ADGB), formed in 1919. Thus divisions in German trade unionism persisted.

The above process mirrored the growth in manual workers as a result of Germany's rapid industrialization, from 3 million in 1913 to about 9.2 million in 1920. At the same time collective agreements expanded to embrace almost twenty per cent of German manual workers by 1914. Such developments should be kept firmly in perspective. Before the First World War, for example, a labour lawyer trenchantly described trade unions as 'free to be outlawed'.[1] After 1918 the right of association appeared at least to be anchored more securely to the legal system through the Weimar constitution. The latter also provided for worker participation in many social and economic issues at plant level (Article 165), as did the *Law on Factory Councils* in February 1920. The state's right to arbitrate in labour disputes was secured at law in October 1923. These basic principles of labour legislation were augmented by the decree on working time in 1923. According to Franz Neumann's essay, *The Social Significance of the Basic Laws in the Weimar Constitution* (1930):

> the social right is far more heavily protected than all the capitalist rights of freedom. While the actual content of the freedoms of private property, trade and enterprise is always subject to restriction by law, the protection enjoyed by the right of association is, quite simply, absolute. Neither federal nor Reich law can in any manner restrict the content of the right of association.[2]

The *practice* could be somewhat less favourable. The committee trying to draft the unified labour laws envisaged in the Weimar constitution (Article 157) ran into opposition and was disbanded by 1924, ostensibly for reasons of finance. In the absence of a secure and uniform code a veritable legal minefield developed. In effect three strands of employment law unfolded in the 1920s. Apart from that implementing

---

1. O. Kahn-Freund, *Labour Law and Politics in the Weimar Republic* (London–Oxford, 1981) pp. 30ff, on the legal framework of trade unions between 1869 and 1933.

2. Essay printed in K. Tribe (ed.), *Social Democracy and the rule of law: Otto Kirchheimer and Franz Neumann* (London, 1987), p. 39.

the revolutionary actions of 1918–19, labour law covered both private contracts and collective agreements. These had to be enforced if need be in court and there the difficulty began.

The early Weimar labour tribunals, rooted in the pre-war era, had strictly limited functions. From the time of the revolution onwards the unions reacted against the anti-worker bias in the regular courts by pressing to extend the jurisdiction of the labour tribunals to embrace all labour disputes, particularly those relating to collective agreements. Ultimately the *Law on Labour Courts* of 23 December 1926 brought about such an extension. At the same time, however, the local tribunals were coupled to two higher levels of appeal, namely the Regional Tribunal and the Reich Labour Court. Since the latter was a division of the Reich Supreme Court, ultimately professional judges and advocates tended to dominate proceedings, with fairly predictable results. Another labour lawyer encapsulated the process neatly in 1931: 'It is symptomatic of the whole approach of the Reich Labour Court that it is positively inclined to have regard to the interests of the employee in *individual* cases, but that it can only bring itself with difficulty to decide in favour of employees when it is concerned with a fundamental principle about which there is a major disagreement between the employers' associations and the trade unions.'[3] In other words the collective spirit enshrined in the constitution was eventually weakened in the courts, in so far as labour disputes fragmented into thousands of individual cases.

THE DECLINE OF THE UNIONS

Trade union power was undoubtedly diminished by the events of 1923. In supporting and indeed helping to manage passive resistance to the French occupation of the Ruhr, the ADGB leaders strove to increase their influence in the political and social sphere through integrating the unions into the nation. They looked in vain for parity of union and employer direction of the planned relief fund (*Ruhrhilfe*) and pressed for the Ruhr defence to be funded by taxation rather than the printing press. Little support came from either government or employers. The hollowness of the ZAG was cruelly exposed, union funds suffered and trade union membership declined thereafter. 1923

---

3. Kahn–Freund, *Labour Law*, p. 132.

therefore inflicted a severe blow to the 'civil truce'. Union leaders faced a still more sustained assault on their position in the second half of the 1920s and had to fight harder than ever to defend the social gains of the revolution. Employers, on the other hand, were bitter that real wage increases from 1924 exceeded productivity growth, making it still more difficult to finance investment either from profits or from capital. On the length of the working day, a focal point of resentment, employers eventually secured the decree of 21 December 1923. According to this the eight-hour day remained the norm but the decree also sanctioned its modification through industry-wide collective bargaining. State arbitration assumed considerable importance under such conditions.

The whole idea behind the tidying up of arbitration procedures under the law of October 1923 was, of course, to prevent serious disruptions of the economy through strikes. Arbitration boards were set up throughout Germany to handle regional conflicts. They were composed equally of management and labour representatives under the neutral chairmanship of *Land* government nominees. In the event of both parties to a dispute rejecting the conclusions of the boards, state arbitrators, appointed by the Ministry of Labour, were empowered to give a binding ruling after due consideration. Between 1924 and 1932 the process was used on no fewer than 76,000 occasions, leading to 4,000 compulsory awards. In this respect the process of state arbitration obviously provided some compensation for the weakening of union power. Nonetheless, the erosion of industrial harmony left the state increasingly exposed in its role as the preserver of peace between worker and employer and, arguably, made both more irresponsible.[4] What was quite certain was that the arbitration service was increasingly resented by the bosses. They provoked the most bitter of all labour disputes in the winter of 1928–9, when Ruhr industrialists rejected an arbitration award favouring iron workers and locked out more than 200,000 employees as a sign of their determination.

In retrospect the Ruhr lockout appears to have been the critical turning point in the social conflict. Although it was resolved through a compromise reducing the wage increase originally made by the arbitrator, it demonstrated the determination of Weimar employers to cut back production and other social costs. A huge burden had already been placed on the public budget as governments paid into welfare insurance to compensate for the crisis in 1923. If the state of the

4.   J. Baehr, *Staatliche Schlichtung in der Weimarer Republik. Tarifpolitik, Korporatismus und industrieller Konflikt zwischen Inflation und Deflation, 1919–1932* (Berlin, 1989).

German economy provided some justification for employers' anxiety about wage rises and welfare payments, their own hard-headed tactics were virtually guaranteed to provoke more resentment from the trade unions. In 1929–30, the latter were further weakened in the struggle over the social insurance system. The costs of this had again escalated as a result of the scheme's enlargement in 1927 and, more dramatically, because of soaring unemployment rates from the winter of 1928–9.

The above combination of factors made it difficult to continue financing the welfare support system as it was modified in 1927. At that point the new Reich Institute for Labour Exchanges and Unemployment Insurance began to administer relief for those able and willing to work but who found themselves without employment through no fault of their own. With almost 3 million unemployed by 1928–9 and relief levels fixed by law, the state increasingly lent money to the Reich Institute, making even more difficult the balancing of the overall budget. The crux of the matter was that unions and employers adopted opposed strategies to deal with the problem, the former clamouring for increased insurance contributions, the latter hell-bent on reducing benefits. This fundamental conflict over principle, rather than the fractional raised rate of unemployment insurance contributions itself, was what brought down Hermann Müller's 'Great Coalition' in 1930.

The drop in trade union membership during the course of the 1920s confirms that not all industrial workers saw eye to eye with the organizations representing them.[5] Yet general wage levels suggest that on the whole Weimar workers did reasonably well through their unions' efforts. Indeed, in the last part of the 1920s pay rises were not always linked to productivity. Pay was still below the highest pre-war levels in 1922 but between 1924 and 1928 real wages exceeded the pre-1914 high point. These figures can be compared with the drop in real income for agricultural workers between 1913 and 1929. Keynes therefore insisted that industrial wage costs were a major factor in the poor performance of German exporters, particularly since there was no labour shortage in the Weimar period. One drawback of such widespread wage demands was that legitimate claims were often not met, with increased dissatisfaction resulting.[6] In fact the rising cost of wages also reflected an annual increase in the labour force of 400,000

5. S. Salter, 'Germany', in S. Salter and J. Stevenson (eds), *The working class and politics in Europe and America 1929–1945* (London, 1990), pp. 99–124.
6. K. Borchardt, 'Wirtschaftliche Ursachen des Scheiterns der Weimarer Republik' in K. D. Erdmann and H. Schulze (eds), *Weimar: Selbstpreisgabe einer Demokratie. Eine Bilanz Heute* (Düsseldorf, 1980), pp. 218ff.

between 1924 and 1930, as well as a change in the ratio of blue- to white-collar workers. This had been 1 : 5.3 in 1907; by 1925 it stood at 1 : 2.8.[7] All in all, the situation looked far bleaker in the last years of the Republic. By 1932, national income had dropped to sixty-two per cent of what it had been in 1928. Unemployment was rampant, most of it in the industrial sector. What inflation might have brought about – continuing a trend observed by some prior to 1914 and during the war – was a greater levelling of pay awards. 'Differentials between adolescents and adults, male and female, skilled and unskilled workers were greatly reduced during the inflation years.'[8]

This view needs qualifying, in so far as men maintained their preferential status in the economy in the years of the Weimar Republic. During the war 75 per cent of the work force in German light industry had been female, the figure in heavy industry being 25 per cent. However, the guidelines for demobilization issued by the War Ministry indicated that women should give up jobs for veterans. Almost half the women at work in the 1920s in Germany were employed in agriculture, often as 'helping dependants'. The census for 1925 showed that although 5 per cent more women were at work than in 1907, the rise was nearer seven per cent for men. 68 per cent of males were employed in 1925 compared with 35 per cent of women.[9]

1930 marked the effective end of collective bargaining and ultimately the ADGB leaders reaped a bitter harvest for their efforts. Even the Christian union leadership, whose strategy had been less overtly in favour of sectional gain, had found it difficult to pursue 'national interests' in the face of reactionary employers.[10] The path which Franz Neumann depicted the unions taking between 1869 and 1933 – from repression via toleration to incorporation – had led to increased participation in public policy, but at the cost of weakening union independence and militancy. It was left to Hitler's regime to complete the emasculation of the German trade union movement after 1933.

7. G. D. Feldman, 'Industrialists, bankers and the problems of unemployment in the Weimar Republic', *Central European History* 25 (1993): 76–96.

8. Kolb, *The Weimar Republic* (London, etc., 1988), p. 163.

9. R. Bridenthal, 'Beyond Kinder, Küche, Kirche. Weimar women at work', *Central European History*, 4 (1973): 148ff. More generally, S. Bajohr, *Die Hälfte der Fabrik: Geschichte der Frauenarbeit in Deutschland 1914–1945* (Marburg, 1979).

10. W. Patch Jr, 'Christian trade unions in the Weimar Republic', *History*, 73 (1988).

As we have seen, the National Socialists *were* able to capitalize on worker discontent, although the party failed to develop any consistent policy on labour prior to 1933. The general under-representation of 'workers' in the NSDAP before 1933 applied to the unskilled rather than the skilled.[11] Such divisions – widened during the depression and accompanied by the insidious fear of declining status – demonstrate that the 'atomization' of the working class detected by historians of the Third Reich was already well advanced by the last years of the Weimar republic. This fragmentation, coupled with the growing demoralization caused by the slump and unemployment, partly explains the rapid collapse of the old framework of industrial relations after 1933. Finally, of course, the violence unleashed by the SA, SS and NSBO from February 1933 softened union resistance.

The *Law on Plant Representative Councils and Business Organizations* (4.4.33) equipped authorities with powers to postpone elections on the works councils in factories until 30 September. The move came in response to disappointing performances by NSBO works council candidates in March and was intended to provide a suitable 'breathing space' to purge the councils of non-Nazi sympathizers. Any lingering hopes entertained by trade union leaders that action would be confined to the political field were dashed by the events immediately following May Day. May 1 itself witnessed a colourful but highly orchestrated demonstration of 'solidarity' between the government and the nation. On the following morning plans for the take-over of the trade union system, drawn up on 21 April, were augmented. The free trade union offices – at that point functioning inefficiently if at all under SA and NSBO supervision – were seized. The voluntary subordination of the liberal trade unions followed shortly. In late June, as part of the National Socialist agreement with the Vatican, the Christian trade unions dissolved themselves.

THE GERMAN LABOUR FRONT

Contemporary Marxist analysis emphasized that of the twin pillars of National Socialist labour policy – terror and persuasion – the latter was arguably more important to Hitler's success in the long term. A thoroughly intimidated and brutalized labour force would not have

---

11. P. Manstein, *Die Mitglieder und Wähler der NSDAP 1919–1933. Untersuchungen zu ihrer schichtmässigen Zusammensetzung* (Frankfurt–New York, etc., 1988), p. 139.

advanced the German economy significantly.[12] In the words of the Marxist, Kahn-Freud: 'The most likely road to fascism in our social conditions is not through force . . . but above all through the ideological integration of the organizations of struggle into a hierarchically ordered national community.'[13] Such an organization was the newly formed German Labour Front (*Deutsche Arbeiter Front* – DAF). Yet DAF illustrated at the same time the curiously improvisational character of the party's labour policies. DAF was itself, for example, part of a much wider effort to head off more extremist pressures coming from the NSBOs. Even when the latter were purged, a key NSBO figure, Reinhard Muchow, continued to work for DAF and radical party plans for labour relations were not finally confronted until the passage of the *Law for the Ordering of National Labour* on 20 January 1934.

Ruler of DAF was Robert Ley. He had already headed the action committee which drew up the plans for the liquidation of the old trade unions. It says as much for the physique of Dr Robert Ley as it does for the qualities of management selection under National Socialism, that he had actually recovered from a plane crash in 1917 which left him with frontal lobe damage, a stammer and an addiction to alcohol. After abandoning his job with IG Farben in the 1920s and immersing himself in the NSDAP he later became *Gauleiter* of Rhineland South, subsequently progressing to become Political Inspector for the party in October 1931. By 1932, still drinking heavily and fighting intermittently, he had become one of the party's two Reich Inspectors, with responsibility for the west and south, including Austria. Subsequently, as Reich Organizational Director, Ley looked after personnel and organizational aspects of the NSDAP and embarked on the quest for self-aggrandizement which was almost *de rigeur* for the Third Reich's leaders.

Indications were very soon forthcoming, however, that the regime had no intention of allowing DAF to become a sort of substitute trade union with the extensive influence over wages and economic policy to which Ley aspired. In the first place DAF incorporated employers as well as workers from November 1933. The regulation of wages had already fallen to the twelve new regional Trustees of Labour, who were made responsible to the Ministry of Labour according to the law on 19 March 1933. *The Law for the Ordering of National Labour*

12. For some of these arguments see A. Sohn–Rethel, *Ökonomie und Klassenstruktur des deutschen Faschismus. Aufzeichnungen und Analysen*, ed. J. Agnoli (Frankfurt, 1973).

13. Kahn–Freud, *Labour Law*, p. 155.

acknowledged the ideal of a 'people's community' and the abolition of class divisions by depicting the workplace in terms of its 'leader' and 'retinue'. Together these formed Councils of Trust. In practice the councils had only an advisory role and the power of decision-making continued to rest with the employer. Disputes within the 'Plant Community' which actually reached the new Courts of Social Honour were relatively few and mainly concerned actions against small businessmen and artisans rather than against large firms.

Naturally enough, Ley's restless personality would not let him give up his ambitions easily. He made his own personal contribution to the institutional chaos of the Third Reich by persuading Hitler to issue a decree on the nature and goals of the Labour Front on 24 October 1934. DAF was thereby allocated grandiose but exasperatingly vague responsibilities in the whole realm of labour relations and social policy.[14] Automatically he clashed with other organizations, notably with that responsible for agriculture, the Reich Food Estate (*Reichsnährstand* – RNS). Under the terms of the 1934 labour law agricultural workers had access to the Courts of Honour in disputes. During such cases DAF, which was viewed by the pro-farmer RNS as 'bolshevik', inevitably favoured the viewpoint of the labourer. Eventually, through the so-called Bückeberger agreement of 1935, the RNS was formally made the part of DAF responsible for agriculture, still allowing RNS members full access to the facilities of Ley's organization.[15] Disputes lingered on, however. Equipped with the recognition of DAF as the 'organization of gainfully employed Germans of hand and head', Ley continued to employ his considerable financial resources in the interests of his own fiefdom. DAF grew from a membership of 4.7 million in 1933 to some 22 million by 1939, by which time its earnings from dues alone amounted to 539 million marks. The associated Bank of German Labour had reserves of 20 million marks by 1938, and a turnover of 15 billion marks. DAF ultimately became the largest National Socialist organization and its investments reached into the insurance, building and many other sectors of economic life.

With such resources it is surprising that Ley was unable to achieve his larger ambitions to determine economic policy. This failure was partly because his own personality made it difficult for him to focus his energy and develop coherent strategies. 'He was adept at chasing

14. Text in J. Noakes and G. Pridham (eds), *Documents on Nazism 1919–1945*, (London, 1974), pp. 435–7.
15. J. Farquharson, *The Plough and the Swastika. The NSDAP and Agriculture in Germany, 1928–1945* (London, 1976), pp. 87–106.

jurisdictions, bits and pieces of power.'[16] More fundamentally, his over-riding obligation to prevent conflict in the workplace restricted any desires he had to enhance DAF's authority by making it a really effective representative for workers. Instead the ideology of the regime imposed on DAF the task of integrating the workers, through keeping them happy and promoting their self-regard. Much of DAF's energy was necessarily channelled into schemes to placate labour, notably through the related organizations, Beauty of Labour and Strength through Joy. The latter in particular generated massive holiday, leisure and cultural projects in the attempt to convince workers that status was more important than pay packets and thus to reduce industrial conflict. That was naturally very much in the interests of the employers. It is striking to note that companies like Siemens had seen for themselves the value of making their work force contented. This particular concern sought to develop a core elite of workers by specifically targeting them with the benefits of material and housing support thus, like DAF, recognizing the family's role in keeping the work force quiescent.[17]

THE CONDITIONS OF WORK

A degree of embourgeoisement undoubtedly afflicted many workers after 1933 as a result of their exposure to DAF's leisure machine. The question as to whether holidays, concerts and improved canteen facilities offset the loss of free bargaining and the introduction of surveillance and intimidation must, however, be purely rhetorical. What is certain is that the much vaunted recovery of full employment in Germany by the mid-1930s was not accompanied by real income rises for most workers. What material benefits accrued, to some workers at least, owed more to general economic forces than to Ley's efforts. Until 1936 the regime made every attempt to keep wages pegged at 1933 levels. It was helped at first by the impact of the depression itself. Gratitude at the return to work after the impact of mass unemployment may have lowered workers' expectations initially. The experience of Bavaria suggests, however, that real wages declined between 1933 and 1936, through a combination of pay reductions, enforced deductions and rising food costs. In general it was not until

16. R. Smelser, *Robert Ley. Hitler's Labour Leader* (Oxford, 1988), p. 300.

17. C. Sachse, *Siemens, der Nationalsozialismus und die moderne Familie. Eine Untersuchung zur sozialen Rationalisierung in Deutschland im 20 Jahrhundert* (Hamburg, 1990).

1939 that real weekly earnings reached the levels of 1929, although a substantial sector of the active labour force was then still working at an hourly rate of pay equivalent to that in 1932.[18] Wages as a percentage of gross national product sank between 1933 and 1939, whereas undistributed business profits were up by 36.5 per cent in the same period. Admittedly, these generally gloomy figures conceal the advantages which some skilled workers could derive, for a time at least, from the shortage of labour caused by Hitler's success in 'solving' unemployment by 1936. The dearth of skilled labour at that point threatened to interfere with the regime's own economic priorities, which is why workers in arms-related industries enjoyed wages rising faster and higher than in other sectors. Even so, skilled workers were prevented from leaving the Reich following the introduction of the Work Book in February 1935.

Conditions came therefore to vary considerably from one branch of industry to another. Whereas DAF strove to improve material conditions and to keep workers happy, the priorities of the Four Year Plan and of the army entailed that more restrictions were placed on labour mobility. Many workers had of course already been locked into low-paid work creation schemes. Thus the *Labour Service Law* of 26 June 1935 made a six-month spell of labour service compulsory for men, for the benefit of public works, arms-related and other projects. Later, on 22 June 1938, the Decree on the Duty of Service virtually conscripted workers for employment on building Germany's western fortifications (Siegfried Line). Such measures did not in themselves prevent labour mobility entirely. It has been estimated that of the total work force of 23 million, just over a million workers were conscripted, often on an irregular basis.[19] In addition a concern to avoid major labour unrest played its part in modifying schemes to direct resources. A good example is that of the decree of November 1939, which enabled men and women conscripted for vital work to operate from their home towns. Some of the holes in the labour market were plugged by simply abandoning in practice the party's ideological commitment to keeping women at their kitchen sinks. By 1936, over 1,200,000 more women were employed than when Hitler had come to power. From September 1939 voluntary labour service for women was replaced by a compulsory scheme. Overall, however, the number of women in work fell until the introduction of a new law enforcing women's working in 1943. The important point is that

18. I. Kershaw, *Popular Opinion and Political Dissent in the Third Reich. Bavaria 1933–1945* (Oxford, 1984), p. 98; Salter, 'Germany', pp. 111f.

19. Noakes and Pridham, *Documents on Nazism*, p. 459.

employment of women never reached the level where it could actually accelerate economic growth.[20]

Another way of avoiding further unpopular direction of German labour was to employ foreign workers on a larger scale to meet Germany's growing production requirements. Hitler referred to the possible use of foreign labour from the occupied East in a meeting of 25 May 1939 but there was nothing resembling a master plan for this until war commenced. In this context it should be kept in mind that even the partial mobilization for war against Poland removed some 4.4 million workers from active engagement in the economy. The invasion and dismemberment of Poland provided the opportunity for the first significant recruitment of foreign labour by the National Socialists. Between May 1940 and October 1941 there was an increase in the numbers of foreign workers employed from 1.1 to 3.5 million.[21] During the war millions of foreigners toiled for Germany, with up to one-third of the work force in the armaments industries being non-German.[22] The turning point towards a really systematic recruitment and allocation of foreign labour came in spring 1942. From 1943, thanks to the support of Goebbels as Plenipotentiary for Total War, Speer at last wrested the allocation from Fritz Sauckel, who then reverted to being merely the *Gauleiter* of Thuringia.[23] By 1944 there were 7 million foreign workers in the Reich. Sheer expedience clearly forced the regime to overcome its fear that such a major influx of alien blood would dilute the party's ideology in the work place. Yet the lot of foreign labour was brutal, the camps in which they were made to live, desperate. The machinery of degradation in this instance could only barely be slowed down by 1943, when minimal efforts were made at that stage to improve foreign workers' productivity in the interests of the Reich's war effort. But countless numbers of them continued to be, literally, worked to death for the Reich.

Most German workers suffered no such fate but their habits, their locale and their places of work were deeply affected after 1933. It is difficult to generalize on the length of the working day but most Germans had to work harder and for longer hours for what they got

20. R. J. Overy, *Nazi Economic Recovery 1932–1938* (London, 1982), p. 60.

21. E. Homze, *Foreign Labour in Nazi Germany* (Princeton, 1967), pp. 28–35. See also U. Herbert, *Fremdarbeiter. Politik und Praxis des 'Ausländer Einsatzes' in der Kriegswirtschaft des Dritten Reiches* (Bonn, Berlin, 1985). For a case study, K.-J. Siegfried, *Das Leben der Zwangsarbeiter im Volkswagenwerk 1939–45* (Frankfurt, 1988).

22. D. Peukert, *Inside Nazi Germany. Conformity, Opposition and Racism in Everyday Life* (London, 1989), pp. 125ff.

23. Homze, *Foreign Labour*, p. 226.

by the end of the 1930s – certainly if comparisons are made with the period before 1929. During the war the average working week rose from 49 to 52 hours by 1943. Eventually, workers – including women – in some key industries were putting in a 60-hour week. They could hardly be said to have enjoyed adequate compensations for these hardships in the shape of improved leisure and consumption. What gains the skilled worker had made were offset from 1941 by the decline in consumer goods and certain types of foodstuffs. Wage rises were often siphoned off by the black market. The adverse impact on worker health has also been recorded.[24]

LABOUR IN THE THIRD REICH

Any discussion of labour and the Third Reich invariably goes far beyond a survey of material conditions, important as these were in helping to explain worker acquiescence. Workers were not only intimidated initially by the action against their unions, but they were also disillusioned with the Social Democratic Party (SPD), which after 1933 became preoccupied with exile politics. The German Communist Party (KPD) tried to encourage worker resistance and to spread information through its leaflets. There were many groups on the left criticizing the government but it remained difficult for them to organize a concerted response to the new regime. It was not until 1935 that the Comintern really threw itself behind the idea of closer collaboration between SPD and KPD in opposing the system. By this time the left was operating largely underground and vulnerable to infiltration, a point best illustrated by the Gestapo's own nickname for one active group of left wing resisters, 'Red Orchestra'.[25] The left was not lacking in ideas or will but in *practical* terms, because of the above factors, 'social democratic and communist resistance to the Nazi regime was of little significance'.[26]

At the same time, even the secret reports published by the exiled SPD (*Sopade*) did not rate the political significance of worker unrest at all highly. This has been put down widely to the mood of resignation in the early years. However, it is unwise to lose sight of the obvious point that the NSDAP *did* also enjoy substantial support even among

---

24. See Kershaw's description of conditions, *Popular Opinion*, pp. 98, 110, 303.
25. See material on the left in P. Hoffmann, *German Resistance to Hitler* (Cambridge–London, 1988), pp. 5ff.
26. Salter, 'Germany', p. 112.

workers prior to 1933. In the second half of the 1930s the labour shortage coincided with increased efforts at surveillance and direction by the government. This combination occasioned a definite surge of worker discontent but the motivation appears again to have been more economic than political. Hitler's personal appeal still extended deep into the working-class ranks until 1941–2, when pessimism at the course the war was taking, together with increased hardship and sacrifice, nourished more widespread and growing scepticism of the regime. The singular fact remains that at no stage did labour indiscipline seriously threaten war production. What disruption there was through absenteeism and stoppages seems to have been caused more by foreign than German workers.

This is not to forget the huge numbers of individual German workers who personally suffered at the hands of the Hitler regime, through internment in concentration camps, enforced exile and death. Working-class opponents and victims of National Socialism were far more numerous than the better-born ones. When war came, the number of workers arrested each month for labour discipline offences rose, by 52 per cent between 1941 and the first half of 1944. Towards the end of this period 2,000 German workers a month were being arrested. Inevitably, there are few extensive records surviving of the many individual workers who stood out against the regime but doubtless many were like Anton Saefkow. Of his private life little more is known than that he was married. Yet this communist worker had a record of political activism in the Weimar Republic and was imprisoned at Dachau between 1936 and 1939. He developed a network in Berlin and beyond, recruiting would-be resistance fighters. The extent of his activities can be seen from the fact that – along with Saefkow – the authorities executed 450 of his fellow conspirators in order to close his network down in 1944.[27]

It is profoundly depressing to have to record that the activity of many such brave individuals found little resonance in general and 'was increasingly isolated even from its own mass base in the working class'.[28] This reality makes it very difficult to interpret the responses of the German working class as a whole in terms of 'resistance', at least if the concept is to retain any significant meaning. Indeed, in this respect there has been a detectable shift in perceptions of German labour in the Third Reich since the publication of the pioneering work of Tim

27. M. Balfour, *Withstanding Hitler in Germany 1933–1945* (London, 1988), pp. 206–8.

28. I. Kershaw, *The Nazi Dictatorship. Problems and Perspectives of Interpretation* (3rd edn, London–New York, etc., 1993), p. 172.

Mason from the late 1960s, where the emphasis *was* very much on German worker resistance and on the regime's alleged failure to integrate workers into the people's community.[29] In fact, the example of skilled labour exploiting its power to interfere with the economic priorities of the regime was anything but an expression of class solidarity and yet another indication, if anything, of the fragmentation of labour in the 1930s. Dissent, rather than resistance, might indeed therefore offer a better general explanatory concept for deviations from the sullen acceptance of the inevitable which characterized large sections of the atomized German working classes in the Third Reich.

Even that fails to exhaust the issue of 'labour in the Third Reich', and there remains one final dispiriting thought to consider. Through pressures as well as through social and leisure incentives, German workers as a whole were inexorably drawn into the system in varying degrees. As war escalated the racialism of the Hitler state, German workers were, for example, either willingly or unwillingly involved in the repression of foreign labour, thus becoming participants in and indeed beneficiaries of the racial hierarchy in the workplace. Even women, responding to a perfectly understandable desire to pursue a career away from the home, were forced into a degree of consensus with the regime's values at work, like it or not. Somehow the scale of this complicity is absent from the temperate and balanced judgement that many if not most workers were 'resigned, but not rebellious' after 1939.[30] It also fails to do full justice to the fact that the working classes, who provided the bulk of the brutal German fighting forces in eastern Europe, maintained a remarkably high morale virtually to the end, at least to the extent of removing all hopes for the elite conspirators against Hitler of finding mass support. Finally, the all encompassing ideological imperatives of the Third Reich are grimly illustrated from the fact that middle-aged, working-class or lower-middle-class 'ordinary men' – hitherto wholly inexperienced in their new craft – manned the murderous Reserve Police Battalion 101 in Poland and that most, though not all, of them became enthusiastic about their war work.[31] Whatever was being done to workers in the Third Reich was clearly not being done in the name of capitalism.

29. Cf. for example T. Mason, *Sozialpoltik im Dritten Reich. Arbeiterklasse und Volksgemeinschaft*, (Opladen, 1980).

30. Kershaw, *Popular Opinion*, p. 110.

31. C. Browning, *Ordinary Men. Reserve Police Battalion 101 and the Final Solution in Poland* (New York, 1993). Cf. O. Bartov, 'The missing years. German workers, German soldiers' in D. Crew (ed.), *Nazism and German Society 1933–1945* (London, 1994), pp. 41–66; A. Luedtke, 'The appeal of exterminating "others". German workers and the limits of resistance', *Journal of Modern History*, 64 (1992): 46–67.

CHAPTER EIGHT

Feeding the Reich; Farmers and Politics

Landowners and farmers no more rushed to embrace the new political order in Germany after 1918 than did the Reich's businessmen. The determination of the landed elites to survive placed a premium on political organization but they were no strangers to this. The inexorable course of German industrialization in the late nineteenth century had long stimulated the great estate holders in the east and north of the Reich to hone their lobbying skills to perfection. In 1893 they set up the powerful *Bund der Landwirte* (Agrarian League). The dominance of the Junkers can be gauged by their securing of protective agricultural tariffs (in 1879 and 1902) which lasted until 1914, blocking less costly imports of foodstuffs for Germany's dairy and livestock farmers of the south and north-west. In short, the estate owners held back domestic production of cheap food at a time when Germany's growing towns demanded it.

Yet the socialist government remained unwilling to mount a frontal assault on German farming interests during the revolution. Total agricultural production in 1918 and again in 1919 was less than half that of 1913. Post-war food scarcity militated against draconian reforms, although the settlement act of 1919 expressed the vision of land in the east being split up for smaller farmers. By 1920 any direct threats to the position of the estate owners, from the government at least, had passed. Nor were the Junkers foolish enough to present their politics as self-serving. Their campaign to reinstate protection was waged on the basis that what was best for them was good for German agriculture as a whole, and therefore for the nation. Superficially, their claim to speak for 'agriculture' was persuasive.

In 1921 the Agrarian League was re-constituted as the *Reichslandbund* (RLB). Within four years it had grown to a membership of

4.5 million. Most of these were family farmers but some 150,000 landless labourers were also included. The RLB offered technical, legal and official support to its members and helped with credit.

The RLB was politically powerful. Of the 102 nationalists (DNVP) in the Reichstag in 1924, no fewer than 52 were also members of the RLB. The League in addition had adherents from the DVP and other splinter parties. It brought out some 200 publications at national and local level and greatly influenced the various chambers of agriculture as well as producer and consumer co-operatives. The German Agricultural Council itself, it has been said, was a virtual affiliate of the League.[1] Other major agrarian interest organizations, notably the Peasant League (*Bauernbund* – 200,000 members) and the Catholic associations (580,000 members), could not seriously rival the RLB. The Peasant League split in 1925, much of its membership subsequently merging with other groups to form the *Deutsche Bauernschaft* in 1927. This, too, eventually drifted into the RLB's orbit.

THE STRAINS WITHIN GERMAN AGRICULTURE

German agriculture as a whole was disadvantaged in the first place by the pace of industrialization and the concomitant growth of the service sector, which inevitably attracted labour. Secondly and notwithstanding this, there were still too many German small farmers to guarantee all of them a satisfactory income. The relative depopulation of eastern Germany was more than offset by the overcrowding in the countryside west of the Elbe. Thus real peasant income rose by only 4.5 per cent between 1913 and 1928, while the national average went up by 45 per cent during the same period. Thirdly, the pre-war protectionist policies militated against the rationalization of agriculture. Tariffs did not discourage inefficient production of grain but they did make the import of fodder and feeds (bran, barley, oil cake) expensive, continuing to retard German dairy and livestock production in spite of rising domestic demand.

The most obvious beneficiaries of Germany's relative agrarian backwardness were therefore its competitors – the intensive producers and exporters of Holland and Scandinavia.[2] In attempting to match the

1. D. Abrahams, *The Collapse of the Weimar Republic*, 2nd edition, 1986, p. 64.
2. In general, D. Gessner, *Agrardepression und Praesidialregierungen in Deutschland 1930–33. Probleme des Agrarprotektionismus* (Düsseldorf, 1977).

price of foreign products, Germany's small farmers worked harder for less. When credit *was* obtained to assist modernization, costs were difficult to recoup in the face of such fierce foreign competition. Complaints of debt and high taxes were legion while fear of foreclosure haunted many a German small farmer. Although the inflation of 1923 wiped out extensive rural obligations, the new agricultural debt incurred (much of it from abroad) amounted to some seven billion marks.[3] Whereas German industry was re-integrated after 1924 this was not true of German agriculture. The gap between industrial and agricultural prices persisted. Under these conditions the pressure on governments to take action grew tremendously. Farmers were perhaps not so much against the Weimar Republic on principle as waiting to see what it could or would do for them.

Flying in the face of much contemporary advice from economists, the politicians of the Weimar Republic drifted towards protectionism. When Luther's first cabinet pushed through the so-called small tariff revision on 12 August 1925, agricultural duties were reinstated, although at levels well below those of 1902. The compromise was made partly to deflect rightist criticism of the free trade platform which became central to Stresemann's foreign policy and which was favoured by Germany's manufacturers and exporters until the end of the 1920s. The decree bringing back the system of import licenses in the following month also ensured that German grain prices would be kept higher. Yet the small tariff concession brought little respite for small farmers. Cheaper foreign food imports continued to be the price paid for access to foreign markets of German manufactured goods. It says much for the influence of the big land owners that they sustained for so long the fiction of acting for agriculture as a whole, when essentially lobbying for their own interests. Admittedly, estate owner and small farmer alike distrusted industry and the 'capitalists' who controlled the marketing of food products from farm to retail outlets.[4] The farming community also united against high taxes and the welfare system these sustained.

It seemed long unlikely, therefore, that the small farmers would find better allies than the Junkers; the latter appeared to be the lesser of several evils. The impression of unity was heightened by the alliance of agrarian organizations in the 'Green Front' from 1929 and by the RLB's attacks on the 'Great Coalition' of 1928. Unqualified victory for the RLB lobby appeared to come with the installation of the

---

3. E. Eyck, *A History of the Weimar Republic,* vol. 2 (New York, 1963), p. 121.
4. Cf. Abraham, *Collapse,* pp. 42–105.

Brüning government and the appointment of Martin Schiele as Minister of Agriculture in March 1930. The estate owners remained major beneficiaries of aid grants to agriculture (*Osthilfe*); Brüning refused to sign the Polish–German economic agreement which would have brought more cheap food to the Reich. When Martin Schiele ceased to please the RLB he too, moreover, fell from grace. Subsequently, von Papen's government offered import quotas on dairy and livestock products, land tax remission of forty per cent, a two per cent reduction of interest charges and the cancellation of turnover tax. The retreat from these commitments to the Green Front by the short-lived Schleicher government from December 1932 was all the more unacceptable to the RLB. Quite apart from reversing von Papen's import quotas, Schleicher expressed his concern for the peasants of the south and west and indicated interest in reactivating the settlement programme. He also developed slight but worrying symptoms of commitment to the export industry. In due course he had to depart.

This view from the top conceals the uneven economic impact on the land of Germany's free trade policies from 1925. After that year agricultural imports rose to over one-third of the gross value of domestic production. Imports of dairy and other processed foods virtually tripled by 1928. The economic realities for medium and small farmers were generally much grimmer than those facing the big estates. Worldwide over-production, together with the withdrawal of American capital and rising urban unemployment in Germany, pushed prices down faster than ever from the beginning of 1928. Between 1927 and 1932 the gap between agricultural prices and those of all other goods and services grew constantly. From 1928 onwards, as the agricultural crisis deepened, less than fifty per cent of farms in the west and one-third of those in the east could cover the interest on their debt from their receipts. The rise in foreclosures from 2,554 in 1927 to 6,200 by 1932 registered more dramatically than anything the plight of the farmers. Yet in 1928, upon the return of the SPD to government with the 'Great Coalition,' the drive for cheaper food was intensified. With ruined profit margins after 1928, small and medium farmers could contemplate estate owners 'afloat on Europe's highest domestic cereal prices'.[5]

The emergence of agitationist factions in the late 1920s, such as the Rural People's Movement, as well as more narrow interest groups like the Christian National Peasants' Party, testified to the growing

5. Abraham, *Collapse*, p. 83.

resentment in the countryside. The mere existence of such bodies contradicts the image of unity on the land so assiduously propagated by the RLB in the 1920s. Peasants had been alienated by the controls and requisitions of the war years and were often bitterly disillusioned by the reality of peacetime after 1918. The longer perspective on this is perhaps even more revealing. By the 1880s and 1890s, when the main peasant organizations had begun to emerge, traditions of deference were already being repudiated.[6] The energy expended by the right-wing agrarian elites in rural politics testifies to their growing concern. Straw-chewing, cap-doffing, tractable peasants were in shorter supply; not idiocy but volatility characterized the German countryside. Peasants were no longer, if they ever had been, merely passive recipients.[7] The radicalism of sentiment could be seen, for example, with the emergence of the Free Peasantry organization at the end of the First World War, in the Rhineland and the Palatinate. One of the leaders of this movement, Franz Josef Heinz, briefly founded a so-called 'autonomous palatinate' during late 1923 and early 1924.[8] Such restlessness, to which the big parties responded with success from the 1890s onwards, provides important clues to the path later beaten by small farmers towards National Socialism after 1928, as the peasantry looked for political cover elsewhere. Perhaps inevitably, they were attracted to those untainted with existing policies.

NSDAP AND AGRICULTURE BEFORE 1933

Rural hardship played a major role in persuading the NSDAP leadership to place greater emphasis from 1928 on winning over the middle classes. However, it should be remembered that the term 'rural' covered artisans, hand workers and others, as well as farmers and there is not very much evidence of a coherent party strategy for the latter before 1930. What Hitler first offered, as his antenna picked up rural distress signals, was reassurance about the NSDAP programme. Point

6. G. Eley, *From Unification to Nazism. Reinterpreting the German Past*, (London, Sydney, 1986), pp. 239–40.
7. In general see R. G. Moeller (ed.), *Peasants and Lords in Modern Germany. Recent Studies in Agricultural History* (London, 1986) and R. J. Evans (ed.), *The German Peasantry. Conflict and Community in Rural Society from the 18th to the 20th Centuries* (London, 1985).
8. J. Osmond, *Rural Protest in the Weimar Republic: the Free Peasants in the Rhineland and Bavaria* (London–New York, 1993).

17 of this had talked of expropriating land 'for communal purposes without compensation'. This, Hitler declared on 13 April 1928, was primarily directed against Jewish companies which speculated in land 'acquired illegally or not managed in the public interest'. Significantly, the party benefited during 1929 from rural perceptions that its 'realistic' tactics were more likely to be successful than those of violent agitationists in the Rural People's Movement, under Klaus Heim and Wilhelm Hamkens.[9] Confirmation that the party was becoming the major beneficiary of the disaffected farming community was provided by its big successes in the Reichstag elections of September 1930, in the Protestant and agrarian regions of Schleswig-Holstein, Pomerania and Hanover South Brunswick.

In 1929 and again in 1930, the party spokesman on agrarian affairs in the Reichstag, Werner Willikens, wrote in the NSDAP *Year Book* on rural problems, his articles probably forming subsequently the basis for the party's official programme for agriculture in March 1930. Apart from criticizing current government shortcomings – taxes too high, fertilizer and electricity too expensive, excessive profit margins for wholesalers and retailers, inadequate protection against food imports – the document envisaged a large settlement programme in eastern Germany. The land for this was to come not from the big estates, as Willikens had first suggested, but from expansion through foreign policy.

There was a stress on the need to reform inheritance laws to prevent further fragmentation of holdings. In addition, land workers were to be helped and rural migration prohibited in order to end the use of foreign farm labour. Finally, the cultural and social standing of the German peasantry was to be advanced. A mixture of large and small estates was acknowledged as important in the quest for greater self-sufficiency, the latter being a central plank of NSDAP propaganda and the party's economic thinking.

DARRÉ'S WORK AND IDEAS

The man responsible for building up the party's agrarian organizational apparatus was not Willikens, however, but Richard Walter Darré. Born to German parents in Argentina, his schooling in Europe included a spell at King's College, Wimbledon. After voluntary service

9. J. F. Farquharson, *The Plough and the Swastika. The NSDAP and Agriculture in Germany 1928–1945* (London, 1976), p. 11.

in the German army during the First World War Darré studied colonial economics and agronomy, receiving his diploma in 1925. Through his involvement with the völkisch right, Darré first met Heinrich Himmler, himself an agronomist. In the late 1920s Darré worked in the Baltic region, including a spell as consultant at the German embassy in Riga during 1928. His first major published work was *The Peasantry as the Life Source of the Nordic Race* (1928). Here he tried to demonstrate that the Nordic races – unlike parasitic Jews – were the fount of European culture. His romanticized view of the peasantry inevitably showed a marked anti-urban bias.

> At the bottom of his heart the true peasant . . . has only a deep and mostly silent contempt for the city dweller or non–farmer . . . The
> peasant directs the farm, he is the head, the others the limbs; but all together they are visibly for the farm. . . . To be a peasant therefore means to have a feeling for the organic interplay of forces in the work as a whole.[10]

In his second volume Darré brought his specialism in animal breeding to bear on human beings, favouring restriction on 'less valuable' community members. The book also argued against speculation in landed property and advocated inheritance law reforms. Significantly, he urged that 'if Marxism is to be overcome in Germany then the flag carrier in this battle will be the German peasant.[11]

Views like this placed Darré close to the official policy of the NSDAP. He made contacts with its Wiesbaden organization in 1928 but when he became a full member is unclear. Nevertheless, by July 1930 Darré had attracted sufficient interest from Hitler to be commissioned to head the NSDAP's new agrarian cadre. Darré promptly argued that this should comprise only agricultural specialists (in practice these were invariably reliable farmers acting as honorary advisers to the party in order to save expense) allowing every regional and local party leader to call up professional advice. The pyramidal structure of advisers at village, district and *Gau* levels built up slowly at first but by spring 1932 the NSDAP's Agrarian Policy Apparatus had become a very large bureaucracy. Through its work the party made striking propaganda advances between 1930 and 1933 and thoroughly penetrated rural organizations, including the RLB itself. In conquering one position of power after another in the RLB Darré aimed not to

10. Cited in B. Miller Lane and L. J. Rupp (eds), *Nazi Ideology before 1933. A Documentation* (Manchester, 1978), p. 105.
11. Farquharson, *Plough and Swastika*, p. 16.

destroy it but 'to take it over as the foundation stone for the eventual NSDAP agrarian organization in the Third Reich.'[12]

Indeed, by December 1931 the RLB had elected Werner Willikens to one of its four presidencies and National Socialist influence increasingly coloured the RLB's campaign against Schleicher in particular who, as we have seen, appeared to be more resistant than von Papen to agrarian pressure groups. On 11 January 1933, the presidium of the RLB duly attacked 'the pillaging of agriculture' whose impoverishment had reached levels 'which were not even deemed possible under a Marxist government.'[13] The NSDAP had clearly profited from the confusion and discontent in agriculture to put across its message about the need for unity to replace the quarrels and divisions of the past. Darré's part in this process was a vital one and on 29 June 1933 he succeeded Hugenberg as Minister for Agriculture while retaining his existing posts.

THE REICH FOOD ESTATE (*REICHSNÄHRSTAND* – RNS) AND THE LAW OF HEREDITARY ENTAILMENT (*ERBHOFGESETZ*)

Darré's new powers derived above all from two laws. The first concerning *The Reich's Responsibility for the Regulation of the Coporatist Reorganization of Agriculture* (15.7.1933) and the second on *The Provisional Organization of the Reich Food Estate and Measures for Market and Price Controls in Agricultural Products* (13.9.1933), as well as a series of supplementary decrees. The new compulsory organization was a huge conglomeration of co-operatives, economic associations and specialist offices in the agricultural sector, covering and regulating all aspects of distribution and production. Darré partly controlled this mammoth syndicate in his capacity as Reich Minister for Food and Agriculture. But the RNS was also a 'corporatist, centralized organization geared to the party's leader principle'[14] and staffed largely from the party's Agrarian Policy Apparatus. Serving under Darré (Reich Farm Leader) were Hermann Reischle (Staff Leader) and Wilhelm Meinberg. The hierarchy continued on down through *Land*,

12. Farquharson, *Plough and Swastika*, p. 20.
13. Cited in M. Broszat, *Hitler and the Collapse of Weimar Germany* (Leamington Spa, 1987), p. 136.
14. M. Broszat, *The Hitler State. The Foundation and Development of the Internal Structure of the Third Reich* (London, 1981), p. 176.

Kreis and local farm leaders. Thus Darré concentrated in his hands the vocational, state and party control of agriculture.

By and large the leadership of the RNS remained professional, if increasingly under party influence. Inevitably, its pretensions to control all aspects of agriculture brought it into conflict with both state organizations and other party authorities. A particularly protracted argument, for example, arose between the RNS and *Gauleiter* Erich Koch (East Prussia) who insisted on absolute party primacy. Koch reacted strongly against the idea of agricultural self-government in his area and argued that RNS officials should devote their energies to turning peasants into National Socialists. The dispute was eventually resolved by conceding the right of Darré's organization to control technical matters. In effect this indicated limits to the *political* control of the RNS. Those were further defined in the clash of the RNS with that other Titan, the German Labour Front, as we have already seen. Darré's interventionism was opposed, often successfully, to Schacht's growing inclination to give more play to market forces.

The party's reverence for peasant ideals was also expressed through the law on entailment. This legislation was – alongside the RNS – the second pillar of National Socialist agricultural policy. Laws preventing the break-up or take-over of farms which had become hopelessly indebted were first introduced in Prussia on 15 May 1933. The legislation was extended to the rest of the Reich in September and applied only to holdings of between 7.5 and 125 hectares. Farms of this size could no longer be split up or seized to meet debts. The burden on the inheriting member of the family was reduced too, by ending the obligation to provide monetary compensation for those unfortunate enough to inherit nothing. Under the new arrangements the honorific title 'peasant' (*Bauer*) was now confined to the holders of *Erbhöfe*. Nothing more earnestly signalled Darré's romanticized elevation of the peasantry – Nordic life source of the nation – than this appellation. Yet from 1936 Darré's position was to become steadily less secure.

It is precisely because his 'blood and soil' views were endorsed by the National Socialist leaders and because the peasant officially remained the 'ideological darling' of the Third Reich, that Darré's slow fall from grace is so interesting to observe. On one level it underlined the need for a tougher personality than he enjoyed to survive the remorseless political machinations going on inside the Third Reich. Yet Darré's personality defects cannot alone account for his decline, any more than can his general ideas. Hitler manifestly continued to share the vision of a great German agrarian domain, where the evils of industrialization could be eradicated. Nonetheless, there was implied criticism in Hitler's secret memorandum accompanying the Four Year Plan, where he cited the inability of German agriculture to feed the population as justification for his expansionist plans for the Reich. The ideological finery bedecking the *Bauer* after 1933 in fact concealed much that was still highly unsatisfactory in German agriculture, and herein lie clues to the eventual failure of the RNS leader.

THE BURDENS OF HONOUR

In propaganda terms, the Third Reich's rulers continued to recognize the importance of sustaining the morale of the farming community, losing by contrast precious little sleep over any possible threat from the rest of the middle classes, as will be clear later. The slump in agricultural prices had dented the confidence of farmers badly but the all-pervasive controls of the RNS at last made it possible to fix prices and to achieve a domestic monopoly for German farmers from 1933 onwards. A rise in farm incomes was therefore very noticeable between 1933 and 1934. Thanks to a combination of state protection, tax cuts and favourable interest rates, agriculture as a whole could be said to be better off than other sections of the community by the mid-1930s. What had been less clear before the NSDAP came to power was the fact that such controls would prove to be double-edged. Thus in 1935, for example, overall restraints on prices and distribution prevented farmers from cashing in on shortages. On general political grounds Hitler stubbornly continued to refuse rises in agricultural prices.

As a result, from 1935 the relative economic position of farmers – as distinct from their much heightened public esteem and standing – began to worsen. In absolute terms, admittedly, farm income rose from 4,200,000 marks in 1933 to 5,600,000 by 1937. As a proportion of *national* income, however, that of farmers fell from 9.7 per cent in 1935 to 7.8 per cent by 1938. Moreover, profits in trade and industry were greater than those in agriculture. While farm income stagnated from 1935, working hours grew longer. Of course this was partly because the regime insisted that farmers increase production in the greater interest of making the Reich more self-sufficient. The battle for production (*Erzeugungsschlacht*), launched by Herbert Backe in 1934, resulted in farming output being one-fifth higher in 1938–39 than it had been ten years previously. In spite of a growing consumption of foodstuffs from 1936 (with the return of full employment), the RNS managed to raise the degree of German self-sufficiency to eighty-three per cent, although the shortfall in fats was still pronounced. In sum it became apparent that the protection and veneration which the peasant enjoyed under National Socialism had a hefty price tag attached to it.

The bald figures on income chart the inexorable shaping of the farming community to accommodate the larger economic priorities driving the regime. Some evidence of this was provided by the continuing ability of the great estate holders to retain most of their land. During the Weimar Republic some 57,547 new proprietors were settled following the settlement act of 1919 and the homestead act of 1920, mostly on very small holdings. In the Third Reich the figure for new settlers was actually lower, namely 20,408. This is all the more remarkable in view of Darré's drive against the Junkers and the regime's propagation of the anti-urban images of a 'wild East' with 'the small homesteader as the cowboy and the Pole as the Indian'.[15] In reality, even the much trumpeted *Erbhöfe* accounted for no more than one third of all German farms. By 1938, 2.5 million of the smallest farms occupied less land than the top one per cent of holdings. Ironically, the regime's drive for self-sufficiency – demanding major investments and rationalization – favoured the larger estate owners, who found it easier to raise credit than small farmers. In addition, Hitler's obsession with conquering Lebensraum may have made him less concerned about the need to provide new settlement opportunities by dismantling existing large estates.[16]

This is not to say that the lot of even the big landowners was ideal. These, too, like all farmers, continued among other things to suffer from the ongoing process of migration from the countryside. As the more attractive pay and living conditions of the towns continued to suck German farm workers from the land, the regime had to resort to the ideologically unsound step of bringing in more foreign labour to till the soil. Voluntary groups were put to work and unmarried women under the age of twenty-five devoted their 'duty year' to agriculture or domestic science. There were regional variations but labour losses affected small farmers more severely. Whilst Junkers shared the indebtedness of all farmers they managed in spite of this to reduce their debts by a greater percentage than could be achieved by

15. D. Schoenbaum, *Hitler's Social Revolution. Class and Status in Nazi Germany* (London, 1966), p. 50.
16. Farquharson, *Plough and Swastika*, p. 148.

either the *Erbhöfe* or the countless farms below the 7.5 hectare threshold. Moreover new debts on the large estates tended to take the form of new investments, compared with the absolute losses suffered on the *Erbhof*. Under such conditions it is easy to see why the *Bauer* has been characterized as 'a farm manager under a quasi-feudalistic contract with the community, the terms of which allowed him to be removed when necessary from having any further say in the management of the property'.[17]

Only in relation to such adverse conditions was the lot of the Junker tolerable. The long-term structural changes in the German economy condemning the farming community as a whole to further hardships were not so much slowed down as disguised by the Hitler regime, at least for a time. In the end a farmer's life in the 'Third Reich Limited' demanded – in exchange for security of tenure and praise – more work for less return. It has been rightly said that conditions were desperate for the small farmer, hard for the middle-sized farmer and only a little less so for estate owners. The regime's overriding preoccupation with rearmament and the expansion of heavy industry meant that less investment was made in agriculture. Although the Ministry of Agriculture enjoyed a large rise in its budget, its spending capacity lagged far behind the Ministries of War, Aviation, the Interior and Justice. In addition there were too many authorities with residual planning powers of their own for Darré to push through any comprehensive restructuring of farming.

In any case, Darré's anti-modern elevation of the *Bauer* as the life source of the nation could also be said to have restricted production, and this too played into the hands of his opponents in the industrial sector. It is not by chance, therefore, that Darré's slide down the slippery pole began around 1936. His own priorities were increasingly challenged by the rapid industrialization demanded under the Four Year Plan, of which the RNS itself became a branch by 1939, and by the intractable economic realities generated through Goering's new authority. Eventually Darré's role in making agricultural policy was usurped by a more formidable agronomist in the party, Heinrich Himmler. From 1938 Darré ceased to head the SS Race and Settlement Office. Himmler's demands for SS-run farms (*Wehrhof*) from 1939, confirmed that emphasis was to continue to be on defence, rather than on the resettlement of farmers favoured by Darré. Herbert Backe, who became food commissioner in the Office of the Four Year Plan, also favoured the notion of the soldier–settler (*Wehrbauer*) being

---

17. Farquharson, *Plough and Swastika*, p. 121.

planted in the East. Backe himself had been steadily siphoning off Darrés own authority since 1936 and finally took over the Ministry of Agriculture from his erstwhile superior in May 1942. Undoubtedly, Backe was more hard-headed and efficient than Darré and also more able to work alongside Himmler. The fact remains that Darré played a central role in co-ordinating production and distribution of agriculture and in making the RNS so efficient. His major failure was in not making it a self-governing organization. By 1939 the RNS's existence was largely justified in terms of facilitating 'the introduction without friction of a wartime food system'.[18]

Wartime differences completed the rift between Darré and Himmler. Darré himself had argued in January 1939 that the occupation of the Sudetenland and Austria had not improved the agricultural situation for the Reich and that taking foreign territory would not help since it did not have what Germany really wanted. However, Darré's aversion to the war coincided with his own fall from favour and his declining political fortunes undoubtedly coloured his views. At the very least, it seems questionable to try to draw a clear distinction between the fundamental ideas systems of Darré the 'racial tribalist' on the one hand and Himmler the 'imperialist with romantic racial overtones' on the other.[19] Darré's vision of a new order was based on applying the RNS model to the restructuring of the economy of Central Europe as a whole. It is true that, unlike the SS leader, Darré did not particularly favour the invasion of Russia, but he was very enthusiastic about the resettlement of 'German lands' in the Baltic and Poland. The blood-and-soil ideas preached by Darré ultimately pointed towards extensive settlements in the East, so that the use of force at some point was surely likely.

Backe in fact subsequently extended Darré's thinking on the role of the RNS and, thanks to the Reich's military victories, was also in a position for a while to contemplate the inclusion of the Soviet Union in the process of reconstruction. Backe had no qualms about distributing 10,000 copies of his failed dissertation on the Tsarist grain trade to his staff prior to the invasion of Russia. The thesis argued that the communists were diverting the area from its natural role as the granary of the continent through forced industrialization. Backe in addition wished to treat south-eastern Europe as a supplementary supplier of cereals and expected the Netherlands and Denmark to furnish dairy products. A flow of industrial goods from the western

18. Farquarson, *Plough and Swastika*, p. 106.
19. A. Bramwell, *Blood and Soil: Richard Walther Darre and Hitler's 'Green Party'* (Bourne End, 1985), p. 130.

European powers, Germany in particular, would be provided in return. This rationalization of the economies of different countries for Germany's benefit has rightly been described as elevating the idea of autarky from national to continental level.

Backe and Himmler accepted with less qualms what such settlement would entail for the 'subject' races currently living in the territories occupied by Germany. Their ready acceptance that the naturally inferior races, in Russia in particular, should be content with a wholly dependent economy illustrated once more the absolute primacy of ideology. At the same time, the schemes considered by Backe and others tended to reinforce the argument that German agriculture could *only* be transformed through victory for the Reich. Until that happy day German farmers and land workers would have to toil for little reward, for Hitler resolutely refused to transfer resources from armaments to agriculture. The question naturally arises as to whether National Socialist agricultural policy as a whole would have worked without the war. It is doubtful. Even though the regime attached great importance to having a contented peasantry as a bulwark against the evils of industrialization, the wider economic priorities of the regime left little room to restore profitability to agriculture after 1935. No amount of official veneration for the *Bauer* could disguise the intractable nature of the problems in German agriculture.

The NSDAP did not seem to have the answer to these problems and could not prevent continuing migration from countryside to town, with the attendant decline of rural labour. Urban life was preferable to the profound boredom and long hours of work even as an independent farmer. All the more was this true for the farm hands, who without a war would have had very little prospect of owning their own holding. Both Darré and Backe showed their awareness of the scale of the problem by postulating massive post-war aid schemes for agriculture. It remains unlikely that any such aid programme could have done the job. What was required was nothing less than the reversal of German industrialization. In truth Germans showed themselves reluctant in the extreme to resettle in the East, even after military conquest. If the Germans were a people without space, Backe suggested in 1933, their own east stubbornly remained a space without people. A final German victory would thus have provided the Third Reich 'with new land when its citizens were busy depopulating part of their existing countryside'.[20] In any event and in the absence meanwhile of the final victory, the law governing German agriculture

20. Farquharson, *Plough and Swastika*, p. 254.

after 1933 appears to have been 'not so much the Law on the *Reichsnährstand* as the law on diminishing returns'.[21]

21. Schoenbaum, *Hitler's Social Revolution*, p. 172.

CHAPTER NINE

The Middle Classes; Angst and Reality

Material decline was certainly one powerful factor influencing the mood of the *Mittelstand* as a whole towards Hitler. More generally, there is much evidence, as in the case of German farmers, for interpreting the electoral behaviour of the middle classes as the reaction of 'losers' in the industrialization process. The NSDAP certainly voiced its dislike of giant combines, expressed sympathy for the suffering of small entrepreneurs and exalted the values of rural life over those accompanying urbanization and industrialization. On the other hand the term 'Mittelstand' covered a very wide range of groups experiencing varying economic pressures. Many profited, at least for a time, from the development of industrial society. Which is to say that as well as economic there must have been other reasons impelling the lower middle classes especially to vote for National Socialism.

In surveying the Mittelstand as a whole, the distinction between 'old' and 'new' elements often appears to have been broadly that which was made between 'productive' and 'unproductive' members of the class. The former would include – as well as the small and medium farmers – artisans and craftsmen, small businessmen, traders and shopkeepers. Professional and political bodies had long developed among the old middle classes. For a while they made do with chambers of handicrafts and trade, with guild organizations and with the existing political parties in late nineteenth-century Germany. Thuringia, however, witnessed an abortive attempt to set up a distinct Mittelstand Party in 1895. The German Mittelstand association enjoyed brief life from 1904. Eventually, in 1911, a more substantial organization was at last born, namely the Imperial German Mittelstand League.[1] These

1. G. Eley, *From Unification to Nazism. Reinterpreting the German Past* (London–Sydney, 1986), pp. 240–1.

were expressions both of an anxiety to preserve status and of a determination to wield political influence.

Meanwhile the development of industrial society and the business of managing the new Germany after 1871 threw up many more aspirants to the Mittelstand, in the form of white-collar workers in the private and public sector. A census of 1907 indicated that there were then already some 2 million private and 1.5 million state employees categorized as white-collar. Between them they had some fifty-three associations in 1913, spanning the entire political spectrum. By the early 1920s white-collar workers seem to have been broadly divided between the socialist General Free Federation of Salaried Employees (AFA), with 69,000 members and the right-wing Trade Union Federation of German Salaried Employees' Organizations (GEDAG), which claimed a membership of 463,000.

Even though many of the 'new' *petits bourgeois* could not easily be distinguished in daily life and conditions of work from the blue-collar sector, the formal distinction between worker (*Arbeiter*) and employee (*Angestellte*) helped to generate a sense of distinctiveness for the Mittelstand as a whole. Thus the class identity of what was in reality a rather disparate group was indeed forged on the ideological–political plane.[2] It was notable in this respect that the active nationalist lobby groups of late nineteenth- and early twentieth-century Germany had also drawn their sustenance from the ranks of the Mittelstand. Organizations such as the Pan–German League (1891) or The Colonial Society (1897) and The Navy League (1898) refute the picture of political passivity still often ascribed to the German bourgeoisie. Finally, in economic terms at least, distinctions between 'old' and 'new' elements of the middle classes were increasingly eroded by the impact of the First World War, the crisis of 1923 and the Great Depression.

It has been suggested that the Weimar Republic witnessed a crisis point in so far as there was a growing asymmetry between the social strength of the bourgeoisie and its political weakness. In fact even the Mittelstand's pre-war function as a social barrier had been weakened as a result of the agreement between industry and labour during the German revolution. In broad terms the political and economic position of the Mittelstand was generally worse after 1918 than it had been during the Empire. Even at that time the new mass pressures coming from the Mittelstand and its organizations sorely tested the ability of

2. I. Kershaw, *Popular Opinion and Political Dissent in the Third Reich. Bavaria 1933–1945* (Oxford, 1984), pp. 111ff.

the established parties to respond appropriately. That the Weimar system found the challenge equally if not more difficult was evident from the 'portentous fragmentation of middle-class electoral loyalties' during the 1920s.[3] Ad hoc political ties were forged with the established parties but the dissatisfaction of the commercial middle classes was all too clear when they formed their own party in Hamburg in November 1925, The Economic Party (*Wirtschaftspartei*). What was said of the new Mittelstand in nineteenth-century Germany, that it occupied the contested zone of German politics, had become true of the middle classes generally by the end of the 1920s.

CASE STUDY – CIVIL SERVANTS

Civil servants provide a valuable illustration at least of the mood of the so-called 'unproductive' Mittelstand in Germany after the First World War. The top leadership will be considered later but the growth of self-doubt and disorientation was certainly quite evident among rank-and-file civil servants. It should be stressed that the term civil servant – tens of thousands of whom were women – covered a wide range of activities, at Reich and regional level. Vast numbers of civil servants worked in the transport and postal systems for example. In Germany, school teachers were civil servants too. Interestingly, they provided many exceptionally active functionaries for the NSDAP, in which party civil servants were statistically over-represented.

Historically, the German bureaucracy evolved from a private contract basis of employment by the princely rulers to the point where, during the nineteenth century, obligation to the *state* became central. The *Beamte* expected more than a mere salary. A formulation of 1880 noted:

> The essence of the German public service lies in the fact that it is a
> lifelong profession, on which one embarks only after a prolonged
> preparation and after renouncing every other commercial livelihood, but
> in which one expects on the part of the state the provision of a level of
> maintenance consistent with one's social status.[4]

---

3. G. D. Feldman (ed.), *Die Nachwirkungen der Inflation auf die deutsche Geschichte 1924–1933* (Munich, 1985), p. 391.

4. J. Caplan, *Government without Administration. State and Civil Service in Weimar and Nazi Germany* (Oxford–New York–Toronto, 1988), p. 4.

Apart from a number of leading offices occupied by 'political' civil servants, such as state secretaries, most *Beamte* enjoyed solid tenure. Within the civil service, however, the insistence on university training for high office frustrated upward mobility to a considerable extent. As a result, although the civil service expanded in size and diversity it experienced an increasingly rigid social stratification. Even during the German Empire the civil service was 'not the homogenous ethical corps it represented to its champions, but an increasingly diverse, expensive and unwieldly bureaucratic apparatus numbering well over a million persons by the outbreak of war'.[5]

War and revolution profoundly affected the *Beamte*. For the duration of the conflict there was a steep decline in pay while living conditions were further undermined by the post-war inflation. Additional imperatives to reduce civil service costs as a whole came from the unprecedented expansion of public administration through war and demobilization. The total complement of civil servants in Reich and Land administrations increased by forty per cent between 1914 and 1923. The decree to reduce Reich personnel expenditure of October 1923 ultimately led to wholesale dismissals in 1924, although for those still employed the upward revision of salaries in the mid-1920s saw pay nearer to 1913 levels than at any time since the war. Nevertheless, the civil service job losses of 1924 generated great resentment and were a key element in the dissolution of the 'consensus' on containing inflation.

Where considerations of material decline overlapped with doubts on status, the danger of disaffection was greater. In order to reduce expenditure, governments sought to limit the numbers falling within the category of *Beamte* – with all that this implied in terms of job security, public regard and recognition. The erosion of the *Beamte* category came partly through the growth of other public sector support work, in connection for example with the expansion of public health and social legislation. In 1913 *Beamte* had held more than eighty-eight per cent of all public sector jobs but by 1927 their share had dropped to almost sixty-seven per cent. The introduction of the merit principle into salary structures in 1920, together with the fact that the lower civil service ranks did better than those higher up in the second half of the 1920s, created additional sources of anxiety about status in some sectors of the civil service. Here was a potential menace for the republican system.

Sufficient diversity of individual conditions remained within the

5. Caplan, *Government without Administration*, p. 13.

bureaucracy to cast doubt, however, on the argument that it was *as a whole* opposed to and obstructive of the new political order. The heightened activity in forging organizational links with relevant interest groups and parties after the war confirms that, on the contrary, 'defensive mobilization' was taking place in the 1920s.[6] This relates to the point made in the opening of this book about the civil service contributing to the functioning of the new political order in 1918–19. War and inflation in effect also helped to mould civil servants into a modern social group, able and willing to defend their interests in industrial society and thus open, as it were, to offers. The civil service unions exemplified this. As well as the German Civil Service Association (*Deutscher Beamtenbund* – DBB) there was, from 1921, the Reich Association of Higher Civil Servants (*Reichsbund der höheren Beamten*), with 60,000 members and, from 1922, the trade union-affiliated General German Civil Servants' Association (*Allgemeiner Deutscher Beamtenbund* – ADB).[7]

After 1919 Weimar governments were forced to tread a narrow line between, on the one hand, demands for the wholesale purging of anti-republican elements in the civil service and, on the other, the constitutional guarantees of individual civil rights. The constitution included a reference in Article 129 to the effect that: 'The vested rights of civil servants are inviolable,' but was less clear on whether or not the civil servant's oath of loyalty committed him or her to the defence of the republican form of government as such. As it turned out, the civil service as a whole provided no support for Kapp's attempted coup in 1920. Moreover, some democratization of the civil service took place in Prussia. Persistent doubts produced, however, an amendment of the *Reich Civil Service Law* (1907) in the form of the *Law Concerning the Duties of Civil Servants for the Security of the Republic* in July 1922. Significantly, the law was passed by the Reich government in the face of some Länder opposition. Henceforth civil servants had a duty to support the republican state and their right to participate in even lawful anti-republican, pro-monarchical activities was restricted.[8]

6. Caplan, *Government without Administration*, p. 17.
7. In general, A. Kunz, *Civil Servants and the Politics of Inflation in Germany, 1914–1924* (Berlin, New York, 1986).
8. Caplan, *Government without Administration*, pp. 38–9.

THE NSDAP'S APPEAL TO THE MITTELSTAND

The NSDAP had been alerted to civil service grievances during the 1920s. The party shrewdly stressed the *Beamte*'s declining status in the Weimar system, dismissively labelling the democratization of the civil service as a 'shabby device' for Social Democratic patronage. It attacked the dismissals of 1924 as a gross violation of the *Beamte*'s traditional right to tenure.[9] With the onset of the economic crisis in 1929 the party's activities in this field increased and *Gauleiter* Jakob Sprenger was given responsibility by Frick to appoint party followers to specialize on civil service issues in each of the *Gaue*. In December 1932 Sprenger's special journal for civil servants appeared (*NS Beamten–Zeitung*). Earlier that year, in May, the party had set up a special department for *Beamte*, rounding off its successful penetration of the civil service associations. The NSDAP's wooing of the civil service reached a peak in the 1932 campaigns, exploiting deep-seated resentment about the reductions in salaries and benefits imposed by first Heinrich Brüning and then Franz von Papen. It was because the civil servants' position was at least relatively favourable in comparison with those of other white-collar groups that they responded above all to the NSDAP's campaigning about the erosion of their elitist *identity*. It is important not to lose sight of the persistent sense of marginalization experienced throughout the middle classes. Their disorientation, manifested in disenchantment with the political system, could readily be translated into militant activism – as Hitler soon realized. Not the least of his appeal to the Mittelstand was his stress on the restoration of clear authority, of established and 'patriotic' values.[10]

Comment has already been made on the sheer range of social groups supporting the NSDAP but with this caveat the extent to which the middle classes dominated is still striking. In Bavaria in 1933 the self-employed (excluding peasants) white-collar employees and *Beamte* (civil servants and teachers) made up forty-eight per cent of the party membership.[11] The relationship between the Mittelstand and the NSDAP is also only too evident from the composition of its Reichstag delegation. In October 1932 this broke down into the following social categories: blue- and white-collar (55), farmers (50), independent

9. T. Childers, *The Nazi Voter. The Social Foundations of Fascism in Germany, 1919–1933* (Chapel Hill–London, 1983), p. 228.

10. On the political activism of the bourgeoisie, P. Fritzsche, *Rehearsals for Fascism. Populism and Political Mobilisation in Weimar Germany* (Oxford–London, 1990).

11. I. Kershaw, *Popular Opinion and Political Dissent*, p. 119.

representatives of trade, handicrafts and industry (43), full-time party functionaries, including editors (29), career civil servants (20), teachers (12) and former officers (9).[12] It is possible to exaggerate the importance of the youthful element in the NSDAP, since many older voters were drawn to it, but most of the party's Reichstag delegates were under 40. Not all middle-class supporters of Nazism were attracted simply by the idea of restored status and nostalgia. The longing for career prospects not blocked by representatives of the ageing oligarchy was a powerful factor for many voters. In this context it should also be noted that the disgruntled ranks of the Mittelstand provided something like 64.2 per cent of university students. Those with more technocratic ambitions were often clearly convinced by the dynamism of the NSDAP that it had far more to offer in terms of a secure and profitable future than the other parties.

The 'check-list' of Nazi propaganda aimed at the middle classes added up to a most powerful and persuasive call, going far beyond restoration of earnings, important as these undoubtedly were. The faithful were to be conducted from the barren confines of modern industrial society; privilege and 'standing' would be restored. Traditional values would be reaffirmed, containing the unwelcome powers of large capitalists on the one hand, 'Marxist' unions and parties on the other. 'The intermediate social strata of an industrial society dominated by big capital and labour would once more become the respected and authoritative centre-ground of a hierarchical, corporatist society.'[13] The marginalization of the 'little man' would be over, people would know where they stood and, on top of all this, their specific economic grievances would be attended to.

This is not to say that the NSDAP's party managers had as sure a touch with white-collar workers outside the civil service during the 1932 campaigns. The party approached these as 'either a subspecies of the civil-service electorate or as a somewhat elevated component of the working class'.[14] The National Socialists were not helped by the popular perception that the NSDAP far preferred women to stay at home, since females constituted a high percentage of the *Angestellte*. The Weimar Republic, the party affirmed, had advanced women's rights but produced 'millions of men without work' as well as 'millions of women without familial happiness'. In the event this ideology was

12. D. Schoenbaum, *Hitler's Social Revolution. Class and Status in Nazi Germany* (London, 1966), p. 38.
13. D. Peukert, *Inside Nazi Germany. Conformity, Opposition and Racism in Everyday Life* (London, 1989), p. 87.
14. Ibid., p. 233.

compromised by economic necessity and manpower shortages, as we have already observed. By contrast the NSDAP was remarkably successful after 1929 in gaining the support of the middle-class pensioners, small investors and rentiers promising 'the revalorisation of your savings and just and adequate retirement care'.[15] In general, however, there is much to suggest that the division between 'old' and 'new' middle classes had become increasingly blurred with the onset of economic crisis. The civil servants and other white-collar workers – who had been in many respects and for some time the beneficiaries of industrialization – were experiencing something like the fear of declining status afflicting farmers, artisans and other 'productive' elements of the Mittelstand, thus helping to forge the sense of a distinctive 'class identity' remarked on earlier.

EXPECTATION AND 'CO-ORDINATION'

Whatever the party's propaganda appeal before 1933, it is difficult to believe that its activists can ever really have identified that closely with the values of their bourgeois supporters. Hitler served early notice in an interview in 1934 of what the Mittelstand could expect: 'The bourgeois must no longer feel himself a kind of pensioner of either tradition or capital, separated from the worker by the marxist idea of property, but must aim to accommodate himself as a worker to the welfare of the community.'[16] Indeed, National Socialist legislation abolished the formal distinction between *Arbeiter* and *Angestellte*. Tough bargaining between the regime and the middle-class organizations and pressure groups was likely to be the order of the day during the process of 'co-ordination' and economic reconstruction after 1933.

The disappointments experienced by career civil servants during this process after 1933 have already been noted, as has the frustration of farmers later in the 1930s. Expectations of the NSDAP were also particularly high in the retail sector by 1933, where the number of outlets had grown by some twenty-one per cent between 1907 and 1925. The rapid expansion of this sector brought about a situation where a high proportion of the large labour force employed in the retail trade was often poorly trained and living on low incomes, freely exploited by the large department and chain stores, as memorably

15. Peukert, *Inside Nazi Germany*, p. 225.
16. Cited in Schoenbaum, *Hitler's Social Revolution*, p. 65.

described in Hans Speier's famous study of white-collar workers written in 1932. He pointed out of 'the saleswoman' that 'she was distinguished from an automaton only through the scrap of personality that satisfied the sovereign demand of the customer on whom she waited. On the job she was on the borderline between human being and disembodied, minimally functioning brain: a vocabulary of thirty words and mastery of the multiplication table sufficed for the execution of her duties.'[17] Not surprisingly, the small businessmen found the competition intolerable and once more the fear of social decline was accentuated.[18] The NSDAP campaign literature and ideology had certainly identified the party with the mood against the department stores and the large consumer co-operative societies and in December 1932 the National Socialist Combat League for the Commercial Middle Classes had been formed under the leadership of Theodor Adrian von Renteln.

The Combat League had of course nothing like the strength of numbers and experience of personnel that Darré for example could bring to bear through his Agrarian Policy Apparatus. Yet the League made initial progress when personnel and organizational changes were forced through in the corporations and associations of handicraft and trade. Individual acts of violence against Jewish businesses and department stores also met some of the grievances of the commercial Mittelstand. By May, von Renteln and Paul Hilland had become respectively president and managing director of the German Industrial and Trade Congress. Legislation was put into place with the *Law for the Protection of Retail Trade* on 12 May 1933. It enlarged the powers of state and local authorities to prevent the setting up of new department or chain stores and to withdraw or refuse existing concessions where unfair competition, insufficient demand or fraud could be demonstrated. However, the law was issued under Hugenberg's auspices. He had already frustrated von Renteln and his collaborator in the Brown House, Karl Zeleny, by having the Reich Commissioner for the Commercial Middle Classes (Dr Wienbeck) installed in the Ministry for Economics. Additional legislation in July authorized the state licensing of businesses. Effectively, this 'imposed a state-regulated control of middle-class commerce in place of free enterprise'.[19] This has rightly been seen as a reflection of Hitler's paramount concern not

17.   H. Speier, *German White-Collar Workers and the Rise of Hitler* (New Haven and London, English edn, 1986), p. 25.

18.   T. Geiger, *Die soziale Schichtung des deutschen Volkes* (Stuttgart, 1932), pp. 72ff.

19.   Broszat, *The Hitler State. The Foundations and Development of the Internal Structure of the Third Reich* (London, 1981) p. 159.

to upset big business. Hugenberg's immediate successor, Karl Schmitt, suspended further corporative reorganization and on 7 August the Combat League itself was dissolved.

In reneging on promises to the Mittelstand the regime was also reacting to the growing public dismay at the rise in prices as a result of often undisciplined and ill planned party attacks on department stores in 1933, together with the prospect of huge job losses arising from their closure. Ultimately, party activists had to accept merely a reduction in the business of the large stores instead of their liquidation. That particular goal was achieved by means of a turnover tax from 1935 (only lifted on 1 April 1940) and the closure of refreshment rooms, catering and handicrafts services in the big stores. The discounts which the stores could offer were also curtailed. In 1935 the turnover of the department stores dropped to 54 per cent of the record turnover of 1928, but slowly recovered to almost three-quarters of that level by 1938. Aryan department stores inevitably profited, too, from the pogrom against Jews and the enforced exclusion of Jewish business rivals.[20] Hostility to the large stores never disappeared from the party ranks but in reality the absolute share of the retail turnover falling to the chain stores was small. A study in 1929 indicated that they took only 4 per cent of this, although their share of clothing and household goods was much higher. Furthermore, by 1928 their relative share of turnover was growing some twenty-two per cent faster than the total volume of retail trade. At the same time retail trade as a whole had only a small share in the economic recovery of 1934–35. The closure of a succession of department stores came eventually through the pressure for war-time savings in trade and retailing.

A similar process achieved party control of the handicrafts guilds and associations by March 1933.[21] Emphasis on the corporative strength of the guilds and an adherence to hierarchical values persisted amongst Weimar artisans and handicraft concerns during the Weimar Republic. Indeed, the depression eventually forced many of the larger craftsmen back to the guilds. Some guild leaders talked aggressively of an economic parliament based on occupational estates. Hopes for a corporatist reorganization of economic life favourable to small business and handicrafts were encouraged by the appearance in early May of the Reich Corporation of German Handicraft and the Reich

20. Broszat, *The Hitler State*, p. 161. Also see M. Ohlsen, 'Ständischer Aufbau und Monopole 1933–34' in *Zeitschrift für Geschichtswissenschaft*, 1 (1974): 28ff.

21. F. Domurad, 'The politics of corporatism. Hamburg handicraft in the late Weimar Republic' in R. Bessel and E. J. Feuchtwanger (eds), *Social Change and Political Development in Weimar Germany* (London, 1981).

Corporation of German Trade. During the summer a General Association of Craftsmen, Shopkeepers and Traders was set up within the German Labour Front (DAF). Eventually, on 15 June 1934 the *Decree on the provisional Reconstruction of German Handicraft* replaced the free professional associations with a system of handicraft guilds with compulsory membership. This was arguably less the outcome of reactionary tendencies than an indication of the pressure for efficiency. By excluding the untrained through compulsory guild membership, many of the less able and smaller workshops could be eliminated.[22] Once again, the Reich Ministry of Economics was the moving force behind the system. While artisans now had their obligatory guild it was therefore firmly under state supervision.

The evidence considered so far would appear to support the argument that the Third Reich eventually sounded the death knell of the aspirations awakened in the old middle classes.[23] The economic drive for full employment and rearmament certainly favoured big business and Hitler was not disposed to allow too much disruption at any level by *any* groups. The chattering classes were given due warning of his displeasure at any uncoordinated interference in the economy during the conference of Reich Governors in July 1933, when he reminded them that the party programme did not sanction 'behaving like fools and turning everything upside down, but setting to with intelligence and foresight'.[24] It should again be emphasized that it is unlikely that the productive middle classes as a whole suffered automatically from the regime's emphasis on large-scale enterprise and rearmament. Many small concerns were involved in the rearmament programme; large numbers of specialist firms served bigger enterprises through the manufacture of components and accessories. In addition the work creation scheme had various aspects which benefited artisans. The latter's compulsory guilds, although state-controlled, kept outsiders away as we have seen and forced through a higher degree of professionalism. It should also be added that National Socialist policies favoured the more efficient firms and that these profited from the collapse of the less able ventures. Finally, although there was disappointment in material terms, there was a compensatory official emphasis on the status and importance of components of the Mittelstand. There were winners as well as losers in the middle-class ranks.

Nevertheless, war brought new setbacks and further decline in the

22. A. von Saldern, 'The old Mittelstand 1890–1939. How "backward" were the artisans', *Central European History*, 25 (1992): pp. 27–51.
23. M. Ohlsen, 'Ständischer Aufbau und Monopole, pp. 29ff.
24. W. Fischer, *Deutsche Wirtschaftspolitik 1918–1945* (Opladen, 1968), p. 79.

176

handicraft sector. Labour shortages worsened as Germany's military position deteriorated from 1942. Civil servants, to return briefly to the 'unproductive' were, or felt themselves to be, afflicted through overwork when war came, and watched the real value of their salaries fall. All this and the public still disliked them. Yet middle-class support for National Socialism had never been explicable in economic terms alone. A depressing measure of commitment to the movement's ideology long characterized the Mittelstand's response to the NSDAP, to its anti-Bolshevism and its anti-Semitism. Of course at the same time *some* members of the middle class displayed uneasiness at the developing persecution of the Jews, while clashes between the state and the traditional values of the family, locality and church continued. Ordinary middle-class experience could not therefore be reduced to a simple either/or, to disobedience or quiescence. Nevertheless, there was no serious resistance to the regime. The Mittelstand's almost pathological aversion to the left helped to ensure that its mercenary grumbling after 1933 never seriously threatened the system. It may well indeed have been the case that from 1943 the increasing alienation of the middle classes, together with that of other social groups, deprived the government of mass support. Doubtless, too, the increased use of terror from then on indicated that the regime's legitimacy might have been dissolving.[25] It remained to the end able to turn a deaf ear to the distressed cries of the middle classes. 'Complaint and compliance,' it has been neatly argued, 'were related characteristics of middle class life in the Third Reich.'[26]

25. Cf. D. Welch, *The Third Reich. Politics and Propaganda* (London, New York, 1993), pp. 120ff.
26. Kershaw, *Popular Opinion*, p. 155.

CHAPTER TEN

Policing the 'People's Community'

Associating the concept of 'policing' with that of Hitler's proclaimed 'people's community' (*Volksgemeinschaft*) highlights the deep ambiguity about the relationship of government to governed in the Third Reich. It could be supposed, for example, that a genuine 'people's community' would not have needed to resort to extensive policing within. Alternatively, it could reveal something of the nature of the policing itself. Finally, policing might be seen largely in terms of excluding or eliminating undesirable social groups from the Volksgemeinschaft in the interests of the favoured majority. Either route leads inexorably to further questions about 'opposition' and 'resistance' and, ultimately, about the wider responsibility for the fate of the Jews.

Even in the middle of war, in June 1942, Hitler's *Table Talk* records him as saying: 'For goodness' sake, don't let us rush to the police every time some small peccadillo raises its head. Don't forget, after all, that it was not by using fear inspired by police methods that we National Socialists won over the people, but rather by trying to show them the light and to educate them.' The statement is wholly consistent with Hitler's concern to avoid the sort of dissension at home which, in his view, had produced the 'stab in the back' in November 1918, but is it accurate? It has been disputed on the grounds that the 'extent of unorganised individual and discrete popular resistance in the years 1943–5' *would* have produced a stab in the back for Hitler had it not been for 'the Gestapo's activities and the fear which they engendered. Police terror stood between the regime and collapse'.[1] The argument

---

1. Cited in T. Mason, 'The legacy of 1918 for National Socialism' in A. J. Nicholls and E. Matthias (eds), *German Democracy and the Triumph of Hitler. Essays in Recent German History* (London, 1971), p. 226.

that police terror was the major factor in accounting for the absence of successful wide-scale popular reactions against Hitler's regime is plausible, although not easy to substantiate. It is difficult to measure 'unorganised' and 'discrete' popular resistance for a start and even harder to trace its agreed aims and strategies, assuming their existence. Significantly, the most extensive accounts of Gestapo action are against the organized resistance groups. It therefore still seems important to emphasize the mixture of terror and persuasion in managing the people's community as a whole. The combination promises to provide answers to the question as to how *any* police force would have been adequate to police Germany, swollen as it was through war and expansion, without extensive compliance from the population. It is helpful first to outline the institutional context of the Gestapo.

THE GESTAPO; LIMITS TO POLICING

Like other Continental countries Germany had a long tradition of police surveillance of political affairs. The work of the Political Police inevitably expanded in the turbulent years after 1918 but the absence of a national police force was widely criticized. The Reich Public Prosecutor was compelled to work through the *Länder*, with their often marked political differences. This situation was finally changed by the emergency legislation following the Reichstag fire on 28 February 1933, allowing the central government to introduce their appointees into the police and justice systems. During the ensuing action taken against the Reich's 'enemies' the 'participation, compliance or accommodation of ordinary citizens' was encouraged from the outset by the widespread fear of communism. Public anxiety on this score diverted attention from the arbitrary arrests and beatings as well as the first 'wild' concentration camps.

The decree of 6 February 1933, replacing police chiefs in Prussia from the ranks of the SA, SS and the Stahlhelm, had been ostensibly directed against police excesses. The process escalated rapidly after the Reichstag fire. In reality the Gestapo was built by relying heavily on modifying and transforming the existing Political Police forces in most of the federal German states. The first 'Secret State Police' (*Geheime Staatspolizei* – Gestapo) were set up in Prussia by Hermann Goering, who as Prussian Minister of the Interior effectively controlled Prussia's police. His appointee, Rudolf Diels, briefly headed the Secret State Police Office, created by a special law on 26 April 1933. Soon the so-called Regional Secret State Police posts (*Staatspolizeistellen* – Stapostellen) spread throughout Prussia until by March 1934 the Prussian Gestapo had become an independent body dealing with anything that was 'political.'[2] The process of transforming the Political Police in Prussia was echoed broadly in Bavaria, where SS Leader and Provisional Police President of Munich, Heinrich Himmler, enjoyed the title of Commander of Political Police from 1 April 1933.

In the ruthless struggle against the Reich's 'enemies' in 1933–4, Himmler gradually assumed control of the Political Police in a series of *Länder*, culminating in his command of the Prussian Gestapo from 24 April 1934. At that point his own protégé, Richard Heydrich, took over the day-to-day running of the office from Diels. Himmler's power was augmented by the unification of all police authority in his hands through a law of 17 June 1936. Henceforth Himmler was the Chief of the German Police. His control of the police forces throughout the Reich was assured, although he remained nominally subordinate to the Minister of the Interior, Frick. Further rationalization followed. The Political Police were combined with the Criminal Police into an overall Security Police (SIPO) and by September 20 all political police forces in Germany were formally under the Gestapo Headquarters in Berlin. The Gestapo's competence was further defined at the expense of the Party Security Service (*Sicherheits Dienst* – SD), which from 7 July 1937 had no real police powers. When the Reich Security Main Office (*Reichsicherheitshauptamt* – RSHA) was formed in 1939 to systematize the organizations concerned with 'security' issues, it had little impact on the powers of the Gestapo. The latter was able to function independently 'outside' the state and could resort to 'special principles and requirements' as well as to normal laws to justify action. 'Despite some appearance to the contrary, the Gestapo could very nearly decide for itself what the law was, act accordingly and ignore objections.'[3]

At the same time, the greater awareness of the conflict-ridden nature of the Third Reich's administration has focused more attention on how policing worked and how the Gestapo could operate so effectively with the comparatively limited resources at its disposal. Except for those in Würzburg–Lower Franconia and Düsseldorf, Gestapo case files have been destroyed. Detailed study of the first region – not notably pro-Nazi – has given a picture of the Gestapo as a compact top group relying heavily on information provided by many

2. R. Gellately, *The Gestapo and German Society. Enforcing Racial Policy 1933–1945* (Oxford, 1991), p. 30.
3. Ibid., p. 42.

individuals and agencies. Membership of the Gestapo itself was remarkably small and even by the end of 1944 stood at only 32,000, of which the 15,500 or so 'executive officials' carried out the real tasks of political policing.[4] In enforcing racial policy in particular, tip-offs provided the major cause of Gestapo investigations. Most of the denouncements came from the lower end of the social scale but all social groups were implicated in the process; informing transcended class barriers. Motives were highly variable and could include personal grievances; only a minority seem to have been prompted by loyalty to the government. Nonetheless, denunciations – together with the ease with which the traditional police forces became acclimatized to the new order – were in effect supportive of the system between 1933 and 1945.

QUALIFYING THE 'SS STATE'

The celebrated pervasiveness of the Gestapo takes on new meanings in this context, which is certainly not to deny the fear that it could instil in its victims. Yet the concept of extensive self-policing indicates also that the terror system of the Third Reich was more open than many have admitted. This idea is in fact a far more uncomfortable one to have to cope with than the argument advanced in the earlier but enormously influential study by H. Krausnick and M. Broszat, *Anatomy of the SS State*. The perfectly understandable concern of these historians – to try to trace 'the day to day practice of totalitarian tyranny' – yielded vital insights into the nature of terror and of the concentration camps.[5] At the same time it gave a misleading impression of the uniformity of policing after 1933 and tended to overlook the extent to which the policed participated in the whole process of controlling 'criminality'.[6] The study also underestimated the degree to which the state rested on several pillars of support, at least until 1937–38, when Hitler more decisively eroded the influence of the armed forces and of key civil service elites. As well as acknowledging more fully the nature of policing in Germany during the 1930s, it is important to give sufficient weight to both the complexity of the power struggle in, and

4. R. Gellately, *The Gestapo and German Society*, p. 44.
5. H. Krausnick and M. Broszat, *Anatomy of the SS State* (London, 1970), p. 14.
6. R. Gellately, 'Situating the "SS State" in a socio-historical context. Recent history of the SS, the police and the courts in the 3rd Reich', *Journal of Modern History*, 64 (1992): 338–65.

the social composition of, the Third Reich. Even if these caveats are kept firmly in mind, then the concept of the 'SS state' still retains explanatory value, in so far as it does at least draw our attention to the centrality of the National Socialist ideology, providing a constant reminder that the 'people's community' was to be built and maintained on a racial basis, to the exclusion of those identified by the Nazis as unfit, unwanted or undesirable.

From this perspective nothing in the long run could have been more destructive of the old order, or more consistent with Hitler's Darwinistic belief that only the fittest (most ruthless) merited survival, than Heinrich Himmler's own path to infamy. His organization, itself far from monolithic, was surely destined to be the eventual victor of the regime's polycratic power struggle. Himmler's achievement, it should be stressed, was extremely hard won; even the SS had to fight constantly to save its corner. At the same time Himmler's example demonstrated that Hitler was not opposed to the concentration of power as such. The cancerous spread of the SS was aided by its encroachment on policing not only throughout the Old Reich but also, and above all, in the conquered and annexed territories beyond Germany's borders.[7] Himmler also secured for himself decisive influence on racial policy in the East as Reich Commissar for Securing Germandom (*Reichskommissar für die Festigung deutschen Volkstums* – RKVD), according to a decree of 7 October 1939. In the course of time SS Special Duty Troops were formed, including the unspeakable SS-Death's Head for the concentration camps. Linked in with the latter were the SS-run economic 'enterprises', based ultimately on a cheap labour force that could literally be worked to death. Also to be emphasized is the creation of the Higher SS and Police Leaders (*Höhere SS und Polizeiführer* – HSSPF). These offices, staffed from 1937 onwards by hand-picked personnel from the former front generation and freikorps, had overall control of the regional SS organization when they finally became active in August 1939. Detailed study of the activity of the HSSPFs confirms once again that the high degree of internal conflict built into the National Socialist governmental apparatus never excluded efficient execution of policy if need be. Indeed, the case of the HSSPFs, who were also appointed to each of the occupied territories, indicates that rivalry and the pressure of action were more rather than less likely to lead to a quick and efficient translation of ideological and racial dogma into practice. HSSPF

7. For a detailed recent study, R. L. Koehl, *The Black Corps. The Structure and Power Struggles of the Nazi SS* (University of Wisconsin Press, Madison, Wisconsin, 1993).

members, who were answerable directly to Himmler, invariably proved to be capable of carrying out the Führer's commands to the letter even against their better judgement.[8]

It is significant that such primacy of ideology was not countered in any significant way by the incidence of self-policing, if the Würzburg–Lower Franconia experience is anything to go by. We have seen that even in this not pronouncedly pro-Nazi region denunciations on racial matters exceeded all others. Moreover, there were many other areas of political and social activity where the ideological purity of the racial state, guarded above all by the SS and Gestapo, became increasingly apparent and which, in more or less direct ways, created the overall policy climate for first excluding the Jews from the Volksgemeinschaft and then eliminating them. As in policing, it was often the case that elements existing before 1933 were incorporated and adapted to very different settings and policy ends in the Hitler state. One important example among all too many is in the general field of public health, where numerous ideas on social engineering to improve the quality of the German race were already being aired in the 1880s.

The work of the founding father of eugenics, Alfred Ploetz (1860–1940), initially attracted public health authorities, social policy makers and biomedical scientists looking to provide a brighter social future. Many of these stressed the social role of medicine and maintained contacts with writers generally critical of society. Most of the discussions by the experts 'occurred initially in a medical and legal context rather than in a narrowly racial context, and showed the force of an independent strain of biological opinions'.[9] In addition, questions were raised by some theorists as to how far the costs of preserving 'life unworthy of life' could be borne by the state, thus raising the idea of enforced killing of the mentally ill. Although the roots of such thought were located in Weimar, it was the Nazi seizure of power which enabled this work to be carried out. Only after 1933 could eugenic thinking be drastically transformed by the new realities of state, so that scientific ideas could be turned into political weapons. Having said this, it is disturbing to note that doctors were Nazified sooner and more thoroughly than other professions in Germany. Eleven per cent of them actually joined the SS, although power struggles and formations within the medical professions helped to determine choices,

8. See R. B. Birn, *Die Höheren SS- und Polizeiführer. Himmlers Verkehr im Reich und in den besetzten Gebieten* (Düsseldorf, 1986).

9. P. Weindling, *Health, Race and German Politics between National Unification and Nazism, 1870–1945* (Cambridge, 1989), p. 397.

as well as ideological convictions.[10] It can safely be assumed that many individuals desired to implement Rudolf Hess's belief that National Socialism was 'applied biology'. Thus adequate behavioural explanations for the enforced Euthanasia programme of the 1930s are provided less by the *nature* of medicine itself than by the state's identification of groups after 1933 'that, in the cost-benefit analysis of Nazi authorities, were useless to the state and hence unfit to live'.[11]

There are all too many instances of social engineering driven by racist policy goals in the Third Reich. The emphasis on *policy* in the public and private sector appears to be vying with if not actually displacing the preoccupation with 'daily life' which characterized the social history of the Third Reich written in the 1970s.[12] Since the stress on policy carries within it the implication that National Socialism was an extreme variant of modern social control, it has also revived arguments about whether or not Hitler's regime was an agent of modernization.[13] It is, however, precisely the barbarity of the ideology and actions informing so much of the Third Reich's social policy that makes it hard to acknowledge the 'racial state' as a modernizing force. At the same time, our understanding of the social reality of the Third Reich is not greatly advanced by assertions that within it there co-existed elements of 'modernity' and 'anti-modernity'.[14] Both components probably co-exist in most societies at some point in their development and it would not be difficult to find them today in a number of countries. The Hitler regime manifestly caused changes in society (including attitudes), if not to the extent that they resulted in a full-scale social revolution, which is defined by fundamental alterations in class structures and relationships.[15] It remains in many ways surprising that so much energy has been devoted to trying to determine how far National Socialism fell short of achieving such a revolution, particularly as defined in class terms which Hitler and his followers explicitly rejected in propagating the Volksgemeinschaft in the first place. There is an obvious risk of underestimating the extent and impact of the Volksgemeinschaft if it is simply measured against

10. H. Kater, *Doctors under Hitler* (Chapel Hill, 1989).

11. Remark of M. Kater in a review, *Journal of Modern History*, 64 (1992).

12. An excellent illustration is provided by C. Sachse, *Siemens, der Nationalsozialismus und die moderne Familie. Eine Untersuchung zur sozialen Rationalisierung in Deutschland im 20 Jahrhundert* (Hamburg, 1990).

13. For an early but important general discussion, R. Dahrendorf, *Society and Democracy in Germany* (London, 1965).

14. M. Burleigh and W. Wippermann, *The Racial State* (Cambridge, 1991).

15. I. Kershaw, *The Nazi Dictatorship* (3rd edn, London, 1993), p. 147.

the paradigm of a 'good' revolution. Interestingly, it is possible for a leading British historian of Hitlerism to insist that the regime itself did *not* bring about social revolution, while recording that: 'Nazism produced a maelstrom of destruction which threatened, then inevitably sucked in, the representatives of the existing social order.'[16]

THE VOLKSGEMEINSCHAFT

The National Socialist version of a Volksgemeinschaft was an explicit rejection of what Germany had become. Defeat in the First World War was seen by Hitler as the sorry and inevitable outcome of the crisis of purpose and morale under the old regime. His deep personal distaste for the pre-1914 social order persisted to the bitter end. In addition Marxism, which in National Socialist thought had engineered the 'stab in the back' in November 1918, had to be confronted and destroyed.[17] Germany's renewal would take place under National Socialism in the form of a united ethnic community; class divisions, as exacerbated by Marxism, would be not so much eliminated as overcome by the stronger ties of blood and race. Hitler was also convinced that healing the internal divisions in German society was indispensable to the restoration of German hegemony in Europe.

The expectations aroused by the NSDAP as it developed electorally helped to create a foundation for the Volksgemeinschaft even before 1933. Although Hitler can be said to have reached the outer limits of his electoral appeal by 1932, he could also justly claim to have been more successful than any other party in breaking down social barriers. It is vital to give full weight to this unprecedented success with the German electorate, for it is an important part of the explanation of the relative speed with which *Gleichschaltung* (co-ordination) took place after 1933. When Hitler proclaimed the end of all parties other than his own, however, he was already beginning to make clear that the Volksgemeinschaft would be defined also by those kept *outside* it. The people's community would manifestly be at the expense of the organized left, which was humiliated and driven underground. It almost immediately became apparent, too, that Hitler had been absolutely serious about confining the community to racially pure Germans, as the NSDAP programme had insisted in 1920. This was bound to have

16. Kershaw, *The Nazi Dictatorship*, p. 149.
17. Mason, 'The legacy of 1918 for National Socialism', pp. 215–39.

dire implications for Jews in particular once the National Socialists had seized power.

It should be recorded that the number of Jews never exceeded 1.09 per cent of the German population between 1871 and 1933, although the proportion of foreign Jews within this increased to twenty per cent by the time of the *Machtergreifung*. Jews were concentrated mainly in cities, being over-represented in business and commerce. It has been argued that Germany was not as bad a place for Jews to live in as other parts of Europe and the world.[18] Yet German Jews had already become more marginalized and were subject to crude stereotyping during the Weimar Republic. Hitler's insistent identification of Jews with Bolshevism was one example; another was that Jews had supposedly been less patriotic in the First World War. Few Jews made it to the very top in either national or local politics during the 1920s, leading some to conclude that the *Machtergreifung* in 1933 merely accelerated the departure of Jews from the centre of public life.[19] It has often been said that anti-Semitism might have been less of a drawing card than once supposed in accounting for electoral support for Hitler in the 1920s, but equally it does not seem to have been much of a deterrent. Those voting for Hitler knew that *some* measures would be taken against Jews and in that respect at least had accepted the prospect of further persecution.

Public hostility to the Jews, of which there were 564,000 in the Reich in the mid-1920s, was a necessary condition of the application of National Socialist racialist policies during the 1930s. Yet anti-Semitism did not lead towards the gas chamber until Hitler's assumption of power and was in that respect a wholly vital but not sufficient pre-condition of the 'Final Solution'. That 1933 brought an immediate hardening of policy was confirmed by the new virulence in the application of anti-Semitic measures.[20] The *Law on the Restoration of the Civil Service* offers an example. In defining what could be considered as 'non-Aryan', it may well have directly affected relatively few civil servants, some 5000 of whom were Jews, but it set a dangerous precedent generally for Jewish doctors, lawyers and other professionals. Intellectual and artistic elites were quick to draw the conclusion that they had best leave Germany fairly quickly, which many did. Jews who were workers (24,000), Angestellte (84,000) or

18. S. Gordon, *Germany and the Jewish Question* (Princeton, 1984), pp. 8–49.

19. P. Pulzer, *Jews and the German State: the Political History of a Minority, 1848–1933* (Oxford, 1992).

20. P. Wende, 'Dislocations and new beginnings; the experience of German-speaking Jews', *Bulletin of the German Historical Institute*, May, 1992, p. 5.

self-employed (110,000) according to the 1925 census immediately experienced a wide variety of discrimination, such as the sudden appearance in welfare offices of posters warning against spending public funds in Jewish shops. In 1933 alone, some 40,000 Jews, mostly young and unencumbered, abandoned Germany. The majority of those remaining soon lost their initial illusions about fighting back with the aid of the law and were forced to create their own self-help organizations. Thus a national body representing German Jews (*Reichsvertretung der deutschen Juden*) was set up in the autumn of 1933. Within a short time a Jewish sector of the economy evolved, providing a network of support and some employment for Jews. Although official violence against the German Jews supposedly gave way to a honeymoon period between 1934 and 1937, their situation actually worsened accumulatively during those years.

In the first place their material and social position was steadily undermined through administrative practice and legislation, notably the Nuremberg Laws of 1935 forbidding marriage or extra-marital sexual intercourse between Jews, and the Reich Citizenship Law. From the end of 1937 anti-Semitic measures became progressively sharper – at which time the number of Jews still living in the Reich had dropped to 350,000. By 1938 Jewish workers were employed almost entirely for German firms while the wealth of the Jewish community as a whole had been halved. The enforced registration of Jewish assets in April 1938 was followed by the familiar escalation of violence in November – inadequately termed the 'Night of broken glass' in many earlier accounts but long since recognized for what it was, a pogrom. More Jews were forced to flee until this avenue was also closed in October 1941. By then, 'The Nazis had largely succeeded in isolating Jewish citizens, excluding them from the "Volksgemeinschaft" in the eyes of the majority of the German population and branding them "enemies of the race".' During this time the 'majority of the population showed indifference'.[21] On the contrary, during the 1930s many Germans favoured restricting the rights of Jews, if the surviving files of the Düsseldorf Gestapo office are anything to go by.[22] Those middle-class beneficiaries of measures against Jews and other 'undesirables' who may have personally regretted what was happening and even reacted with dismay and sympathy, allowed their instinct for survival and their exaggerated fear of Marxism to keep most of them from meaningful opposition, as we have seen.

21. Wende, 'Dislocations', p. 122.
22. Gordon, *Germany and the Jewish Question*, p. 208.

It is all too obvious, then, that the notion of a Volksgemeinschaft was exploited by the regime after 1933 as a device for political coercion. The obvious gaps between day-to-day reality and the proclaimed people's community have caused many to conclude that the Volksgemeinschaft was no more than a facade masking ongoing class conflict in an officially 'classless' society. As war approached, the government's insistence on a united and harmonious society barely concealed warnings against dissension and the prosecution of 'selfish' interests.[23] There remains, however, a logical objection to interpreting discontent as proof of the absence of a 'proper' Volksgemeinschaft, since *by definition* the concept assumed that individuals and groups might have to give up something for the good of the majority. The truth is that the 'people's community' being forged was simply a very depressing one. Individuals retreated into what has been described as non-political privacy in reaction against public rhetoric, but since this secured the passive consent required by the government its effects *were* political.[24] What, for instance, is to be made of the poster in an Essen library in 1937, welcoming the decline of indiscriminate reading by the public as a sign of healthy recovery? Faced with such evidence, it is far from clear even that the 'internal emigration' of intellectuals and artists and their pursuit of non-controversial topics were, as some have insisted, indications of the hollowness of the people's community. Trying to find ways in which the people's community was not fully realized diverts attention from the insidious way in which a 'community of compliance' became a stark reality. Moreover, the community was also defined by the benefits which the German public as a whole derived from it. One telling and depressing example is the way in which the Reich's mass tourism followed in the wake of Germany's annexation and expansion.

The community of compliance never precluded scattered but surprisingly wide dissent and defiance by ordinary Germans – often with tragic results for those concerned. Dissent or 'nonconformity' are more apt descriptions than resistance of most of these acts of opposition. They could include circulating leaflets, helping the victims of National Socialism, unobtrusive and minor obstruction such as spreading rumours, even – in the case of youth – listening to the great American (and Jewish) jazz clarinettist, Benny Goodman. More seriously, there were also strikes, although the limits to what the

23. Mason, 'The legacy of 1918 for National Socialism', p. 225.
24. Cf. D. Peukert, *Inside Nazi Germany. Conformity, Opposition and Racism in Everyday Life* (London, 1989), pp. 208ff.

working classes as a whole achieved to oppose the regime have been noted. Suicides, which rose to 18,600 a year between 1933 and 1935, removed many from the impact of Hitler's regime while some 400,000 Germans, mostly Jewish, emigrated between 1933 and 1939.[25] The persecution of hundreds of thousands of Germans by the Hitler regime serves to illustrate that their dissent and nonconformity must have been widespread. Resistance, defined as an organized and sustained attempt to destroy the government, was not. This was partly because spheres of conflict and opposition remained largely isolated from each other while, in addition,

> many aspects of Nazism enjoyed a popularity extending far beyond Party die-hards. Economic recovery, the destruction of 'marxism', the rebuilding of a strong Germany, territorial expansion, foreign policy and military successes, all seemed, before the middle of the war, stunningly impressive to millions. They found their embodiment in Hitler's personal popularity, boosted by propaganda into a leadership cult of great potency. The apparent 'achievements' of the regime both disarmed criticism and created an atmosphere in which opposition was unable to reckon with any broad base of growing popular disaffection that could have proved dangerous to the regime.[26]

RESISTANCE WITHOUT THE PEOPLE

In such a context organized resistance could only arise from within those same German elites who had enjoyed such a problematic relationship with the NSDAP before 1933. The traditional forces of conservatism in Germany had sought since the 1890s to harness the 'new right' – groups claiming to locate their authority in the *Volk* rather than in the state or the person of a monarch. Hugenberg's decision to join forces with Hitler was on one level a culmination of this long-term goal of right-wing activists. That Hugenberg entered Hitler's coalition, against the advice of those of his colleagues who had already become disillusioned with their new Chancellor, is further evidence of the tremendous uncertainty afflicting German elites. Although German conservatives favoured an authoritarian polity over the Weimar system, many of them distrusted Hitler intensely.

25. M. Balfour, *Withstanding Hitler in Germany 1933–1945* (London–New York, 1988), p. 60.
26. Kershaw, *Nazi Dictatorship*, p. 172.

Moreover, one opponent, Ewald von Kleist-Schmenzin, a key figure in the ultra-conservative Main Association of German Conservatives, warned a friend about the dangers of *any* collaboration with the National Socialists by urging: 'Do not think that when you board an express train, the driver of which is deranged, you can somehow take over the controls.'[27]

Most conservative elites, however, did eventually go along with the régime with varying degrees of reluctance and compliance to secure their interests. In working with Hitler to restore Germany's economy and power many must have stifled doubts about the less acceptable faces of National Socialism, perhaps hoping in the last resort that the civil service, the courts and the armed forces would prove effective barriers against a wholesale restructuring of German society. In reality the civil service was not likely to become a focal point of sustained opposition to the government. Thus Franz Gürtner, Reich Minister of Justice from 1933 until his death in 1941, professed his aim to preserve the state of law and aimed to keep the police and judiciary distinct. Yet he was compromised by his innate distrust of liberal jurisprudence in the first place and a personal inclination towards right-wing authoritarian government. In embarking on self-coordination in order to preserve the principles of the law, the judiciary effectively worked in favour of the regime. The ideas system of National Socialism inexorably penetrated the legal system as jurists struggled to transform the law 'in the spirit of National Socialism'. Ultimately, Gürtner was wholly unable to prevent the loss of power of the ordinary courts to the SS and Gestapo.[28] As to the army, the revolutionary implications of Hitler's seizure of power were momentarily cloaked by the ruthless action taken against Ernst Röhm and other SA 'extremists' in 1934. Military leaders were persuaded to believe – or *wanted* to believe – Hitler when he depicted the party and the army as the two pillars of German society. The resistance was ultimately and absolutely dependent on the German army's support for protection of any new government which would be formed after Hitler had been toppled, and this is central to the discussion of *Widerstand*.

On the one hand, the military generated the dramatic bomb plot which came very near to killing Hitler on 20 July 1944. Much earlier,

---

27. Cited by J. Noakes, 'German conservatives and the Third Reich: an ambiguous relationship', in M. Blinkhorn (ed.), *Fascists and Conservatives* (London, 1990), p. 76.
28. Cf. K. Anderbrügge, *Völkisches Rechtsdenken: zur Rechtslehre in der Zeit des Nationalsozialismus* (Berlin, 1978), p. 24. See also L. Gruchmann, *Justiz im Dritten Reich 1933–1940. Anpassung und Unterwerfung in der Ära Gürtner* (Munich, 1988).

in autumn 1939, the Chief of the General Staff of the Army, General Franz Halder, carried a loaded pistol in his pocket and thought about shooting Hitler during his conferences with him. In March 1943 members of Field Marshal Günther von Kluge's staff made an abortive attempt to blow up Hitler's personal aircraft during the Führer's visit to the Russian front. Later in the same month Colonel Rudolph Baron Christoph von Gersdorff tried blow himself up with Hitler while showing the latter round an exhibition of captured war material in Berlin. His attempt culminated with him hastily defusing the primed ten-minute fuses in a lavatory after Hitler had dashed through the exhibition rooms in little more than two minutes. Other army volunteers were prepared to kill Hitler. Until von Stauffenberg's famous attempt in July 1944, the difficulty of bringing a volunteer together with his quarry continued to baffle and frustrate the conspirators. Moreover, the actions of these exceptional individuals cannot conceal that the armed forces as a whole were not likely to generate widespread resistance to Hitler.

One of the first serious post-war studies of the German army in politics, written between 1949 and 1952, deliberately set out 'to show the extent and the responsibility of the army in bringing the Nazis to power, for tolerating the infamies of that regime once it attained power, and for not taking the measures – at a time when only the army could have taken them – to remove that regime from power'.[29] However, by the time the study was first published in 1953, the author himself detected a risk of the German army's record being whitewashed as a result of the then West Germany being brought into a new European security system directed against the Soviet Union.[30] In due course the conservative historians of the Federal German Republic produced the picture embedded in the popular mind; namely that of an essentially honourable, though misguided German officer corps, reluctantly following an all-powerful leader, Adolf Hitler, but emerging in 1945, and in sharp contrast to the SS, with their shields relatively untarnished. Thus equipped with less painful historical antecedents, the new Bundeswehr fitted more comfortably into NATO.[31] Very little now remains of this picture, following the

29. J. W. Wheeler-Bennett, *The Nemesis of Power. The German Army in Politics 1918–1945* (London, paperback edition, 1961), p. x.

30. Ibid., p. 701.

31. See in particular G. Ritter's *The Sword and the Sceptre: the Problem of Militarism in Germany* (London, 1972); cf. W. H. Carr's introduction to K-J. Müller, *The Army, Politics and Society in Germany 1933–1945. Studies in the Army's Relation to Nazism* (Manchester, 1983), p. 3.

detailed archive work during the 1960s and 1970s. The predominantly hostile criticism of the army's role in politics was taken up once more; there was a stronger emphasis than before on the dynamics of the armaments process, on the obsession of the German armed forces with their modernization and on their consequent drive for military autonomy.[32] This approach modified the view of the Reichswehr as being automatically against the Weimar Republic, which could be accommodated, however, for just as long as it could finance the expansion and transformation of the armed forces.

Following the economic crisis from 1929, only a government led by Hitler appeared to offer prospects for funding on that scale. From 1933 the German officers duly worked actively to secure the autonomy of the armed forces. Both the Army High Command (von Fritsch and Colonel Ludwig Beck) and the Armed Forces Command (von Blomberg and von Reichenau) agreed on this policy, although the latter embraced more completely the concept of a wholly professional army in an age of mechanized warfare. Newer officers also identified the Hitler state as the optimum vehicle for prosecuting such warfare. Crucially, co-operating with Hitler provided what many regarded in any event as the only way for the military elite to form a pillar of the new Reich and to have a decisive influence over the government. For many officers this expectation fully justified the abandonment of key aspects of their tradition. Some naturally welcomed the new ethos after 1933 more readily than others. In the event, Hitler was soon in a position to exploit to the full the military imperatives of obedience when, following the shake-up of the German foreign office and the army in January–February 1938, he assumed for himself the office of Supreme Commander of the Armed Forces.

The old War Ministry was replaced by the new High Command of the Armed Forces (*Oberkommando der Wehrmacht* – OKW), staffed by selected supporters. Loyal General Keitel became Chief of OKW, with largely administrative functions; the more pliable Walter von Brauchitsch replaced the disgraced von Fritsch as Chief of Army Command. In this manner Hitler decisively undermined the position

---

32. F. L. Carsten's study, *Reichswehr und Politik 1918–1933* (Cologne–Berlin, 1964) was an important landmark on the army and politics. On the dynamics of rearmament, M. Geyer, *Aufrüstung oder Sicherheit. Die Reichswehr in der Krise der Machtpolitik 1924–36* (Wiesbaden, 1980); 'Professionals and Junkers. German rearmament and politics in the Weimar Republic' in R. Bessel and L. Feuchtwanger (eds), *Social Change and Political Development in Weimar Germany* (London, 1981); 'The dynamics of military revisionism in the interwar years. Military politics between rearmament and diplomacy' in W. Deist (ed.), *The German Military in the Age of Total War* (Leamington Spa, 1985), pp. 100–51.

of the military elites, who were already thoroughly compromised by their participation in the regime's consolidation and rearmament. From this perspective even the figure who came to represent for many the 'centre' of resistance, Chief of the General Staff of the Army, General Ludwig Beck, 'must be regarded as one of the representatives of the Reich's traditional ruling elite whose rapprochement and co-operation with the leadership of the Nazi movement in 1933 constituted the Third Reich'.[33] Against this background Beck's resistance was in truth sparked by his disillusionment at the failure of the military to become an equal partner in the Hitler state. Paradoxically, his desperation in trying to prevent Germany risking premature war in 1938 derived from his support for Hitler and from his fear that the Führer was being badly advised. Since Beck had a major share in forging Hitler's military instrument and in furthering the European arms race it is difficult not to agree that when he too resigned in August 1938, 'the dilemma of his rearmament policy and with it the hopeless contradictions of great-power politics, backed by the military, had caught up with him.'[34] It has been said that the military, like the civil service, was in effect reduced to a functional elite in the Third Reich, and thus incapable of generating widespread resistance. However, that does not account for, let alone excuse, the ideological attraction that developed between National Socialism and the armed forces, which led so many of the latter to behave in a brutal manner indistinguishable from that of the SS in Eastern Europe during the war and to play a major role in the Final Solution.

There were of course less horrible examples of ideological affinity, which nonetheless also made resistance less effective than it might otherwise have been. National Socialism shared with the German military and conservative forces a fundamental rejection of Bolshevism, as well as a distaste for the 'extreme' form of democracy which they believed had ruined the Weimar Republic. Even the intermittent meetings of the Kreisau Circle between 1941 and 1943 thus produced plans for a post-Nazi reconstruction which revealed a distinct uneasiness with political parties. A paternalistic streak ran through the circle's ruminations on the threats posed by mass population centres and the need for a new spiritual integration of society. Goerdeler's own extensive reports and proposals echoed the Kreisau Circle's conviction that a future chancellor's cabinet should not be over-dependent on Reichstag support. The upper house in Goerdeler's

33. Müller, *Army, Politics and Society*, p. 60.
34. Ibid., p. 94.

scheme of things would have taken the form of a Reich Chamber of Corporations, consisting of the leaders of industry and commerce, of the churches, universities and trade unions. A different, somehow more worthy Volksgemeinschaft seems to be implied in this proposal. The brothers Berthold, Alexander and Claus Schenk Count von Stauffenberg explicitly desired to see a 'true' German Volksgemeinschaft replace the perverted National Socialist version. Other major figures, like Ulrich von Hassell and Johannes Popitz, assumed the need for a period of military government following Hitler's overthrow. In the preliminary constitution drafted by Popitz between 1938 and 1943 we read: 'The deep corruption of public life makes necessary the imposition of martial law until further notice and the transferral of executive power to the armed forces.'[35]

This overlap between the political thinking of the resistance and that of the government could be seen also in the matter of Germany's territorial extent. It must be emphasized that Beck and his successor from 1938 until 1942, General Franz Halder, who were both persuaded to contemplate Hitler's removal, initially hoped that the Allied Powers would accept border rectifications in eastern Europe in Germany's interest. Dietrich Bonhoeffer was one of the few resisters who saw defeat and occupation as vital for Germany's own good. Other key figures like Helmuth Count von Moltke (heading the group named after his Kreisau estate where important resistance meetings took place), Carl Goerdeler (Mayor of Leipzig 1930–37, Reich Price Commissioner until 1934) – perhaps the main underground opposition leader – as well as figures further to the right developed plans for post-war reconstruction involving among other things the restoration of Germany's pre-1914 borders with Poland. Winston Churchill's perfectly logical response from January 1941 was to adopt a policy of absolute silence on peace overtures from the German opposition to Hitler. His consequent demand for unconditional surrender demonstrated that: 'The minimal requirements for a national German government were thus incompatible with the Allied war aims.'[36]

The strong religious conviction which coloured the work and ideas of key individuals in the resistance raises questions about the role of the Churches, which were relatively privileged after 1933 in not being 'co-ordinated' by the regime. While distrusting the Weimar con-

35. P. Hoffman, *German Resistance to Hitler* (London, 1988), p. 68.
36. Ibid., p. 104; K. von Klemperer, *German Resistance against Hitler. The Search for Allies Abroad, 1938–1945* (Oxford–New York, 1992), pp. 436–7. Cf. H. Mommsen, 'Der Kreisauer Kreis und die künftige Neuordnung Deutschlands', *Vierteljahrshefte für Zeitgeschichte*, 42 (1994): 361–77.

stitution, both Catholic and Protestant Churches had been formally correct republican partners. Catholics, since the unity of their Church derived from canon law, were more resistant to National Socialism than Protestants who, with their synodal organization, were divided amongst twenty-eight regional Churches (*Landeskirchen*). The general resistance of the Catholic electorate to National Socialism persuaded Hitler to concentrate in 1933 on at least eliminating 'political Catholicism'. The Concordat between Rome and Berlin of 20 July 1933 thus left the Catholic Church in Germany with limited control over education and communal institutions in return for the Vatican's recognition of the Hitler regime.[37] Hitler's endorsement in April 1933 of the breakaway German Christians (May 1932) confirmed his inclination to control the German Evangelical Church too.

The German Christians, who were strongly anti-Semitic, supported the National Socialist agenda as the political reflection of 'true' German Christianity. Under their newly elected 'Reich Bishop', Ludwig Müller, they notionally formed the unified Protestant 'Reich Church'. In reality, the German Evangelical Church continued to oppose the incompetent Müller's efforts at centralization. The Pastors' Emergency League, set up by Martin Niemöller and others to assist those sacked or arrested in Prussian churches, evolved into the Confessing Church by April 1934. At its first Synod at Barmen on 29–31 May 1934, it roundly asserted the spiritual authority of the Churches and their right to control their own affairs. Although the Confessing Church subsequently claimed to be the only legitimate Church in Germany, divisions persisted within the German Evangelical Church as a whole. Müller's plans were frustrated and in spite of Hans Kerrl's appointment as Reich Minister for Church Affairs on 16 July 1935, the Protestant Church was not fully co-ordinated. A more sustained drive to undermine Church autonomy was made in 1937 but the regime modified its attempts to Nazify the Church during the war, if chiefly in the interests of preserving social harmony.

Difficult questions arise about the Church's wider role in the Volksgemeinschaft and its ultimate failure to become more of a threat, as an institution, to such a manifestly un-Christian regime. A Gestapo memorandum from 1935, on the struggle between the German Christians and the Confessing Church, found the latter potentially more dangerous, because its emphasis on the Church was likely to nourish more inner opponents of National Socialism.[38] Nevertheless,

---

37. K. Scholder, *The Churches and the Third Reich. Volume 1: 1918–1934* (London, 1987), p. 227.

the Gestapo assessment emphasized the loyalty to the state of *both* German Christians and the Confessing Church. It might be more accurate to say that the Protestant Church as an institution sought refuge in being apolitical, whereas only its most courageous individual resisters could accept the inexorable logic of opposing the regime by force if need be. A harsh judgement, based on personal interviews with former members of the Confessing Church, affirms that the Churches refrained from criticising the National Socialist regime because they agreed with it and not simply from a desire to be apolitical.[39]

The fact that neither the German Evangelical Church nor the Confessing Church barred party members was justified on the grounds of influencing the regime, but it is equally evident that the clergy as a body worried about the loss of direction in the secular and pluralist Weimar Republic. Protestant support for the NSDAP in the later Weimar elections has already been remarked. All too many in the German Evangelical Church welcomed the restoration of Germany's honour in 1933 and the good will towards the revival of national Christianity was evident in the words of a number of prominent Protestant theologians. One remarkable example is that of Gerhard Kittel, who in spite of being an expert on the relationship between the teaching and language of Jesus and his contemporary Jewish world, yet went on to become a leading light in Walter Frank's research department on the Jewish question. Anti-Semitism as such was not alien to the German Evangelical Church either, and the 'Aryan' paragraph imposed by the Reich Church was resisted not so much because of its insistence on pastors and their wives being free of Jewish blood, but because it threatened the independence of the Churches.[40] The moral confusion is neatly encapsulated in the following words: 'Christianity was German culture. Christianity was middle-class morality. Christianity was respect for authority. Christianity was law and order . . . so many Christians mistook the Nazi movement for a religious movement.[41]

There is little doubt, admittedly, that the Church as a whole played a major part in alienating sections of the German population from the spirit of the regime. However, like other key institutions in the Third Reich, the Church's contribution to meaningful resistance was made by its individual members. It must never be forgotten that the leading

38. Victoria Barnett, *For the Soul of the People. Protestant Protest against Hitler* (Oxford, 1992), p. 68.
39. Ibid., p. 72.
40. Ibid., p. 35.
41. R. P. Eriksen, *Theologians under Hitler* (Yale, 1985), p. 46.

figures in the German resistance to Hitler took their opposition to the point of sacrificing their own lives. In the face of such bravery a dispassionate critique of their political ideas must seem heartless.[42] It remains a vital task if the resistance is to be properly assessed, neither monumentalized nor undervalued. The onset of war transformed the Volksgemeinschaft into a community of defence against a hostile world and it is significant that policing became ever more stringent. What would have become of the people's community without the war is an open question, the discussion of which is still fraught with difficulty. The ambiguity of the relationship between National Socialism and German conservatism, in all its manifestations, is fundamental to that discussion. That Beck and others trod a path towards disillusionment and resignation after enthusiastically supporting Hitler's government in 1933 helps to explain why some historians insist on treating resistance as part of a continuum including passivity, partial affirmation and participation.[43]

42. Cf. justified reactions of R. J. Evans to critics of his reviews of books on the resistance, 'Furtwängler and the German resistance', *Times Literary Supplement*, 11 December 1992.

43. In general, M. Broszat, *Nach Hitler. Der schwierige Umgang mit unserer Geschichte* (Munich, 1978).

CHAPTER ELEVEN
The 'Racial War' and its Legacy

THE GENESIS OF THE 'FINAL SOLUTION'

What should we make of Hitler's speech to the Reichstag on 30 January 1939, when he predicted the annihilation of the Jewish race in Europe in the event of a war? It is still difficult to prove that he was then wholly clear in his own mind about how, when or even if his prophecy would be fulfilled. What he was not implying was that the position of the Jews would improve if war did not break out. Five years of Nazi peacetime rule had already demonstrated the commitment of the NSDAP to attacking the Jews and destroying their position in Germany. Within the party there was widespread anticipation that war would definitely make life much more difficult for the Jewish population, and so it proved. During the Polish campaign the special task forces (*Einsatzgruppen*) entrusted with operations behind the German front lines summarily executed Jews, as well as destroying the Polish intelligentsia, the clergy and nobility. Although objections from the armed forces temporarily interrupted this butchery in September, military government was ended on 26 October, giving the SS a free hand. Poles and Jews continued to die during their expulsion from the two new eastern *Gaue* to Hans Frank's General Government, in order to make room for Germans being resettled from the Baltic states and Soviet-occupied Poland.[1] Frank

---

1. Cited in J. Noakes and G. Pridham (eds), *Documents on Nazism, 3: Foreign Policy, War and Racial Extermination* (Exeter, 1988), p. 1055. Cf. W. Lenz, 'Vom politischen Schicksal des baltischen Deutschtums: Welches Mass an Freiheit besassen die beiden letzten baltischen Generationen?' *Jahrbuch des baltischen Deutschtums in Lettland und Estland* (1959), pp. 62–9.

observed of the deported Jews in November 1939: 'The more that die the better.' Alongside deportation and from the outset, the *possibility* of execution confronted Jews who now fell under the control of National Socialists. This necessarily casts doubt on the argument that the increasingly urgent but incompetently managed deportations brought about the shift from numerous but largely uncoordinated murders to the systematic extermination of the Jewish population throughout Europe – the 'Final Solution'.[2]

More challenging is the view that the final solution was the outcome of 'pure improvisation', arising from the cumulative radicalism and competitive zeal within the movement, which expressed itself in ever more violent forms in response to growing pressure from the National Socialist leadership.[3] Why radicalization should in itself have finally pushed policy in the specific direction it took, rather than in some other, is less obvious. As to the wild assertion that Hitler only *heard* in October 1943 about the mass extermination of Jews being conducted by his functionaries from 1941, the less said the better. That, too, derived support from the failure of historians to find a written order directly from Hitler initiating the final solution.[4] There are obvious objections to most attempts to explain the final solution as the outcome of policy evolution, even accepting that Jewish emigration in the 1930s gave way to ill-planned and forced resettlement from 1939, first targeting the Lublin area of Poland and later, after the defeat of France in 1940, Madagascar.[5] However, to move from resettlement to mass extermination, first of Russian Jews during the attack on the Soviet Union in 1941 and then of European Jewry, demanded a qualitative and quantitative leap such as to imperil the concept of 'evolution'. It can only be satisfactorily explained by positing a definite decision or decisions for genocide taken sometime in 1941 by the highest authority, namely, Hitler.

Trying to determine exactly when the order for the 'Final Solution' was made might seem insensitive to the memory of its victims. This is far from being the case. The issue keeps the spotlight on policy-making, thereby subjecting the motivation of all those directly concerned to closer scrutiny. The supreme indifference of the party's

---

2. In particular, M. Broszat, 'Hitler und die Genesis der "Endlösung". Aus Anlass der Thesen von David Irving', *Vierteljahrshefte für Zeitgeschichte*, 25 (1977): 739–75.

3. H. Mommsen, 'Die Realisierung des Utopischen: Die "Endlösung der Judenfrage" im Dritten Reich', *Geschichte und Gesellschaft*, 9 (1983): 381–420.

4. As propounded by D. Irving, *Hitler's War* (London, 1977).

5. On the evolution of policy, C. R. Browning, *The Path to Genocide. Essays on Launching the Final Solution* (Cambridge, 1992).

top leadership to the fate of vast swathes of human beings – including apart from Jews the Gypsies, Poles, homosexuals, perverts, the mentally ill and other so-called misfits – is striking, long before mass extermination established itself. Faced in November 1940 with complaints from his *Gauleiter* in Poland about having to absorb so many deportees, Hitler bluntly voiced his expectation that their realms would be wholly German within ten years. 'He would not ask questions about the methods they had used.'[6] Nothing less than this degree of hostility could be expected of Himmler – from 1939 also Reich Commissioner for the Strengthening of German Nationality (RKVD) – or of the personnel of the SS controlled RSHA managing the deportations, or of Heydrich, let alone his *Einsatzgruppen*, or finally, of the Higher SS and Police Leaders controlling the occupied areas in the east.

Such personalities created a climate which made certain that deaths would continue to attend resettlement, particularly for the Jews, who in their ghettos at Łódź and Warsaw were already being singled out for particularly harsh treatment. Even the abortive Madagascar option, which envisaged shipping off Jews to a deeply hostile environment with no visible means of support, demonstrated 'a willingness to exterminate, admittedly not by resorting to shooting or gas, but by relying on the forces of nature'.[7] What was actually 'evolving' within the party and SS policy-making apparatus outlined above was an awareness that chosen policies could at last be implemented; that the violence already endemic to the entire resettlement process could be escalated with impunity. This was all the more so when the early restraints arising from Hitler's hope of securing British recognition of Germany's continental dominion fell away during the course of 1940 and initial consideration was given to planning the attack on the Soviet Union. Feasibility studies during 1940 further desensitized feelings, since fatalities in the order of 30 to 40 million Soviet citizens were projected. And of course, the armed forces leaders were directly implicated in the planning, deepening Hitler's ascendancy over them.

He pointedly reminded his commanders, on 30 March 1941, that what was involved in a war against Russia was the 'struggle between two *Weltanschauungen* . . . It is a war of extermination.' In due course the notorious directive for the troops, of 19 May 1941, enjoined 'ruthless action' against Bolshevik agitators, guerrillas, saboteurs and

---

6. Cited in Noakes and Pridham, *Documents on Nazism*, 3, p. 1081.
7. H. Graml, 'Zur Genesis der "Endlösung" ' in W. H. Pehle (ed.), *Der Judenpogrom 1938. Von der 'Reichskristallnacht' zum Völkermord* (Frankfurt, 1988), p. 169.

Jews and the 'total elimination of all active and passive resistance'.[8] Actually the German military leaders shared Hitler's conviction that the Soviet Union was the source of Jewish–Bolshevism. The unflagging commitment of the National Socialist leadership to anti–Semitism arises time and time again from the exchanges between the personnel involved in the deportations and uncoordinated killings between 1939 and 1941.[9] The conflict with Russia did not cause the fight against the Jews to be intensified, but rather provided the ideal opportunity for genocide, and was indeed perhaps even integral to that policy.

That no written orders by Hitler to commence mass extermination of the Jews of Europe have been discovered is hardly surprising. The system of administration in the Third Reich made it perfectly straightforward for Hitler to point Himmler, Heydrich and company in the required direction. Their loyalty to Hitler and their own wholehearted devotion to the party's ideology ensured that the rest would follow. Much of the evidence relating to the extermination programme was destroyed; major decisions were conveyed orally; profound secrecy about the ultimate aims was enjoined on all those involved in the process. Establishing the existence of Hitler's order must, therefore, rely on the use of as much detailed circumstantial evidence as possible. Just as the fact of a stone being hurled into a pond can be inferred from the ripples it makes, so a whole series of actions and statements by Himmler, Heydrich, key figures in the RSHA and leaders of the *Einsatzgruppen* in 1941, indicate that significant impulses were coming from on high. Hitler's decision most certainly could not have been taken later than mid–September 1941, around the time of his call for a Jew-free Reich by the end of the year. Only weeks later, on 10 October, the first trainloads of *German* Jews for ghettos in Poland and the Baltic culminated in executions for those unable to work on their arrival.[10] That resettlement was still seen as a solution to the Jewish question at that point is doubtful in the extreme, particularly since deportees were destined to end up in or near battle zones where millions of deaths in action against Russia were contemplated.

A major difficulty in accepting an autumn date as a starting point is that executions on an epic scale had begun as soon as the four

8. Noakes and Pridham, *Documents on Nazism*, 3, p. 1090.
9. Cf. E. Goldhagen, 'Weltanschauung und Endlösung. Zum Antisemitismus der nationalsozialistischen Führungsschicht', *Vierteljahrshefte für Zeitgeschichte*, 24 (1976): 379–405.
10. On this see P. Burrin, *Hitler and the Jews. The Genesis of the Holocaust* (London, 1993).

Einsatzgruppen entered Russia on 23 June behind the German battle lines. Ostensibly they were carrying out the aim that Hitler mentioned to his generals at the end of March, of liquidating the communist political leadership. The idea that Hitler might have secretly decreed the elimination of the Jews at the same time therefore has its advocates. Others favour May, the month in which Heydrich finished assembling the *Einsatzgruppen* destined for action in Russia.[11] These were immediately subjected to progressive conditioning against the racial enemy and their leaders told by Heydrich on 14 June: 'Judaism in the East is the source of Bolshevism and must therefore be wiped out in accordance with the Fuehrer's aims.'[12] On 2 July 1941, in clarifying the tasks of his three thousand assassins for the benefit of the four Higher SS and Police Leaders appointed to Russia, Heydrich confirmed that executions would also include all Jews 'in the service of the Party or the State'.[13] This caveat meant little to the killers, it is clear. Once the mood of the times gripped the *Einsatzgruppen*, women and children soon joined their adult male victims. In the process the army – anxious to use the services of the *Einsatzgruppen* – frequently behaved in ways indistinguishable from theirs in finishing off 'partisans' behind the front. The advantages of action against partisans, as Hitler observed in July, was that it provided the perfect excuse to kill anyone who opposed the Reich.

The horrendous death toll exacted by the *Einsatzgruppen* against Russian Jews during the late summer of 1941 marked a new phase in implementing racial policy. It is therefore difficult to see their work other than as one of the streams feeding into the full-scale final solution – the highly organized action to kill *all* the Jews of Europe. There was temporal overlap at the very least, for Goering (nominally overseeing the Jewish problem from the start of the war) authorized Heydrich at the end of July 1941 'to make all the necessary preparations with regard to organizational, technical and material measures for a complete solution of the Jewish question in Europe'. In the event, the Berlin meeting, where Heydrich wanted to discuss the

11. H. Krausnick and M. Broszat, *Anatomy of the SS-State* (London, 1970), p. 77, favours March. Recent advocates of a date in May include R. Headland, *Messages of murder: A Study of the Reports of the Einsatzgruppen of the Security Police and the Security Service 1941–43* (New Jersey, 1992); M. Housden, 'Population, economics and genocide. Aly and Heim versus all-comers in the interpretation of the Holocaust', *Historical Journal* 38, 2 (1995): 479–86.

12. H. Höhne, *The Order of the Death's Head. The Story of Hitler's SS* (London, 1972), p. 329.

13. Document printed in Noakes and Pridham, *Documents on Nazism*, 3, pp. 1091–2.

formidable logistics involved, could not be arranged until 20 January 1942 (Wannsee conference). Although the word itself is missing from the records, extermination was on the minds of all key personnel, as the transports of German Jews worsened the conditions in the packed ghettos. The *Gauleiter* of Warthegau, Arthur Greiser, asked Himmler and Heydrich for trained executioners to clear his area of Jews; Hans Frank, whose General Government was bursting at the seams with most of the deported Polish Jews, anxiously sent his State Secretary, Dr Bühler, to sound out Heydrich before telling his own officials about the coming 'big meeting'.

It is striking that at this briefing for his aides Frank made cynical and dismissive remarks specifically about resettlement before observing: 'With respect to the Jews, therefore, I will only operate on the assumption that they will disappear.'[14] Two days later, on 18 December, Hinrich Lohse's anxious query about the economic impact of indiscriminate executions of Jews in his domain was answered by the *Ostministerium*: 'The Jewish question has probably been clarified by now through verbal discussions. Economic considerations are to be regarded as fundamentally irrelevant to the settlement of the problem.'[15] The participants of the Wannsee Conference, meeting 'to achieve clarity in basic questions' had little doubt that execution, somehow and somewhere, would follow after the evacuation of the 11 million Jews who came 'into consideration' for the task ahead.[16] The fit evacuees could look forward only to being worked to extinction for the Reich's war effort, eventually being 'dealt with accordingly' if they failed to die at the workbench. By clear implication the rest would perish at once.

The disturbing process of gradually speeding up and streamlining the process of executions – so striking a facet of the final solution – can be said to have begun before the Wansee conference, with Lublin Police Chief Odilo Globocnik's commission from Himmler in the autumn of 1941. Globocnik was to liquidate the 2.5 million Jews crammed into the General Government, later dubbed the 'Reinhard Action'. Even before this began, Jews were cleared from the Łódź ghetto in the Warthegau using the mobile gas vans first operating on the Euthanasia programme initiated in April 1940. This had disposed of well over 70,000 mentally defective German men, women and children before the main programme was halted in August 1941. When SS *Hauptsturmführer* Herbert Lange brought his expertise in

14. Noakes and Pridham, *Documents on Nazism*, pp. 1126–7.
15. Ibid., p. 1098.
16. Cf. Graml, 'Zur Genesis der "Endlösung" ', p. 171.

gassing to Łódź at the beginning of November, his ghastly vehicles were parked at an isolated mansion at nearby Chelmno, thereby setting up the world's first production line for murder. The first permanent gas chambers were installed by Globocnik at Belzec, and operated from 17 March 1942 to December of that year. Other death camps followed at Sobibor, working from April 1942 to 14 October 1943, and Treblinka, which carried out executions from autumn 1942 to 19 August 1943. In addition, the large camp at Majdanek in the Lublin neighbourhood had gas chambers installed in the autumn of 1942. The largest extermination centre was at Birkenau, part of the huge Auschwitz complex in Upper Silesia, where the new killing agent – prussic acid gas or Zyklon B – was much quicker and executions could be speeded up. Not until 27 November 1944 did Himmler order the end to the mass murder of European Jews and the destruction of the gas chambers and crematoria.

THE CHALLENGE OF EXPLAINING GENOCIDE

Only too aptly, Goering observed in 1942 that this was not the Second World War but a racial war. The horror of the extermination of between four and six million Jews has presented daunting problems of historical interpretation. On the one hand it was absolutely imperative for as full a record as possible to be built up of the fate of the actual victims of the final solution once the war ended. A vast literature exists – from survivors and eyewitnesses as well as from historians – from which the relentless cruelty of the death camps can readily be described. This record is still being added to, reminding us that Jews from 22 European countries were systematically rounded up for later destruction by the National Socialists and that, in addition, Jews from Asia, Africa and the Americas were trawled into the net purely because they happened to be in the wrong place at the wrong time. Equally, more attention has been given to the way in which some Jews resisted, even in hopeless circumstances. Both Sobibor and Treblinka ceased operations prematurely due to difficulties caused by the inmates.[17] Other 'unknown' death camps are still being uncovered, such as that at Berga, a German village situated on the old Czech border.[18] Many more will emerge with the availability of former

17. H. Langbein, *Against all hope: Resistance in the Nazi Concentration Camps 1938–45* (London, 1994).
18. M. Bard, *Forgotten Victims. The Abandonment of Americans in Hitler's Camps* (London, 1944).

Soviet archives, for as yet very little work on the final solution has given detailed coverage of the fate of Soviet Jewry. How can we dispute the need for the record to be as complete as possible in face of Holocaust-deniers having held their 12th annual conference in southern California in September 1994? Their propaganda makes the importance of teaching and scholarly research on the subject self-evident.[19] How this is done presents problems, in so far as the record of atrocities by itself can anaesthetize the reader, as those who have taught the subject can testify.[20]

Something like this point was made in the deposition which Helmut Krausnick and Martin Broszat prepared for the first large-scale trial of concentration camp staff in a German court, in 1963: 'For some the whole Third Reich business can be summed up in the word Auschwitz; they are incapable of seeing further than the stark fact that this hell on earth actually happened.'[21] This reaction appeared to be in spite of, rather than because of, the preoccupation with the death camps and the machinery of terror in studies of the Third Reich after the Second World War. The dominance of 'totalitarianism' as an explanatory concept in the 1950s did little to counter the narrowing of focus. Paradoxically, more was producing less in terms of under-standing. The broadening of studies in the 1960s, discussed earlier in this book, at last promised to locate the crimes against the Jews in the political and socio-economic realities of the National Socialist regime, so that the con- nection could be seen 'between the form of political tyranny adopted and the mass crime called for by its ideology'.[22] However, preoccupation with the structures of the Hitler state ran the risk of 'trivializing' National Socialism by underrating the role played by the aims and wishes of the National Socialist leaders. This is not to deny the contribution of structuralist studies to our understanding of the genesis of the 'Final Solution', exposing in more detail the way in which rivalry between the authorities involved was itself a major source of momentum.[23] Nonetheless, the pronounced radicalization of Jewish policy which declared itself from spring 1941 had to be driven

19. Cf. remarks of D. Cesarini, 'Extermination in negative', *Times Higher Education*, 7 October 1994.

20. S. Totten, 'The use of first-person accounts in teaching about the Holocaust', *The British Journal of Holocaust Education*, 3 (1994): p. 171.

21. Krausnick and Broszat, *Anatomy of the SS State*, p. 13.

22. Ibid., p. 13. Cf. the remarks of W. Sauer, 'National Socialism. Totalitarianism or fascism?' *American Historical Review*, LXXIII (1967): 404ff.

23. Cf. T. Mason, 'Intention and explanation: A current controversy about the interpretation of National Socialism' in G. Hirschfeld and L. Kettenacker (eds), *Der 'Führerstaat': Mythos und Realität* (Stuttgart, 1981), p. 34.

by individuals making personal decisions. Although Hitler's were the most important, they depended utterly on a commitment to genocide on the part of his co-workers. Nothing less than this, permeating the managers and executors of the policy, can account for the ensuing quest for efficiency in the liquidation process and for the extraordinary way in which the murders continued, even when the defeat of Germany loomed in the final stages of the war. Indeed, it then seemed as if the final solution had become more important than the war itself.

The renewed insistence on the centrality of genocide in the Third Reich – not just of the Jews but of the Gypsies – is also reflected in a surge of studies of the relationship between the final solution and other facets of National Socialist planning for reconstituting German society on a biological basis. Thus compulsory sterilization of those with hereditary diseases in 1933 was followed by the persecution of a variety of anti-social elements 'on the grounds that their economic costs, their disutility and their "racial" danger to the community were biologically determined and thus irredeemable'.[24] Euthanasia, if arguably removed from the comprehensiveness and ferocity of the final solution, must appear as yet another stream contributing to genocide. This is readily apparent from the progressive refinement of gassing techniques which link the murder of the mentally 'unfit' with that of Jews and Gypsies.[25] It does seem to be stretching coincidence too far, for example, that the work of the personnel from the Berlin euthanasia centre at Tiergarten 4 tailed off just in time for the opening phase of industrialized murder in the East, or that Belzec, Treblinka and Sobibor enjoyed the services of Christian Wirth, veteran of no fewer than five euthanasia centres in the Reich. Moreover, euthanasia continued after the formal 'end' of the programme alongside the implementation of the final solution.[26]

More problematic is the assertion that the policy of resettlement itself (rather than its chaotic mishandling) – which co-existed with executions of deportees from the outset – played a crucial role in creating a climate for the final solution. The argument maintains that the dearth of large towns and industries in East Europe made the land

24. Cf. the late T. Mason's personal re-evaluation in his *Social Policy in the Third Reich. The Working Class and the 'National Community'* (Providence, Oxford, 1993), pp. 279ff.

25. H. Friedländer, 'Euthanasia and the Final Solution' in D. Cesarini (ed.), *The Final Solution. Origins and Implementation* (London, 1994), pp. 55–6.

26. See in particular, M. Burleigh, *Death and Deliverance: 'Euthanasia' in Germany c. 1900–1945* (Cambridge, 1994).

over-populated, so that plans for settling Germans in the region necessarily entailed huge population transfers and annihilations. By 1940, university research on demographic issues was increasingly being fed into the equation, giving academics the opportunity to concretize the vague dreams for the east. Many of these advisers shared with policy-makers the dislike of compromise and looked for rapid and bold solutions. Inevitable clashes of opinion about the costing and viability of schemes mutated, as it were, into arguments for and against extermination, thus creating interdependence between resettlement and extermination policies.[27] Since eastern Europe was mainly populated by non-Jews, population economics do not, however, entirely explain why Jews were the primary targets of genocide. To the question 'Was the Holocaust the product of some modernising and general instrumental rationality or a uniquely anti-Semitic action?', one must still say yes to the second alternative.[28] Moreover, as with those academics whose tireless 'scholarship' demonstrated the fundamental right of Germany to Polish territory,[29] the resettlement experts are very obviously a degree removed from the doctors and other trained medical personnel involved in euthanasia, even though 'resettlement' was also linked in practice to mass murder.

All of this touches once more on questions of guilt. It has been said that 'A man may reproach himself for having been politically mistaken or having shown himself a coward, but between him and the man who actively and wholeheartedly participated in the regime's dirty business there is a difference not of degree but of kind.'[30] In reality there *are* degrees of 'participation', although at some point actions indeed become different in *kind* from those at the beginning of the scale. The *Einsatzgruppen*, the SS in the concentration camps, many of the *Wehrmacht* units, the experts in gassing, doctors involved in euthanasia and other executioners were very obviously at the wrong end of any measure of human endeavour, and their behaviour hardened as they got used to murder. And what of the 'ordinary' men who followed behind the *Einsatzgruppen* for further clearing up operations? Men such as those in Reserve Police Battalion 101, too

---

27. G. Aly 'Erwiderung auf Dan Diner', *Vierteljahrsheft für Zeitgeschichte*, 41 (1993): 621–38, replying to critic of G. Aly, S. Heim, *Verdenker der Vernichtung. Auschwitz und die deutschen Pläne für eine neue europäische Ordnung* (Frankfurt–M 1993).
28. M. Housden, 'Population, economics and genocide', p. 486.
29. M. Burleigh, *Germany turns Eastwards. A Study of Ostforschung in the Third Reich* (Cambridge, 1988).
30. Krausnick and Broszat, *Anatomy of the SS State*, p. 14.

old for active service, mainly working- or lower middle class and with no experience at all of what would today be called racial cleansing, but who after their very first action on 13 July 1942 in a Polish village went on to notch up a total of 83,000 executions by November of the following year? That at the most 20 per cent of these men refused orders is an alarming confirmation of how effectively the regime and its leadership had transmitted their values.[31] Yet this brings the issue back to the relationship between those actively carrying out genocide and the wider German public which sustained the regime throughout the war. Another consequence of the growth in research on genocide and its context has been to chip away at the comforting thought that although most German adults had some idea of some aspects of what was happening, 'the enormity of the crime and its moral dimension made it inconceivable'.[32]

Apart from the fact that various civilians came across instances of mass shootings, the soldiers serving in the east who either witnessed or participated in them provided the main source of information. Soldiers also came to know about gassing, although the relative absence of first hand experience for most of them produced distorted stories of how it was actually done and what effects it had on the human body. That such information rippled outwards to civilians is quite clear, as witness the memory of a Berlin woman who, with other passengers, heard soldiers on their train talking about 10,000 Jews being buried at a site in Poland. War against the Soviet Union conditioned the German public to hearing about atrocities and at least some civilians came to recognize that Jews in particular were being singled out. Some at least of the German clergy deliberately tried to counter the pointed avoidance of basic information, and used their position to make sure that knowledge was acquired and absorbed. A letter from the Archbishop of Württemberg directed to Hitler on behalf of 'countless Germans' insisted: 'The steps taken in the occupied territories have become known in our homeland. [They] are widely discussed and burden most heavily the conscience and strength of countless men and women among the German people who suffer from it more than from their daily sacrifices.'[33] However, the regime's call for total war early

31. Again, see C. Browning *Ordinary Men. Reserve Police Battalion 101 and the Final Solution in Poland* (New York, 1993).

32. H. Mommsen, 'Was haben die Deutschen vom Völkermord an den Juden gewusst?' in W. H. Pehle (ed.), *Der Judenpogrom 1938. Von der 'Reichskristallnacht' zum Völkermord* (Frankfurt–M, 1988) p. 200.

33. The quotation and most of the points in this paragraph rely on D. Bankier's interesting article, 'German public awareness of the Final Solution' in D. Cesarini (ed.), *The Final Solution*, pp. 215–27.

in 1943 exploited Germans' fears of revenge by international Jewry and stressed that, conversely, German victory would bring the annihilation of the Jews. In sum, the view that 'very little is known about the extermination at the time, or that only unsubstantiated rumours about the Jews' fate circulated in Germany, is untenable. Second, on the basis of the available evidence it is equally untenable [to suggest] that the German people failed to comprehend the significance of the Nazi's genocidal policy'.[34]

LIVING WITH GENOCIDE

It is bad enough to contemplate the work of the active executioners in the carrying out of the final solution; to realize that, for example, only a small number of *Einsatzgruppen* personnel suffered nervous breakdowns and that very few of the shooting units demanded a transfer;[35] that the members of police battalion 101 who did not take an active role in the slaughter appear to have suffered little punishment, raising the question as to what *might* have happened if more had acted so; that the technicians of murder in the death camps were obsessed by perfection and a smooth-running process; that so much co-ordination was required between so many agencies to ensure the transportation of Jews from all over Europe; that so few in the Third Reich stood out strongly against racial murder. When one considers that even the desperate actions of Jews under the threat of death could disrupt killing operations, it becomes even more depressing to ponder the might-have-beens of key members of society and government raising objections. For example, the German generals in Belgium and France showed less inclination than their counterparts in the Balkans to comply wholeheartedly with SS actions to round up Jews for deportation. Even then, delays to Eichmann's executioners were occasioned mainly by actions of the native populations, so that salvation came for Belgian and French rather than stateless Jews. As to Italy, although Mussolini ordered the surrender of the Jews under Italian-controlled areas in Yugoslavia, Greece and southern France, his minions 'did nothing in the most officious possible way', causing hold-ups until the summer of 1943.[36] The Chief of the Italian General

34. Bankier, 'Public awareness' in Cesarani, *Final Solution*, p. 225.
35. R. Hillberg, *The Destruction of the European Jews* (Chicago, 1961).
36. J. Steinberg, *All or Nothing. The Axis and the Holocaust 1941–1943* (London, 1991), p. 59.

Staff made plain that anti-Jewish excesses were incompatible with the honour of the Italian army, 'a sentiment one would have wished to hear from the mouth of a German General'.[37] Of the two Axis allies it has been said that, at least in their attitude to the Jews, 'they inhabited different moral universes'.[38]

Even though 'Hitler's shadow' is a long one, Germans in the former German Democratic Republic managed to avoid it by claiming that their rejection of capitalism had purged them of any guilt by association with its agent, National Socialism. This convenient route to repressing responsibility was not open to West Germans. Instead, the latter pleaded toleration of Hitler for patriotic purposes during the war and lack of opposition through fear, which still left the knowledge of genocide to be lived with. On this subject a study of children of some of the Nazi executioners concluded:

> After the war, there was a widespread illusion that one could smooth over the actuality of the Holocaust by framing it 'rationally' as a problem to be solved – by carrying out de-Nazification, bringing the decision-makers and the perpetrators to trial, building a democratic welfare society in Germany and making economic and legal restitution to the victims. But the shadow of the Holocaust became longer the more successful these measures were . . . [they] helped society distance itself from the Holocaust, as though one could be infected by getting too close to such an eruption of evil, but it was like covering a volcano with cement.[39]

Many leading historians of the former West Germany did what they could to counter this, by insisting, to take one example, that 'the Third Reich should be judged by its worst crimes, and these did not happen just by chance, due to unforeseeable or unmanageable situations, but as a consequence of clearly defined ideological propositions'.[40] Such judgements did not of course make it any easier for Germans to come to terms with the period of their history which witnessed Hitler waging a racial war to the point of the Reich's own destruction. This knowledge made it difficult to create any historical meaning endowed with a perspective for the future.[41] It is that need

37. Höhne, *The Order of the Death's Head*, p. 364.
38. Steinberg, *All or Nothing*, p. 219.
39. D. Bar-On, *Legacy of Silence. Encounters with Children of the Third Reich* (Cambridge, Mass. and London, 1989), p. 5.
40. K. Hildebrand, 'Monokratie oder Polykratie? Hitlers Herrschaft und das Dritte Reich' in Hirschfeld and Kettenacker (eds), *Der 'Führerstaat'*, p. 97.
41. W. Benz, 'Warding off the past: Is this a problem only for historians and moralists?' in P. Baldwin (ed.), *Reworking the past* (Boston, 1990), pp. 196ff.

which is addressed by the appeals in the last few years for the 'historicization' of National Socialism. What this demands is a deliberate and sustained effort to shake off the historiographical gloom hanging over Germany after 1933; to avoid dwelling only on the origins of war and genocide and instead to consider the expectations aroused by National Socialism, of upward mobility, or of recovery and renewal; or even, for example, to acknowledge the DAF-sponsored drafts of 1941–2 for universal social insurance regulations as anticipating the successful social legislation of West Germany. In sum, we are expected to keep in mind that not all historically significant developments in the Third Reich served the regime's ends.[42]

The idea arouses some sympathy, in so far as it stresses the importance for Germans of preserving access to the total memory of the Third Reich, and not just the awful bits. The trouble is that while this does not in itself make knowledge of the final solution any easier to live with, it might just help to push it to the back of people's minds again. Isn't this risk surely present in the assertion – by no less a historian than Martin Broszat – that the historical reality of the Hitler era is in danger of being submerged beneath monuments of the Holocaust?[43] In reality, as already indicated, it was the knowledge of the latter which was in danger of fading amidst the research from the 1960s on the socio-economic realities of the Hitler state, on its structural complexity and on its day-to-day life (*Alltagsgeschichte*). Allowing the memory of the final solution to fade meant that the guilt and shame of the period were not in fact ever fully articulated even in West Germany and certainly not in the then German Democratic Republic.[44]

An alternative suggestion for helping Germans to come to terms with their past involves setting the Third Reich's genocide in the context of other examples throughout history. Thus Ernst Nolte insisted on drawing comparisons between Germany's actions and American policy in Vietnam, or on arguing that the final solution was born out of the fear of what might befall Germany in the event of a communist victory. 'Auschwitz is not primarily a result of traditional anti-Semitism. It was in its core not merely a "genocide" but was above all a reaction born out of the anxiety of the annihilating occurrences of the Russian revolution.'[45] From this perspective the

---

42. M. Broszat, 'A plea for the historicization of National Socialism' in Baldwin, *Reworking*, pp. 77–87.

43. Ibid., citing a letter from Broszat to S. Friedländer on 4 December 1987.

44. Benz, 'Warding off the past', p. 211.

45. E. Nolte, 'Between myth and revisionism? The Third Reich in the perspective of the 1980s' in H. Koch (ed.), *Aspects of the Third Reich* (London, 1985), p. 36.

defeat of Germany in Russia meant the loss of the 'European centre' and focused world attention on German crimes rather than on those committed by the Soviet leadership. 'Stalin who was pursuing similar goals and using comparable methods (to Hitler) had beaten back the assault of the Nazis in the "Great Patriotic War" and was one of the victors . . . He ordained silence.'[46] Another example of genocide referred to in this debate about the nature of the final solution (*Historikerstreit* – battle of historians) was the murder of a million Armenians by the Young Turks following the overthrow of Sultan Abdul Hamid in 1908. In this instance of genocide, as with that of the Nazis, revolution had opened the way to policies of mass extermination; in each case the onset of war freed the rulers from taking account of domestic and foreign opinion.[47] The comparison soon breaks down with the realization that when it came to pursuing the final solution the quest did not stop at the borders of Germany.

The *Historikerstreit* was in effect about the uniqueness or otherwise of the mass exterminations of European Jewry, rather than about denying that they took place. The predominantly West German historians who argued for developing a new perspective on the Third Reich's racial slaughter were far removed from Holocaust-deniers, in that they fully accepted the actuality of genocide against Jews and Gypsies. Nevertheless, in pleading for the historicization of the Third Reich the danger arose that the full distinctiveness of the final solution would not be properly recognized. As it turned out the 'battle' was remarkably uneven and did not even spread all that far beyond the confines of the German historical guild. Moreover those continuing to insist on the uniqueness of the final solution – in its quest for technical perfection and in its prosecution of murder against an entire race by a highly advanced industrial society – enjoyed undeniable superiority of numbers in Germany. Fears that the neo-conservative German historians who sparked off the *Historikerstreit* would encourage extreme rightists were not entirely misplaced, but the major effect of this 'historians' battle' was to stimulate fresh historical research on the final solution. Revealingly, this appears to be less concerned with structural and other impersonal forces but seeks to uncover 'the complete

46. K. Hildebrand, *German Foreign Policy from Bismarck to Adenauer. The Limits of Statecraft* (London, 1989), p. 250. Cf. U. Herbert and O. Groehler, *Zweierlei Bewältigung. Vier Beiträge über den Umgang mit der NS-Vergangenheit in den beiden deutschen Staaten* (Hamburg, 1992).
47. R. Melson, *Revolution and Genocide. On the Origins of the Armenian Genocide and the Holocaust* (Chicago, 1992).

character of the personal motives of those centrally involved' in the final solution.[48]

It is very clear from this that the moral impact of the Nazi era is far from exhausted. That will continue to be the case now that German re-unification has taken place. The Nazi period was the last period of *common* history for the former 'two Germanies'. Moreover the historical treatment of the Third Reich diverged in important respects for most of the time in divided East and West Germany. Thus even assuming that the Hitler era *could* become something purely 'historical' in the way that conservative German historians have demanded, much time will have to lapse and a great deal of common research and synthesis will be required to achieve that end. Even then, this can never make any less harsh the reality that the Third Reich culminated in racial murder on an unprecedented scale. To respond to the earlier quotation of Krausnick and Broszat (see p. 205), Auschwitz *was* indeed the Third Reich. While the political and psychological burden on Germany of this legacy can be expected to diminish with the passage of time, this is not the case with the *historical* challenge of explaining how the Third Reich functioned in the way that it did and why it produced the Holocaust. The hope that Germany's national identity will be more securely based by producing a more 'balanced' view of the Third Reich is therefore a distinctly forlorn one. The starting point for such an identity remains permanent recognition of the catastrophe which was the Third Reich, coupled with a constant search for what caused it to come into existence. An analogy has been made between the Nazi state and Chernobyl. 'The Chernobyl blow-out . . . was not a "works accident" arising out of the blue, without structural, systemic causes and undetached from human errors and miscalculations. A different kind of reactor, or different management of the reactor, could well have prevented, or substantially reduced the risk of, disaster . . .'[49]

This is a fruitful comparison, but only if expert examination of the causes of the catastrophe also draws sufficient attention to good practice, and this has obvious implications for the study of the Weimar Republic. It is still escaping from the conceptual poverty inflicted by its being viewed for so long as a mere ante-room to the National Socialist state. The Republic is a much better candidate for 'historicization' than the Third Reich will ever be, in so far as its

---

48. Cf. comments of M. Housden, 'Between memory and denial: Hans Frank and the use of personal testimony in the study of those compromised by the Holocaust', *The British Journal of Holocaust Education*, 3 (1994): p. 142.

49. I. Kershaw, *The Nazi Dictatorship* (3rd edn, London, 1993), p. 215.

various and genuine achievements have been seriously undervalued in the determined quest to track down every slightest sign of the terminal disease falling on Germany in 1933. The present study has deliberately tried to counter this by following specific themes right through the 1920s and 1930s, so that factors predisposing German development towards National Socialism can be juxtaposed with those which pointed in different directions, making plain just how much effort the NSDAP had to expend to destroy the political system in which it grew.

CHAPTER TWELVE

The Quest for German Hegemony in Europe

The *Berliner Börsen-Courier* commented of Locarno: 'Things are looking up for Germany because things are looking up for Europe.' Almost exactly the reverse applied some three years later with the onset of the World economic crisis. On 29 November 1929 the Reichstag admittedly defeated Hugenberg's campaign to force the government to reject the Young Plan and key clauses of the Versailles treaty, but Stresemann did not live to see it. The fragmentation of the domestic basis supporting *Verständigung* made it harder than ever for his immediate successor, Julius Curtius, to cope with the extreme right, particularly after the NSDAP's electoral breakthrough in 1930. Curtius soon succumbed to pressure by attacking France for refusing further treaty changes in November 1930 and by pursuing, in vain, his scheme for a customs union with Austria.[1] Carl von Schubert had already been posted to Rome and in his place as State Secretary was Bernhard Wilhelm von Bülow. Although firmly wedded to peace, the latter official was a far more vigorous advocate of Germany's great-power status. All of this was quite enough to re-awaken French fears and to threaten the entire basis on which Locarno had been erected. It fell far short of pleasing Hitler.

POLICY BEFORE POWER

Foreign policy issues played a major role for the NSDAP from the first polls it fought alongside the nationalists in 1924. It shared the extreme

---

1. W. G. Ratliff, *Faithful to the Fatherland. Julius Curtius and Weimar Foreign Policy* (New York, 1990), pp. 75–7.

right's belief in the electoral importance of exposing the government's subservience to the Versailles powers, and Hitler personally was deeply preoccupied with foreign affairs. He was only able to reach a truly national audience, however, through his participation in Hugenberg's Front with the German nationalists, the Stahlhelm and the Pan Germans. His very earliest utterances on foreign policy late in 1918 did little to distinguish him from other ultra-nationalists. All alike were prepared to demand war against France to reverse the peace settlement. Soon, however, Hitler began to ask himself what specific alliances might bring about the defeat of the French. To take one example, his advocacy of Italy as an ally as early as August 1920 initially arose from his conviction of that country's natural hostility to France. Subsequently his inclination was reinforced by Mussolini's 'march on Rome' in 1922.[2] Hitler was even prepared to offend German nationalists by arguing for the abandonment of the Germans in the Tyrol to secure Italy's support. This was no mere daydreaming. By 1922 Hitler had already become part of the network of unofficial contacts fostered by Mussolini's henchmen in Germany, thus also conflicting with the official German policy line of avoiding close collaboration with the fascists.[3]

Hitler took an equally independent line over Russia and Britain, the two other powers most prominent in his reflections. He may have shared briefly the expectation in Germany that Russia could help revise Versailles. Nonetheless, in December 1919 he could be heard voicing his resentment that Russia should enjoy eighteen times as much land as Germany per head of the population.[4] The NSDAP's Russian expert, Alfred Rosenberg and the Baltic German, Max-Erwin von Scheubner-Richter, almost certainly influenced Hitler's thinking on Russia as a source of 'living space'.[5] Yet Hitler also had Brest–Litovsk as a precept for this within his own lifetime. During the course of 1920 he gradually became more insistent that the Jews were the real force behind Bolshevism. His long-standing anti-Semitism, nourished in pre-war Vienna, fused with his thinking on Russia. Any alliance with the latter was precluded for Hitler until the 'infection' had been removed. What doubts Hitler had were probably reinforced by the dwindling prospects for a restoration of the 'white' Russian

---

2. E. Jäckl, *Hitlers Weltanschauung* (Tübingen, 1969), p. 187.

3. J. Petersen, *Hitler, Mussolini. Die Entstehung der Achse Berlin–Rom* (Tübingen, 1973), p. 10.

4. Jäckl, *Hitlers Weltanschauung*, p. 39.

5. See material in G. Stoakes, *Hitler and the Quest for World Dominion. Nazi Ideology and Foreign Policy in the 1920s* (Leamington Spa, 1986), pp. 64 ff.

opponents of Lenin by 1921. At the time the Rapallo treaty was signed Hitler once more distanced himself from republican and nationalist alike by arguing: 'Soviet Russia is not the last straw which Germany can clutch like a drowning man, but a lead weight which pulls us further down into the depths.'[6]

It may well be that Hitler had never at any point seriously favoured post-war Russia as an ally, but this was certainly the case by December 1922. At that time he told the co-owner of the Munich paper *Neueste Nachrichten*, Eduard Scharrer: 'Germany would have to adopt a purely continental policy avoiding damage to English interests. The destruction of Russia with the help of England would have to be attempted. Russia would provide sufficient land for German settlers and a wide field of activity for German industry.'[7] The remark reflected another lesson drawn by Hitler from his critique of Wilhelmine policy, namely that Germany could not be a great land power and a great sea power at the same time. Winning 'England' as an ally and thus detaching it from France, it became clear by the time *Mein Kampf* was completed in 1926, would allow the defeat of the latter and thus clear the way for a successful war for *Lebensraum* against Russia. By contrast, as we have seen, the Locarno arrangements rested on a fundamental community of interests in Franco-British policies towards Germany. Finally, it was more than likely that, once having dominated Europe, Hitler would sooner or later – as an aspirant world leader – turn his hostility against Britain and its empire and, ultimately, against the United States.[8]

The amount of ink spilled in inferring such a foreign policy 'programme' from close textual analysis of all Hitler's writings and speeches before he seized power has been matched by that of the proponents of Hitler the opportunist – a man allegedly exploiting chances as they arose after he became Chancellor of Germany. Hitler's 'opportunism' in foreign affairs (a concept to which we shall return) *might* help to explain why he came to embark on a war at a time not of his own choosing, although economic, international and structural

6. G. Stoakes, 'The evolution of Hitler's ideas on foreign policy 1919-1925' in P. Stachura (ed.), *The Shaping of the Nazi State* (London, 1978), p. 31.
7. Cited by H. A. Turner, 'Hitlers Einstellung zu Wirtschaft und Gesellschaft vor 1933' in *Geschichte und Gesellschaft*, 2 (1976), p. 94. For further discussion of 'England' see A. Kuhn, *Hitlers aussenpolitisches Programm. Entstehung und Entwicklung 1919–1939* (Stuttgart, 1970), pp. 95, 99, 100ff; A. Hillgruber, 'England's place in Hitler's plans for world domination' in *Journal of Contemporary History*, 9, No 1 (1974), p. 11.
8. Cf. K. Hildebrand, *The Foreign Policy of the Third Reich* (London, 1973), p. 21; G. L. Weinberg, 'Hitler's image of the United States' in *American Historical Review*, 69 (1964), pp. 1006–11.

factors were also crucial; it cannot account for the direction of his policy. The durability of his views on the European powers before and after 1933 is quite remarkable and it is anything but surprising to trace connections between his contempt for the communists and Jews of Russia in the 1920s and his regime's murderous behaviour in the east after 1939. Hitler's tactical skill as a politician was always tempered by his remarkable and tenacious world view. In this respect it is impossible to agree that 'most of what passed for "Nazi" ideas on foreign policy were in reality a re-hash of policies pursued by Germany between 1914 and 1918, cloaked (sic) in Hitler's stridently anti-Semitic world view.'[9] In truth, the surviving Wilhelmine elites continued on the whole to advocate re-establishing Germany's borders of 1914, whereas Hitler quite deliberately warned readers of *Mein Kampf*: 'The boundaries of the year 1914 mean nothing at all for the German future.' His distaste for the discredited elites in industry, agriculture, politics and the army, who had had their chance only to throw it away, extended to their opinions on foreign policy. One of the purposes behind the second part of *Mein Kampf* was to emphasize the need for fresh paths for Germany. Hitler aimed to overcome any resistance to his foreign policy within the NSDAP and 'to gather our people and their strength for an advance along the road that will lead this people from its present restricted living space to new land and soil'.

The NSDAP's presence in the Hugenberg Front and its role in exacerbating the political crisis in Germany after 1929 brought the party ever nearer to the making of foreign policy. Brüning's aim to placate the extreme right through a more forceful assertion of German interests over reparations and disarmament was therefore almost certainly unrealizable. Hitler's foreign policy precepts were an integral part of the NSDAP's attack on the Weimar Republic, the overthrow of which constituted the first essential step towards a new foreign policy. All the more ironic that Hitler profited from Brüning's success in having reparations buried at the Lausanne Conference in 1932, as he did from the ground work undertaken during Brüning's term of office on questions of German rearmament. The latter issue provides an excellent example of the way in which Hitler applied 'in a ruthless fashion the diplomatic, political and military instruments made available from Brüning to Schleicher, for a policy with which neither Brüning, Papen nor Schleicher . . . would have identified themselves'.[10]

9. Stoakes, in Stachura (ed.), *Nazi State*, p. 44.

10. M. Salewski, 'Zur deutschen Sicherheitspolitik in der Spätzeit der Weimarer Republik' in *Vierteljahrshefte für Zeitgeschichte* 22 (1974), pp. 138ff. In general see also G. Wollstein, *Vom Weimarer Revisionismus zu Hitler* (Bonn, 1973).

Part V of the Versailles Treaty, justifying German disarmament to facilitate similar action by the Allied Powers in due course, had always offered a hostage to fortune. Since the Allies refused to honour their commitment, Brüning's formal claim for parity of treatment effectively brought the issue of German rearmament onto the agenda, in keeping with his assurances to Hitler on 6 October 1930.[11] This was the context of Brüning's formal invitation to the other powers to join his country in 'disarmament' at the opening of the International Disarmament Conference in Geneva in February 1932. France insisted on its own security being assured before abandoning its existing superiority in land armaments. However, by dint of great effort and under threat of Germany's withdrawal the conference finally agreed, on 11 December 1932, to recognize Germany's claim to 'equality of rights in a system which would provide security for all nations'. Schleicher had in fact already approved a scheme for the rebuilding of the peace-time army, to be completed in three stages by March 1938, effectively beginning Germany's secret rearmament. With British support an elaborate draft disarmament convention was put to the Disarmament Conference on 16 March 1933. However, Hitler had informed his cabinet on 8 February that rearmament would have first priority for the next four to five years.[12] The sort of expansion he envisaged could not be achieved through negotiation at the conference table. Using French objections to the proposals of 16 March as his pretext, Hitler took the not inconsiderable risk of abandoning the discussions on 14 October 1933, at the same time removing Germany from the League of Nations. Yet rather than continuing from this point to survey German diplomacy in the 1930s, the analysis will focus on central themes and issues.[13]

The thicket of conflicting agencies which comprised 'government' in the Third Reich thinned only somewhat when it came to making foreign policy. Hitler, whose confidence in the conduct of policy naturally grew with office, made free use of Ribbentrop's counsel from the outset. Nonetheless, the *Auswärtiges Amt* (AA) continued to be useful to Hitler in the day-to-day conduct of diplomacy, particularly in the early years of the regime, when he maintained some semblance of wanting to negotiate with the other powers. Nor was there an

11. H. Brüning, *Memoiren 1918–1934*, Bd 1 (Stuttgart, 1970, paperback), pp. 203–5.

12. *Documents on German Foreign Policy, 1918–1945*, Series C, vol 1 (London, 1957–), Document No. 16.

13. For fuller coverage of German diplomacy in the 1930s see J. Hiden, *Germany and Europe 1919–1939* (2nd edn, London, 1993).

excessive influx of outsiders into the AA before Konstantin von Neurath was supplanted by Hitler's foreign policy adviser, Joachim von Ribbentrop, in February 1938. Even then the new Foreign Minister took less than a third of the staff from his own personal office (*Dienstelle Ribbentrop*) with him. The marginalization of those who were not 'one of us' was, however, by then profound. Hitler also sanctioned the activity of a number of other organizations and units concerned with foreign policy issues, notably the party's Foreign Policy Office (*Aussenpolitisches Amt der NSDAP* – APA), under the ideologist Alfred Rosenberg, and the *Volksdeutscher Rat* under Karl Haushofer.[14] These and other advisers and units were not conceived as substitutes for the AA, but they illustrate that 'diplomacy' was merely an aspect of National Socialist 'foreign policy'. Although there was room for party and unofficial organizations to be involved in foreign policy in its broadest sense, the major lines of action – on which Hitler believed the leader must always concentrate his energy – were fundamentally determined by his own will and ideas. It is difficult to think of a foreign policy issue where – in so far as decisions lay within Germany's power – Hitler's preferences were not accepted. Equally striking is the stubbornness with which he tried to impose his conceptions in the face of external obstacles. Hitler's often remarkable display of mind ignoring matter accounts for both his diplomatic successes and his risible failure to see the full picture in the world outside, well illustrated by his ultimately comprehensive misreading of British attitudes towards the Continent.

THE VAIN PURSUIT OF BRITAIN

True to his early thoughts, between 1933 and 1935, 'Hitler tried all possible ways and means, conventional or otherwise, of reaching an alliance with England.'[15] Britain's readiness to mediate Franco-German hostility during the Disarmament Conference was indeed evident in its signature on 7 June 1933, with Germany, France and Italy, of a pact affirming in the most general terms the need for co-ordinated revision

---

14. Cf. P. Seabury, 'Ribbentrop and the German Foreign Office', *Political Science Quarterly*, 66 (1951): p. 553; L. Hill, 'The Wilhelmstrasse in the Nazi era', Political Science Quarterly, 82 (1967): 570; H-A. Jacobsen, 'Zur Struktur der NS-Aussenpolitik 1933–1945' in M. Funke (ed.), *Hitler, Deutschland und die Mächte. Materialen zur Aussenpolitik des Dritten Reiches* (Düsseldorf, 1978), pp. 137–86.

15. Hillgruber, 'England's place in Hitler's plans', p. 13.

of the peace treaties. Hitler's confidence was bolstered by the failure of French Foreign Minister Louis Barthou to encircle Germany in the spring and summer of 1934 by means of an *Ostlocarno*. In this instance Hitler profited from the conclusion – against *Auswärtiges Amt* advice – of a non-aggression pact with Poland (24 January 1934). Apart from the adverse impact it had on relations between France and Poland, the agreement indicated Hitler's indifference to the sensitivities of the USSR. It meant, too, that he could afford to be more sanguine about the Franco-Soviet pact of mutual assistance on 2 May 1935 (below).

Yet what good will Hitler could draw on in Britain was never unqualified. The NSDAP had before 1933 been identified in the Foreign Office as a group worth preventing if possible from securing power. As the nature of Hitler's government became clear after 1933, British public opinion 'would accept nothing in the nature of an Anglo-German alliance or axis'.[16] The British White Paper on Defence of 4 March 1935 criticized the military preparations by the National Socialists, while shortly afterwards the French announced plans to increase compulsory service and to reduce the age of conscription. Together with the Italians, the British and the French – in April at Stresa – collectively condemned Hitler's re-introduction of national service on 16 March 1935. All the same, Britain was naturally wary of costs. Resources were already committed to the protection of empire, at a time when France's strategy focused primarily on the defence of its own frontiers. 'The problem in Paris,' it has been said, 'was not so much knowing one's enemy as knowing oneself. Until April 1939 there was no will to stop Hitler by force.'[17] It was precisely the undefined nature and extent of Britain's 'continental commitment' which demanded that negotiations also continue with Hitler. The Anglo-German Naval Agreement of 18 June 1935 must be seen in this context. The agreement 'restricted' Germany's naval tonnage to 35 per cent of that of Britain and accepted the Reich's right to equal submarine tonnage with that of the Commonwealth. The terms were more than adequate for the time being for Hitler to keep the promise he had already made to Admiral Raeder in March, to rebuild the navy systematically come what may.

Although the naval agreement upset France, the core of mutual self-interest in Anglo-French relations, attested by Prime Minister Baldwin's celebrated observation that the British frontier lay on the

16. W. N. Medlicott, *British Foreign Policy since Versailles* (London, 1968), p. 127.
17. A. Adamthwaite, 'French military intelligence and the coming of war 1935–9' in C. Andrew and J. Noakes (eds), *Intelligence and International Relations 1900–1945* (Exeter, 1987), p. 194.

Rhine, remained. That talking with Hitler did not preclude British preparations to meet a threat from Germany was also apparent from the conclusions of the Defence Requirements Committee in autumn 1935. Proposals for increasing military preparedness and expanding the air force 'constituted the first serious programme to enable the British armed forces to take part in a major war against their most probable adversaries'.[18] What was left of the Locarno structures vanished with Hitler's huge but successful gamble in remilitarizing the Rhineland on 7 March 1936. It enabled Germany to begin constructing effective defences in the West, emptying what little practical content remained of the alliances between France and her eastern allies, Poland and Czechoslovakia. The threat to France and the prospect of greater German control in eastern Europe remained as ever profoundly inimical to Britain's long-term interests. Additional pressure which Hitler applied by raising the question of colonial revisions increased the strain. Prospects for a general settlement of issues between Germany and Britain – which the British Foreign Minister Eden had contemplated at the close of 1935 – thus declined sharply.

In 1936 developments in the Mediterranean widened the gap between London and Berlin. The first concerned the Italian–Abyssinian conflict in the winter of 1935–6, culminating in King Victor Emanuel of Italy becoming Emperor of Abyssinia on 5 May 1936. The second related of course to the outbreak of the Spanish Civil War in 1936, where the *Auslandsorganisation* of the NSDAP played a decisive role in the face of the *Auswärtiges Amt's* attempt to resist German engagement. Ideology played a major part in Hitler's decision to intervene and was wholly consistent with his determination to prevent the spread of communist influence in Europe. He hoped that 'in the final conflict for the reorganization of Europe, which was certainly to be expected, Spain would not be in the camp of Germany's enemies but most likely the friend of Germany'.[19] Hitler's support of Franco secured for the Reich supplies of important raw materials through nationalist Spain – particularly iron ore and pyrites – while Italy, through its own engagement on behalf of Franco's Spain, came slowly but surely into the Third Reich's orbit. Finally, the Western powers were distracted from Hitler's diplomacy in eastern Europe. Yet any assessment of the strategic gains accruing to Hitler

---

18. M. Howard, *Continental Commitment. The Dilemma of British Defence Policy Between Two Wars*, Penguin edn (London, 1974), p. 115.

19. H-H. Abendroth, *Hitler in der spanischen Arena. Die deutsch–spanischen Beziehungen im Spannungsfeld der europäischen Interessenpolitik vom Ausbruch des Bürgerkrieges bis zum Ausbruch des Weltkrieges* (Paderborn, 1973), p. 36.

from intervention must take into account that by forcing the French and the British together, Mediterranean developments dealt another crippling blow to Hitler's original hopes for agreement with both Italy and Great Britain at France's expense.

Events in the Far East added to the strain in Anglo–German relations. Hitler had certainly had advice from within the party that Britain would react badly to the rapprochement between Germany and Japan, which he argued was necessary to fight communism (Anti-Comintern Pact, November 1936). Yet the British were long since committed to building up their Singapore base and Rosenberg warned Hitler as early as 1934 that he risked driving them 'right into the arms of the French. England regards Tokyo as more dangerous than Moscow.'[20] Hitler persisted in his chosen course. The AA joined the debate, fearing the loss of the balance it had worked for between Germany's interests in China and those in Japan.[21] Once more ideology triumphed over diplomacy. In this instance strategic considerations also seemed to be overlooked. Following on from the pioneering work of a German advisory mission in China during the 1920s, under Colonel Max Bauer, Germany's rearmament programme might well have expected to derive advantages from access to the raw materials of China, which produced more than fifty per cent of the world's tungsten. However, in return Germany was expected to help China in its looming conflict with Japan and this did not accord with Hitler's priorities. No less a figure than the former Reichswehr Chief, Hans von Seeckt, had urged after missions to China in the early 1930s: 'Germany might lose nothing by siding with Japan, but has far less to gain.'[22]

That Hitler could still ask of Ribbentrop, as Ambassador to the Court of St James in 1936, to 'bring back England' while embroiled in Mediterranean and Far Eastern policies which threatened Britain's strategic position, demonstrates either an inability fully to comprehend British attitudes or, more plausibly, growing indifference to them. A note of exasperation now frequently coloured his remarks about the United Kingdom. Ribbentrop, following his unsuccessful sojourn in London, doubtless reinforced the Führer's growing impatience with the inability of the English to realize on which side their bread was

20. Cited in A. Kuhn, *Hitlers aussenpolitisches Programm. Entstehung und Entwicklung 1919–1939* (Stuttgart, 1970), p. 188.

21. In general, J. P. Fox, *Germany and the Far Eastern Crisis 1931–1938. A Study in Diplomacy and Ideology* (Oxford, paperback, 1985).

22. W. C. Kirby, *Germany and Republican China* (Stanford, California, 1984), p. 119.

buttered. On 13 September 1937 Hitler made his first public acknow-ledgement that 'England and France do not want to see in Europe any readjustment of the balance of power in Germany's or Italy's favour.'[23] A few weeks later, on 5 November 1937, when he secretly re-affirmed to his Commanders-in-Chief his ultimate intention to use force if need be to secure *Lebensraum*, France and Britain were depicted as 'our enemies, who both hate us'. Nevertheless, Hitler argued that Britain would not actively resist when Germany eventually moved against Austria and Czechoslovakia. The thinking recorded in this so-called 'Hossbach memorandum' was extraordinarily risky under the circumstances.

THE IMPERATIVES OF FOREIGN TRADE

To the political obstacles in the way of German–British rapprochement by the late 1930s must be added a number of daunting economic hurdles. The story begins in the late 1920s, when the system of free trade agreements on which the Locarno order was founded began to unravel with the drift towards protectionist trade blocs.[24] The British move towards imperial preference had its counterpart in Germany's growing desire to consolidate a sphere of economic influence in eastern and south-eastern Europe (where Britain nonetheless continued to compete with Germany after 1933). The region had long been targeted by France, too. Much French capital investment was pumped in during the 1920s. With the onset of the World crisis and the fall of agricultural prices, however, the states of eastern Europe were increasingly drawn towards powers providing secure outlets for their agricultural produce and raw materials. They offered in return at least some prospect of new markets for manufactured exports. Although Weimar governments slowly relinquished free trade policies after 1928 and moved towards a new system of preferential bilateral foreign trade agreements, their domestic power base did not permit them to exploit this changing situation fully. The demand from the mighty German agricultural lobby for protection against East European agricultural products was unrelenting, while powerful international resistance showed itself towards German policy initiatives, exemplified by Brüning's abandonment of plans for a German–Austrian customs union

23. Cited in Kuhn, *Hitlers aussenpolitisches Programm*, p. 209.
24. In general, L. Knipping, *Deutschland, Frankreich und das Ende der Locarno–Ära. Studien zur internationalen Politik in der Anfangsphase der Weltwirtschaftskrise* (Munich, 1987).

in 1931. Unlike previous German Chancellors, Hitler was able to accommodate the objections of German landed interests within his wider agricultural policy, while Schacht's 'New Plan' of 1934 facilitated a fresh trade offensive through its extensive import controls, export subsidies and currency arrangements.

It is said that Schacht's 'New Plan' merely 'systematized into deliberate policy a set of trading devices which were already widespread'.[25] The argument somewhat underestimates the importance of the economic theory espoused by leading National Socialists before 1933, with its emphasis on a future *Grossraumwirtschaft*. National Socialist ideology deliberately fostered an aggressive redefinition of German economic interests and the breaking away from the damaging fluctuations of the liberal–capitalist order. To this end Hitler was prepared to accept economic policies which disregarded the Western powers. If bilateralism *was* a 'straitjacket' on German trade policy it was one which the regime itself deliberately chose to don.[26] The bilateral treaties of the 1930s were steps towards building an autarkic bloc, conjuring up memories of Brest–Litovsk and war, rather than anything that can be derived from Weimar's foreign trade policy. The conclusion of such trade agreements with Hungary (23 February 1934) and Yugoslavia (1 May 1934) essentially depended on access to Germany of mainly agricultural products in return for exports of German manufactured goods. In effect, currency-free exchanges were initiated. The impact of these bilateral 'clearing agreements' could soon be measured. By 1936, for example, Germany had 27 per cent of Yugoslav foreign trade. The combined share of that trade by Britain, France and Italy had been reduced from 30 per cent in 1933 to 13 per cent, although British *capital* investment in the region as a whole remained important for some time, accounting for example for as much as 67 per cent of the Greek foreign debt as late as May 1940.[27]

German economic dominance of the Balkans really began to manifest itself in 1938–9, when not only Yugoslavia but also Romania,

25. A. S. Milward, 'The Reichsmark Bloc and the international economy', in G. Hirschfeldt and L. Kettenacker (eds), *Der 'Führerstaat': Mythos und Realität* (Stuttgart, 1981), p. 295.

26. Cf. J. Radkau, 'Entscheidungsprozesse und Entscheidungsdefizite in der deutschen Aussenwirtschaftspolitik 1933–40' *Geschichte und Gesellschaft*, 2 (1976), pp. 33–65.

27. H-J. Schröder, 'Südosteuropa als "Informal Empire" Deutschlands, 1933–9'. Das Beispiel Jugoslawien', *Jahrbücher für Geschichte Osteuropas* 23 (1975), p. 84. See also W. S. Grenzebach Jr, *Informal Empire in East-Central Europe. German Economic Policy towards Yugoslavia and Romania 1933–1939* (Stuttgart, 1988). For the contrasts between Weimar and the 1930s see H-P. Höpfner, *Deutsche Südosteuropapolitik in der Weimarer Republik* (Frankfurt–Berne, 1983).

Hungary and Bulgaria were coming more firmly into the Third Reich's economic orbit. Until the outbreak of the war there was perhaps some credibility to Germany's claim that it respected individual national economic development, leaving room in the words of one historian, for a 'buoyant federation of market-integrated developing economies under German leadership'.[28] Yet inequality was built into the relationship, in so far as the weaker economic partners in the region were compelled to increase both their agricultural exports and the products of their extractive industries in order to pay for expensive German commodities. This burden must be set alongside German investment in the regional infrastructure and transport of south-eastern Europe, in the form of technical goods and services. After 1939 and after 1941–2 in particular, the increased exploitation of regional resources was soon to subordinate the entire region completely to the German war effort.[29]

The political implications of the Third Reich's economic penetration of eastern Europe had long been recognized in London. For example, Britain's new trade agreements with the Baltic states, negotiated in 1934, explicitly recognized the German challenge by promoting British exports more aggressively. Within the Foreign Office officials like Laurence Collier argued that Britain adopt something akin to the German clearing agreement strategy to counter the Reich's commercial penetration of eastern and south-eastern Europe. For a time from 1934 onwards the British had some success in defending their interests in the Baltic and Scandinavia but Treasury resistance, combined with the economic orthodoxy of other British ministries, prevented Collier's recommendations from being adopted as policy.[30] The important point is that National Socialist foreign trade policy from 1934 *already* conflicted with Hitler's professed wish for friendship with Britain; those who had formerly been Germany's best customers were most disadvantaged by the Third Reich's pursuit of bilateral treaties. In the economic as in the political arena, Hitler took some to time to acknowledge the unpalatable fact that Britain was not willing to give the Third Reich a completely free hand in eastern Europe. Yet the Four Year Plan impelled German trade policy further along the same lines in order to achieve the degree of self-sufficiency

---

28. A useful essay is by A. McGelligott, 'Reforging Mitteleuropa in the crucible of war' in P. Stirk (ed.), *Mitteleuropa. History and Prospects* (Edinburgh, 1994), pp. 129ff.

29. For a detailed study of one area see H. Fleischer, *Im Kreuzschatten der Mächte. Griechenland 1941–44*, 2 vols (Frankfurt, Berne, New York, 1986).

30. Cf. J. Hiden and P. Salmon, *The Baltic Nations and Europe* (London, 1994), p. 100.

felt necessary to wage successful war. It made still more remote any prospect of a lasting Anglo-German rapprochement.

HITLER'S OBSESSION WITH RUSSIA

The seriousness of Hitler's ultimate failure to win over Britain may be seen from his earlier conviction that on the 'English alliance' depended the final confrontation with the Soviet Union. About this – the evidence is simply overwhelming – Hitler thought continuously. His secret memorandum on the Four Year Plan reiterated his belief in the inevitable reckoning with Russia. Throughout the 1930s he returned repeatedly to the theme of the 'great showdown' and to the need to exterminate Stalin and his followers.[31] In August 1939 he was to proclaim with considerable frustration: 'Everything I do is directed against Russia; if the west is too stupid and blind to grasp this, I shall be forced to reach agreement with the Russians, to attack the west and then, after its defeat, turn against the Soviet Union with my combined forces.'[32] Much later he came to recall with real bitterness the way in which Britain's stubbornness prevented Germany from being 'secure in her rear' and thereby frustrated his great task, 'the mission of my life, the *raison d'être* of National Socialism, the destruction of bolshevism'.[33]

As it was, Hitler accepted the risks of running down the relationship with Russia after 1933, even though he felt that his regime was vulnerable to a strike from a foreign power (he had chiefly France in mind) during its early months. Virtually everything Hitler did contradicted the official German policy line of 'business as usual' between the Reich and the USSR. The National Socialist rationale for this public stance was that the brutal action against communism inside the Reich had eliminated the dangers inherent in any German–Soviet relationship. In reality that action might itself justly be seen as the beginning of the 'showdown' with Stalin and his followers. For their part the Soviet leaders chose to complain not about the fate of the KPD but about Rosenberg's anti-Russian ranting.[34] In September

---

31. Cf. various remarks in E. Fröhlich (ed.), *Die Tagebücher von Joseph Goebbels. Sämtliche Fragmente*, 4 vols (Munich, New York, etc., 1987), vol. 2, p. 622, entry of 9 June 1936; vol. 3, p. 378, entry of 22 December 1937.

32. C. J. Burckhardt, *Meine Danziger Mission* (Munich, 1960), p. 348.

33. H. Trevor-Roper (ed.), *The testament of Adolf Hitler* (London, 1951), p. 17.

34. J. Hochman, *The Soviet Union and the Failure of Collective Security, 1934–1938* (Ithaca, London, 1984), p. 24.

Hitler again upset the *Auswärtiges Amt* by rejecting any suggestion of restoring the German–Russian friendship. His insistence on improving relations with Poland – over objections from top German military leaders and of Foreign Minister Konstantin von Neurath – contributed to the decision of the Soviets to demand the closure of joint Soviet–German military operations on the Kama river and at Lipetsk.[35] Following the non-aggression treaty with Poland the atmosphere between Berlin and Moscow cooled rapidly. Karl Radek pointedly replied to a query about his uncustomary silence on the subject of the Polish corridor: 'Why should I toot into Hitler's horn?' In May, after conversations with Hitler, Nadolny resigned his post in dismay, to be replaced by Count Friedrich Werner von der Schulenberg. Although economic links persisted, political relations between Germany and the USSR were put 'on hold'.[36]

There are obvious pitfalls in seeing the Third Reich's foreign policy exclusively in terms of what Hitler himself wanted, intended or planned. Quite apart from foreign reactions, the influence of domestic German economic factors and the unfolding internal dynamics of the regime in the 1930s contributed to the growing sense of haste, of time running out, on which Hitler often remarked during his final, beleaguered stand in his bunker. Yet it is impossible to escape the conclusion that 'structural' conditions played havoc with the timing of Hitler's policy largely *because* of his tunnel vision in formulating policy goals in the first place. Party organizations impinging on foreign policy either reinforced his own inclinations or became less influential. Alfred Rosenberg, who depicted Bolshevism as 'the highest form of Jewry' and whose APA was important for the ideological schooling of the emerging Nazi, lost his appeal for the NSDAP when his commitment to autarky wavered and he began to talk instead of how to increase foreign trade through a network of small, independent states allied with Germany. At that point his deficient administrative skills, weak personality and insufficient private means could not save him from marginalization.[37] Much more in tune with Hitler and much more influential was Goebbels's Ministry for Enlightenment and Propaganda (*Reichsministerium für Volksaufklärung und Propaganda*), with its central drive against Bolshevism and a director who in 1936 privately reiterated of Nazism and Bolshevism: 'One or the other must finally vanish.'[38] That

35. Hochman, *Soviet Union*, p. 25.
36. G. Hilger and A. G. Meyer, *Incompatible Allies* (1953), pp. 256–74.
37. See S. Kuusisto, *Alfred Rosenberg in der nationalsozialistischen Aussenpolitik 1933–1939* (Helsinki, 1984).
38. Cited in Jacobsen, 'Zur Struktur der NS-Aussenpolitik', p. 160.

was a remote possibility still in 1937 but – as the Hossbach memorandum indicated – the cumulative effect of Hitler's personal efforts *had* brought the Third Reich to the point where it threatened the vital interests of both Soviet and British empires.

Indifference to what the latter might or might not do had, as we have seen, supplanted Hitler's original hope for an alliance. In spite of this Hitler continued to allow Soviet–German relations to remain in limbo, taking curiously little cognizance of Russia's stumbling advances towards the allies after 1933. In September 1934, Russia finally joined the League of Nations; in 1935 Soviet–French and Soviet–Czech mutual assistance pacts were signed. The readiness of the USSR to defend Czechoslovakia in the event of a German attack was admittedly a highly qualified one, depending on prior action by France. Nor did the Franco-Soviet pact, ratified on 27 February 1936, have any real military teeth. In addition, Hitler was as aware as anyone of the astonishing purges weakening the Soviet Union. On the other hand, Ribbentrop's term of office as ambassador in Britain had shown him that the British government had not the remotest interest in joining an anti-Soviet coalition.[39] Indeed, the once unthinkable prospect of the Soviet and British empires combining their resources against Nazism had become fractionally less remote by 1938. Ribbentrop implicitly acknowledged this in his famous 'Notes' for the Führer of 2 January 1938, where his insistence that Britain would oppose 'an overwhelmingly strong Germany' on the continent helped to persuade him that it would be important to ensure Russia's neutrality.[40]

That was in keeping neither with Hitler's plans for living space in the east at Russia's expense nor with his growing preoccupation with determining optimum conditions for German military action. The *intent* behind this (rather than his erroneous prediction about simultaneous action against Austria and Czechoslovakia) is what makes the Hossbach memorandum interesting, particularly when taken in conjunction with the shake-up of the AA and armed forces in early 1938. Anxious about Germany at some date losing its armaments advantage, Hitler insisted in effect that there was a window of opportunity for the Reich (which would close after 1943–5). The Hossbach memorandum recorded Hitler arguing that 'the world was expecting our attack and was increasing its counter-measures from year

39. Cf. K. Hildebrand, *German Foreign Policy from Bismarck to Adenauer. The Limits of Statecraft* (London, 1989), p. 144.

40. Cf. M. Bloch, *Ribbentrop* (London–New York, etc., 1992), citing Ribbentrop's memo, p. 148; K. Hildebrand, *The Foreign Policy of the Third Reich* (London, 1973), p. 58.

to year. It was while the rest of the world was still fencing itself off that we were obliged to take the offensive.' He was, moreover, prepared to risk taking action against Czechoslovakia and Poland at any suitable moment thereafter.[41] Ten days later, in a private after-dinner talk with Goebbels, Hitler registered satisfaction with the progress of disarmament and the pair agreed – in discussing the 'show-down' with Bolshevism – that Germany would be 'completely ready' by 1938.[42]

In the *Ostpolitik* both of Weimar governments and of the Hitler regime there was natural, indeed inevitable linkage between their respective policy goals towards Russia and those towards the states lying between the two major powers. However, nothing illustrates the fundamental distinction between Weimar and Hitlerian foreign policy more clearly than the Third Reich's stark reduction of issues in eastern Europe to a subset of the overriding concern with Russia. The region's prime importance as a basis for future conquest comes out in Hitler's chilling remark to Hermann Rauschning that Poland, the Baltic states, Hungary, the Balkan states, the Ukraine, the Volga Basin and Georgia were to become an alliance of vassal states, with no army, no separate foreign policy and no separate economy.[43] It made little sense to expend too much energy in the meantime on frontier disputes between Germany and Poland.[44] 'Friendship' between these two also checked the threat of closer relations between northern and south-eastern Europe, facilitating the Reich's economic penetration of the latter region. As to the two major principles of German Baltic policy articulated by Foreign Minister Julius Curtius in September 1931, namely to prevent Estonia, Latvia and Lithuania from joining a Polish-led bloc and to stop them becoming dependent on Russia, the latter above all preoccupied the Reich after 1933. The German–Polish pact was perceived in Moscow as deeply threatening to the system of non-aggression treaties which Russia had built with the Baltic states by 1932, and the latter clearly assumed growing strategic and economic importance in German planning for war as the thirties wore on.[45]

Long-term plans for conquest inevitably threatened to transform the

41. For the full text, J. Noakes and G. Pridham, *Nazism 1919–1945. Vol. 3. Foreign Policy, War and Racial Extermination* (Exeter, 1988), pp. 680–7.

42. *Die Tagebücher von Joseph Goebbels*, vol. 2, 15 November 1937, p. 726.

43. H. Rauschning, *Hitler Speaks* (London, 1939), p. 41.

44. Cf. remarks of G. Weinberg, *The Foreign Policy of Hitler's Germany. Diplomatic Revolution in Europe 1933–36* (Chicago–London, 1970), pp. 1–24.

45. H. E. Volkmann, 'Ökonomie und Machtpolitik. Lettland und Estland im politischenö–konomischen Kalkül des Dritten Reiches (1933–1940)', *Geschichte und Gesellschaft*, 2 (1976): 471–500.

position of German minorities in Poland, Czechoslovakia, the Baltic states and elsewhere. They were increasingly subjected to the propaganda of the Third Reich and evidenced a sometimes cautious but inexorable drift towards National Socialism. This should not be exaggerated, in so far as only some six per cent of Germans living outside the Reich had joined the National Socialist party by 1937.[46] However, the concern here is with the intentions of the Reich's policy-makers and these viewed the *Auslandsdeutsche* in terms of the 'fifth columns' which Stresemann's policy had, in practice, tended to prevent.[47] An important landmark was reached when SS–Obergruppenführer Werner von Lorenz was appointed in January 1937 to build up an Ethnic German Liaison Office (*Volksdeutsche Mittelstelle* – VOMI). The various rival state and party offices hitherto concerned in one way or another with the *Auslandsdeutsche* – including the party's *Auslandsorganisation* (AO), Rosenberg's *Aussenpolitisches Amt* (APA), The Association for Germandom Abroad (*Verein für das Deutschtum im Ausland* – VDA) – were now vulnerable to VOMI. The latter rapidly developed into a centre of SS power, although theoretically subordinate to Ribbentrop.[48] VOMI's activities 'tied the ethnic German organizations closer to the changing foreign policy of the Third Reich'.[49] It was not by chance that the radicalization of nationality policy in 1937 also 'came about at the moment when Hjalmar Schacht's resignation . . . and the new economic course made it plain that the Reich would follow the policy of autarchy until it won increased living space'.[50] The cumulative indicators that 1938 was anticipated by Hitler and his entourage as a year of high drama on the international stage are quite impossible to overlook.

STRATEGY AND FOREIGN POLICY

National Socialist foreign policy embraced risk from the outset. The image of a 'peaceful' Third Reich, fostered by the regime's early

46. Jacobsen, *Nationalsozialistische Aussenpolitik 1933–1935* (Frankfurt, 1973) p. 602.

47. See the official pamphlet, E. Ehrich, *Die Auslandsorganisation der NSDAP* (Berlin, 1933–8), pp. 7–8 with its dismissive comments about the Weimar Republic's policy.

48. H. Höhne, *The Order of the Death's Head. The Story of Hitler's SS* (London, 1969), pp. 253–5.

49. M. Burleigh, *Germany turns Eastwards. A Study of Ostforschung in the Third Reich* (Cambridge–New York, etc., 1988), pp. 161–2.

50. Jacobsen, *Nationalsozialistische Aussenpolitik*, p. 608.

propaganda, barely concealed the fact that the actual initiatives – the treaty with Poland, the departure from the League of Nations and the Disarmament Conference – all had aggressive implications, and were perceived as deeply disturbing by contemporary governments. They provide evidence of Hitler's determination to create room for German action at *some* time. At any rate, they should not be seen in terms of a peaceful 'phase' giving way to a more aggressive phase after 1936. Nor is it possible, as we have seen, for economic policy or indeed armaments policy to be neatly divided into such periods. In all aspects – diplomatic, economic and military – a helpful image is that of a series of curves rising more or less together. However, in 1937–8 the foreign policy curve, to complete the image, suddenly rose much faster. The suggestion that this acceleration was caused primarily by domestic and economic pressures inside the Third Reich is superficially appealing, for a number of indicators revealed problems. However, these were likely to be worsened rather than resolved by war. It was therefore the potentially threatening configuration *outside* Germany – as the Hossbach memorandum recognized – which prompted Hitler to move forward at a faster pace in eastern Europe. The economy then eventually had to catch up, as it were. Much the same thing happened in Germany's strategic thinking, particularly since before 1937 Britain had not been actively considered as a possible target.

Germany's relatively weak strategic position when Hitler came to power mirrored the state of its armed forces. Internal studies had long predicted that 1931 would be critical for the German army. These assumed that some 2.8 million men would be needed in the event of another war and that after 1931 Germany would no longer be able to rely on reserves from the First World War. The reserves yielded by the 100,000-man 'Versailles' army would not make up the shortfall. Assuming a lengthy period to train troops, Germany had to step up rearmament by 1931 even to maintain its security at the level of the 1920s.[51] Army leaders therefore pushed hard for unilateral restructuring of Germany's military forces and for a large professional strike force, based on short-term military service and equipped with advanced weapons. Effective planning for the 'big army' can be said to date from the new cycle of armaments beginning in 1934, following the decision of Hitler and Schacht in May of the previous year to provide fiscal cover for eight years of rearmament. The initial emphasis in rearmament was on the Reich's *defensive* capacity but restoring this was

51. 'Die organisatorische Lage für eine personelle Heeresverstärkung vom Jahre 1931 ab'. Cited in M. Salewski, 'Zur deutschen Sicherheitspolitik,' p. 133.

conceived from the outset as the first step in a two-stage plan, leading to war readiness at the end of the eight-year period (1942–43).

The heightened external risk to which the Reich was exposed by Hitler's diplomacy, and indeed by Germany's unilateral rearmament itself, caused an acceleration of the programme from 1935.[52] By the autumn of 1936 the army had grown to thirty-six infantry and three armoured divisions. The development of the latter and their successful trials in summer 1935 further blurred the distinction between 'defensive' and 'offensive' elements in the Reich's strategic planning. The trend was a triumph for key elements in the armed forces who had long stressed mobility as a substitute for numerical smallness within the context of the Versailles restrictions.[53] Thus a memorandum by Beck, dated 30 December 1935, observed: 'Strategic defence can only be successful if it can also be carried out in the form of an attack. For this reason an increase in offensive capacity represents a simultaneous strengthening of defensive capacity.'[54] The remilitarization of the Rhineland in 1936 was a critically important factor in the development of 'defence through offence' because it improved protection for the Ruhr area, on whose production Germany's military leaders relied heavily for re-equipping the armed forces. (Conversely, it will be recalled that for the French the *strategic* importance of maintaining bridgeheads on the Rhine had been paramount in the 1920s.)

The earliest operational planning naturally considered the threat of a two-front war. Thus *Plan Red* – drawn up in 1935 – assumed an attack from France with support from Czechoslovakia. At that point, the feasibility of a lightning pre-emptive strike against the Czechs was appraised (formalized in *Plan Green* in 1937) chiefly to enable the army to be switched westwards for the decisive conflict with France. The incorporation of both *Plan Red* and *Plan Green* in the military directive of June 1937 continued to give precedence to dealing with France. However, a note of stark urgency was injected into the war games when planning emphasis was changed to give priority to an attack on Austria and Czechoslovakia, shortly after the meeting recorded by Hossbach. General Jodl, Chief of Operations Staff at the High Command of the Armed Forces (OKW), altered the June 1937

52. Cf. the excellent analysis by M. Geyer, 'The dynamics of military revisionism in the interwar years. Military politics between rearmament and diplomacy' in W. Deist (ed.), *The German Military in the Age of Total War* (Leamington Spa, 1985), pp. 119–21.

53. Cf. W. Murray, *The Change in the European Balance of Power 1938–1939. The Path to Ruin* (Princeton, 1984), pp. 29ff.

54. Cited in Noakes and Pridham (eds), *Nazism 1919–1945, vol. 3*, pp. 677–8.

directive, noting that the 'further development of the *diplomatic* (my italics) situation makes "Operation Red" increasingly less likely than "Operation Green" ... The main emphasis of all mobilisation is now to be placed on "Operation Green".' The directive of 7 December 1937 giving effect to this change considered waiting for some years for the political situation in Europe to develop in Germany's favour, but stressed that if 'a situation arises which, owing to Britain's aversion to a general European war, through her lack of interest in the Central European problem and because of a conflict breaking out between Italy and France in the Mediterranean, creates the probability that Germany will face no other opponent than Russia on Czechoslovakia's side, then "Operation Green" will start *before* the completion of Germany's full preparedness for war'. The offensive was to make sure 'that the solution of the German problem of living space can be carried to a victorious conclusion even if one or other of the Great Powers intervene against us'.[55]

The prospect of sudden attacks in the east had obvious implications for the Luftwaffe, which had developed from very unpromising beginnings in 1933 – secretly at first – under Erhard Milch, State Secretary for Air. By the end of 1933 some 2 million workers were employed on airfield and factory construction as the administrative and industrial base of the air force was put into place. The news about the German air force also became public in March 1935. Meanwhile, the Luftwaffe's officer corps expanded from the 300 transferred to it from the army in 1933 to the 15,000 on active duty by the year 1939. Key individuals, notably the first Luftwaffe Chief of Staff, General Walther Wever, were of critical importance in developing the air force as a source of close support for the army, under a doctrine practised with some success during the Spanish Civil War. As in other air forces there was a strong belief in the value of strategic bombing. It was felt in the 1930s, however, that the German air force was not up to an attack on Britain or Russia, if perfectly adequate for action against Prague or Warsaw. The increased risk of conflict with Britain thus placed even greater demands on the Reich's resources. The Luftwaffe was therefore forced to develop in the long run as a strategic weapon for long-range attacks, as well as carrying out its vital support of the army.[56]

Naval planning also had to struggle to keep up with the decisive shift of pace in Hitler's foreign policy. By 1933 the German navy was

55. *Documents on German Foreign Policy*, Series D, vol. III, pp. 635–7.

56. Cf. R. Muller, *The German Air War in Russia* (Baltimore, 1992); H. Nowarra and H. J. Kens, *Die deutschen Flugzeuge 1933–45. Deutschlands Luftfahrt–Entwicklungen bis zum Ende des Zweiten Weltkrieges* (Munich, 1977).

outdated and below even the strength permitted by the Peace Treaty.[57] Naturally, the domestic political factors limiting the construction of armoured cruisers at the end of the 1920s were removed with Hitler's arrival in government. On 1 April 1934 the Commander-in-Chief, Admiral Raeder, was instructed to replace existing plans for a one-front war with Poland with those for a possible conflict including Russia and France and to be ready for action within the general armed forces framework in five years. The limits set by the Anglo-German naval agreement of 1935 threatened no serious restriction on German naval building before 1940. As well as the continuing construction of the armed cruisers, the navy opted for smaller submarines, but more of them, to keep within the ceiling of the 1935 treaty. Submarines could be used effectively against French shipping in the Mediterranean, while the North Sea was regarded as crucial to maintaining German dominance and trade links in the Baltic. Interim directives of the navy prior to 1937 reveal that war against Britain was seen as virtually suicidal by Raeder.[58] This premise, too, was destroyed by Hitler's identification of Britain as an opponent. In 1937 he insisted – against his experts – on the building of a huge battle fleet to be ready by 1944, the resources for which were eventually made available in January 1939 (Z-plan).[59]

The sense of urgency pervading the armed forces from 1937 was manifestly a reflection of foreign policy priorities largely determined by Hitler with the support of key figures in his entourage. During the series of crises in 1938 some of the latter, notable Goering, were undoubtedly anxious to avoid if possible the risk of war breaking out with Britain. However, Goering's complete dependence on Hitler virtually ruled out any systematic attempt to develop alternative foreign policy concepts, quite apart from his own personal commitment to the regime's ideology and his central role in the rearmament process.[60] The Chief of Army General Staff, Ludwig Beck, was compromised by his own readiness to contemplate war as an extension of policy, and troubled mainly by the fear of Germany losing a conflict by embarking on it prematurely. Yet, as we have seen, Hitler appeared to doubt that time would ever be on Germany's side. He rightly suspected that the

---

57. Cf. W. Bernhardt, *Die deutsche Aufrüstung 1934–1939. Militärische und politische Konzeptionen und ihre Einschätzung durch die Allierten* (Frankfurt am Main, 1969), p. 38.

58. Cf. M. Salewski, *Die deutsche Seekriegsleitung 1933–1935* (Frankfurt, 1937), p. 30. Also, J. Dülfer, 'Determinants of German naval policy 1920–1939' in W. Deist (ed.), *Germany in the Age of Total War*, pp. 152–70.

59. J. Dülfer, 'Der Beginn des Krieges', in *Geschichte und Gesellschaft* (1976): 465.

60. Murray, *The Change in the European Balance*, p. 361.

Reich might not achieve overwhelming superiority simply through the processes of rearmament. The lightning attacks injected into operational planning from 1935 evidenced an impatience with orthodoxy which characterized Hitler's whole approach to strategy. It was vital from this perspective to augment Germany's materials and armaments basis through first incorporating Austria and Czechoslovakia, particularly since the Four Year plan had not freed the Reich from its dependence on imported raw materials and strategic metals.[61] As a result of the *Anschluss* alone, following Hitler's triumphant entry to Linz on 12 March, the Reich acquired not only valuable ores and additional steel capacity but some 44 million marks worth of foreign exchange reserves. The full strategic and material advantages to be gained from attacking Czechoslovakia were temporarily denied to Hitler by the Munich settlement in September 1938. They duly fell to the Reich with the 'Rape of Prague' on 15 March 1939, leaving Poland cruelly exposed to renewed pressure to accommodate Germany's claims to Danzig and the Polish corridor.

THE LIMITS TO 'OPPORTUNISM'

The military directives accompanying these momentous and all too familiar events, including the order to prepare for attack on Poland (*Case White*) on 3 April 1939, confirm the impression of strategy scrambling to keep pace with policy. An obvious example concerns the insertion of the phrase in the final directive for *Plan Green* (28 May 1939) about Hitler's 'unalterable decision to smash Czechoslovakia by military action in the near future', instead of the original reference to the fact that it was *not* Hitler's intention to do this without provocation. In this case the 'provocation' had been Czechoslovakia's partial mobilization on 20–21 May 1938.[62] Later, in the knowledge of the Anglo–French decision in March 1939 to guarantee Poland, but before the Nazi–Soviet non-aggression treaty, Hitler observed: 'A conflict with Poland – beginning with an attack on Poland – will only be successful if the west is out of play. If that is impossible, then it is better to fall on the west and thus deal with Poland at the same

---

61. See J. J. Jaeger, *Die wirtschaftliche Unabhängigkeit des Dritten Reichs vom Ausland dargestellt am Beispiel der Stahlindustrie* (Berlin, 1969), pp. 305ff.
62. Drafts in *DGFP*, Series D, vol. II, pp. 300–2, 358.

time.'[63] Is this evidence of incurable 'opportunism'? Hitler's most recent biographer insists of the crises unfolding in 1938 and 1939 that, although strategic considerations were 'uppermost' and economic necessity 'scarcely less important':

> Hitler's decisions and policy adjustments were opportunistic – to invade Austria when Schuschnigg unexpectedly called a plebiscite, to merge Austria into Germany only in the light of the delirious reception he encountered in Linz, to destroy Czechoslovakia at the earliest opportunity when Czech mobilisation . . . made Germany look foolish and to attack Poland only when diplomatic overtures had been repulsed and the British guarantee had been made.[64]

Of course, opportunities *can* be seized in order to further established strategies. However, doing so would make Hitler seem remarkably like most previous German leaders, the very suggestion of which brought widespread vilification for A. J. P. Taylor, whose famous book on the origins of the Second World War played down Hitler's ideas system and argued that his foreign policy was 'that of his predecessors'. Hitler's first important biographer, Alan Bullock, tried to resolve what he saw as a dilemma by ascribing to the Führer's foreign policy a combination of 'consistency of aim with complete opportunism in method and tactics.'[65] The newer biography already referred to essentially repeats this approach: 'Within the bounds of his unchanged long-term objective – the struggle for Lebensraum – and within the narrowing range of options imposed by economic and military-strategic considerations, Hitler's foreign policy decisions in 1938–9 remained highly pragmatic and opportunistic.'[66] But the qualification – 'within the bounds of his unchanged long-term objective' – is absolutely paramount; so much so that it threatens to empty the term 'opportunism' of any real meaning. Hitler's single-mindedness by 1939 made his 'opportunities' *less* extensive than they should have been in the prevailing international disarray, and conjured up the prospect at last of a coalition against the Third Reich. He had actually brought himself to the point where he was presented with an opportunity he could barely refuse to accept. Since the directive for attacking the Poles was taken in the full knowledge of the British guarantee, Hitler

63. Cited in G. Schreiber, 'Der Zweite Weltkrieg in der internationalen Forschung', *Aus Politik und Zeitgeschichte*, B 32–33 (1989): 27.

64. I. Kershaw, *Hitler* (London, 1991), pp. 147–8.

65. A. Bullock, 'Hitler and the origins of the Second World War', in E. M. Robertson (ed.), *The Origins of the Second World War* (London, 1972), p. 193.

66. Kershaw, *Hitler*, p. 147.

faced the very strong probability that only agreement with the USSR might deter Britain from keeping its promises. We appear to be seeing opportunism of a kind comparable to that arising from a drowning man accepting a straw, but Hitler put himself in this position by being determined to move against Poland in accordance with the timetables now driving him.

The immediate price he paid was to consign the eastern parts of Poland along with the Baltic states to the Soviet sphere of influence, under the terms of the Nazi–Soviet pact of 23 August 1939 and the two secret protocols attached to this (23.8.39 and 28.9.39). However, since Poland would be the glacis from which Germany could attack Russia later, the Ribbentrop–Molotov pact might well be seen as directed against Russia and accordingly categorized as a 'not yet-aggression treaty'.[67] Although Germany gave up Lithuania to the Soviets as well as Estonia and Latvia, it gained more of western Poland from the bargain with Stalin, subsequently facilitating more effective German preparations in German-occupied Poland for an eventual invasion of the USSR. For his part, Stalin was relieved of the immediate fear of a conflict on Soviet soil, which the Anglo-French–Soviet discussions in the summer of 1939 had failed to allay owing to British reluctance to abandon the Baltic states. At the same time Stalin divested himself of any obligation to co-operate with the capitalist states in defending the status quo in East Europe. His cynicism matched that of Hitler, in so far as the pact was anti–British and anti-Polish rather than pro-German, even though for the moment Stalin allowed German–Soviet economic collaboration to exceed the USSR's own best interests. In the event, Hitler *was* spared a two-front war for the time being by his rapid defeat of Poland within six weeks of the attack of 31 August 1939.

However, a brief overview of the main theatres of war at once illustrates how Hitler's options began to narrow as a result of his own determination to attack Poland in 1939. Britain's subsequent declaration of war immediately presented Germany with the most daunting policy imperatives. They may be glimpsed in Hitler's 'Directive No. 6 for the Conduct of the War' of 9 October 1939:

> Should it become evident in the near future that England, and, under her influence, France also, are not disposed to bring the war to an end, I have decided, without further loss of time, to go over to the offensive. Any

67. R. Ahmann, *Nichtangriffspakte: Entwicklung und operative Nutzung in Europa 1922–1939. Mit einem Ausblick auf die Renaissance des Nichtangriffsvertrages nach dem Zweiten Weltkrieg* (Baden-Baden, 1988), p. 641.

further delay will not only entail the end of Belgian and perhaps of Dutch neutrality, to the advantage of the allies; it will also increasingly strengthen the military power of the enemy, reduce the confidence of neutral nations in Germany's final victory, and make it more difficult to bring Italy into the war on our side as full ally.[68]

At first things appeared to go well and astonishingly, by the summer of 1940, Belgium, Holland, Luxemburg and France *had* all been defeated. En route, Denmark and Norway were successfully occupied, thus securing the way to the Atlantic.

When Italy finally declared war on the Allies on 10 June 1940 extra pressure could be applied. Thus 'Operation Felix' was designed to capture Gibraltar and to exclude Britain from the Mediterranean by early 1941. Disappointingly for Hitler, the plan was frustrated by General Franco's refusal to allow German troops into Spain. Parallel schemes to attack Egypt with Italy's aid were also shelved when the latter became embroiled in a conflict with Greece, which required Germany's support and ended with the defeat of Greece and Yugoslavia by 23 April 1941. This of course incidentally helped to secure south-eastern Europe for any future offensive against the USSR. However, the planned invasion of England (Operation Sea Lion) had to be abandoned by September 1940 because of the Luftwaffe's failure to secure air supremacy in the Battle of Britain. Though driven from the Continent, the English were therefore undefeated and, to Hitler's chagrin, wholly unwilling to entertain peace overtures from Germany. The arrival of massive American aid for Britain by 1941 had to be reckoned with, but more immediately worrying for Hitler was the prospect of Britain persuading the Russians to reconsider their position.

Ironically, Stalin's first interview with a foreign ambassador since his reception of Ribbentrop in August 1939 proved to be with Sir Stafford Cripps, on 1 July 1940. Although Anglo-Soviet relations remained cool and inactive for some months yet, it became obvious that Russian as well as British interests were threatened by the tri-partite pact signed between Japan, Italy and Germany on 27 September 1940. Unlike Britain, Russia was given the option of joining this arrangement in November 1940 but the scheme foundered on Balkan and Baltic issues. Russia had gained Bessarabia and Bukovina from Romania in June 1940 but disliked Germany's influence in Hungary, Romania and Slovakia, which all adhered to the Tripartite Pact.

68. H. R. Trevor-Roper (ed.), *Hitler's war directives 1939–45* (London, 1966), p. 50.

Following Russia's failure to defeat Finland in the 'Winter War' and the subsequent Soviet occupation of the Baltic states in the summer of 1940, Stalin was also affronted by the Finnish–German agreement of September that year. This allowed German troops transit rights through to Norway and the presence of German troops on Finnish soil to protect through traffic. What was really at stake was Hitler's own determination to secure the vital raw materials of northern and southern Europe. Thus Molotov's pointed demand for satisfaction of Russia's vital interests in the Balkans and the Baltic as a condition for joining the Tripartite Pact was unlikely to be met. Instead it may well have strengthened Hitler's resurgent desire to attack Russia before it was too late. German intelligence led him and his generals to believe that such a campaign would be relatively easy to win.[69]

The preliminary studies of the feasibility of an attack were ordered by Hitler on 21 July 1940, although the final directive for 'Operation Barbarossa' was not issued until 18 December 1940. German armed forces had then to be prepared 'even before the conclusion of the war against England, to crush Soviet Russia in a rapid campaign'. The enticing prospect beckoned of killing two birds with one stone, since the defeat of Russia was expected to end British hopes of bringing the USSR into a coalition against the Third Reich. Once the Russians were beaten, Hitler informed his military commanders on 9 January 1941, then either the English would give in or Germany would be able to continue fighting Britain under more favourable circumstances. The draft directive for the conduct of the war, drawn up by General Walter Warlimont of the Armed Forces Operations Staff at OKW on 11 June 1941, makes plain what enormous stakes were riding on the defeat of the USSR. Assuming this would eliminate any threat on land to Germany and Italy, because they would then control the Continent, there was to be a shift in German arms production towards the navy and air force and the resumption of the struggle against Britain in the Mediterranean and Near East.[70] It is worth stressing that although Russia was indeed in a position to strengthen its own position in East Europe and could threaten Germany economically as well as militarily, there was little indication of Stalin being drawn into a war with National Socialism. Admittedly, this does not dispose of the argument that Hitler thought this *could* happen and that therefore strategic considerations were uppermost in his final decision to attack the

69. B. Wegner, 'The tottering giant. German perceptions of Soviet military and economic strength in preparation for Operation Blau (1942)', in Andrew and Noakes (eds), *Intelligence and international relations*, p. 293.

70. Trevor-Roper, *Hitler's War Directives*, pp. 130–4.

USSR. However, his subsequent and absolute fixation with holding out in Russia come what may, the appallingly brutal nature of the war in the east and, finally, the sinister political objectives spelled out in instructions to the troops, suggest that ideological and strategic arguments were inextricably linked from the very outset of the war against Russia. When Hitler informed Mussolini of his reasoning on the eve of the invasion of Russia, he also confessed how irksome the previous collaboration with the Soviet Union had been for him. In some way or other, he wrote, 'it seemed to me a break with my whole origin, my concepts and my former obligations. I am happy now to be relieved of these mental agonies.'[71]

The *va banque* side of Hitler's personality (often confused with opportunism) was at once exposed by the fact that he drew on all available units – a total of well over 3 million troops – for Operation Barbarossa. Stalin paid dearly for his insistent refusal to believe reports that an attack would be coming, so that huge German advances were made into Russia along three main (northern, central and southern) fronts, profiting from the surprise element to destroy half the Russian air force on the ground in the opening two days. Meanwhile, Rosenberg, designated head of the wartime administration for Russia, divided his *Ostministerium* into a Reich Commissariat Ostland (for Northern Russia and the Baltic) and one for Southern Russia and the Ukraine, the former under Hinrich Lohse, the latter under Erich Koch. By August, however, many of the problems haunting Operation Barbarossa had already surfaced; huge German casualties, over-extended supply and communications lines and equipment ill suited to the Russian terrain, a seemingly endless supply of Russian troops to replace those lost in battle. All of these difficulties were exacerbated with the onset of autumn and its rains. Following a Russian counter-offensive on 5 December, the German armies suffered a reverse before Moscow but, because of Hitler's insistence on 16 December that the German lines remain firm, faced the first of their long and terrible winters. Disagreements between Hitler and his generals on strategy had already become apparent in August, with the former giving priority to securing the northern and southern fronts and access to vital foodstuffs and raw materials, rather than acceding to demands to concentrate on taking Moscow. On 19 December Hitler's grip on overall strategy was strengthened when he accepted the resignation of the Commander-in-Chief of the Army, Field Marshal von Brauchitsch, and personally took over his post. Whether *Blitzkrieg*

---

71. Cited in Noakes and Pridham, *Documents on Nazism*, vol. 3, p. 817.

was ever designated a coherent and planned strategy, or was merely a convenient description of Germany's early wartime victories applied after the event, it had little meaning now. Nothing could disguise the fact that the Third Reich was now fighting for its existence on two fronts. In November 1941, as the German eastward advance slowed, Hitler proclaimed: 'I have never used the word "Blitzkrieg" because it is a very stupid word.'[72]

Until this point the war had been mainly European, with peripheral theatres in Africa, but it now became both global and total. One of Hitler's assumptions had been that the destruction of Russia would enable Japan to move decisively against the United States, thus discouraging the latter from entering the European war. However, it was precisely the existence of the Tripartite Pact between Japan, Germany and Italy which helped to convince the Americans that war in Europe and war in Asia were one and the same thing. The position of Japan was actually weakened by the abrogation of the Nazi–Soviet pact, since it ended Tokyo's grandiose dream of coalescing Japan, Germany, Italy and the USSR as revisionist powers against an Anglo-American coalition.[73] Although the Russians now resorted to an alliance with the Allies, the Japanese military refused to abandon the Axis and to reorient towards collaboration with the United States of America. That would also have meant Tokyo abandoning its war in China. When Pearl Harbor was attacked on 7 December 1941 a point of no return had been reached by the Japanese. Hitler's own declaration of war on the USA on 11 December 1941 appears at first glance to confirm the 'lack of realistic, hard-headed appraisal of risks, strengths, weaknesses and economic factors in German strategic directives'.[74] Arguably, however, Hitler simply accepted that there *was* no alternative to prosecuting the war to a finish. An agreement on the joint conduct of war was signed by the tripartite powers on 11 December, and on 18 February 1942 agreement was reached dividing operations into zones along 70 degrees longitude, with Germany and Italy looking to the west of this, Japan to the East.

In fact the Japanese, heavily engaged with the Allies in the Far East, failed to meet German requests for support against Russia in 1942–43. In spite of some success in renewed major offensives towards Leningrad and on the southern front towards the Donbas and Caucasus oil fields, by 19 August the fateful battle for Stalingrad had been

---

72. M. Domarus, *Hitlers Reden und Proklamationen*, (Würzburg, 1963), II, p. 1776.

73. Cf. A. Iriye, *The Origins of the Second World War in the Pacific* (London, 1987), p. 140.

74. Murray, *The Change in the European Power Balance*, 361.

engaged. During the ensuing months massive losses were sustained on the Axis side and the final reverses in the winter of 1942–43 deprived Hitler of most of the territory his armies had gained from the summer offensive. The chances of victory in Russia bringing pressure to bear on Britain became remote in the extreme, not least because the Axis suffered reverses at about the same time in the theatres of war where they confronted the West directly. In North Africa, Rommel's *Afrika Korps* was forced to retreat after the second battle of El Alamein in Egypt on 23 October 1942. This was followed by the landing of US and British troops in Algeria and Morocco in early November (Operation Torch), forcing General Pétain's government to capitulate and causing Hitler to occupy Vichy France on 11 November. The German navy might have hoped to contain these events but it was dependent on resources to be made available only after Russia's defeat. Although Hitler's displeasure at the ineffectual performance of the German surface fleet became apparent with the decision to build more U-boats, these concentrated on disrupting Allied supply lines in the Atlantic under Admiral Dönitz (also Commander-in-Chief of the navy after Admiral Raeder's resignation early in 1943). Yet even there the use of new location devices by the Allies, and the celebrated 'Ultra' decoding of the ciphers for the command of U-boats in Berlin, made attacks on Allied convoys increasingly dangerous. The turning point in the Battle of the Atlantic came in May 1943, when no fewer than 41 U-boats were lost.

Meanwhile matters went from bad to worse in the Mediterranean, when the Grand Fascist Council in Italy dumped Mussolini in July and the succeeding military dictatorship under Marshal Badoglio reached an armistice with the West on 3 September 1943. Although Hitler was able to re-install Mussolini in the same month the Allied advance up the peninsula continued following their landings at Salerno. In containing problems in the Mediterranean Hitler was forced to divert vital resources from the war in the east where, having held out at the battle of Kursk, the Russians returned to the offensive, retaking Leningrad by 26 January 1944, then going on by May to liberate the Crimea and to drive the Germans out of the Ukraine. Although a chunk of the original central section as well as the Baltic states were still held by the Germans, the opening of the Second Front in the west on 6 June 1944 ensured that the immediate fate of Hitler's Reich would be determined at the moment its adversaries in East and West met on German soil. Although delivering a last shock to the Allies with the Ardennes offensive in December 1944, Hitler committed suicide and his successor Admiral Dönitz made unconditional surrender on 7 May 1945.

This outcome was the result of pursuing policies *in spite of* objective difficulties. Looking back, it can be seen that Germany was compelled to take huge risks to secure its early victories, having initially clear advantages only in the air. It had been imperative for Hitler to escape from this position as quickly as possible. An economic reordering of Europe might have been attempted, but the attack on the USSR and the ensuing shift to total war left little prospect for orderly economic development. The Third Reich was then committed to channelling all economic activity into the prosecution of the war. Yet even drawing with disregard for life and limb on foreign labour from the countries it occupied, the Third Reich could not hope to match the industrial power of the United States once that was fully mobilized, and therefore could not really expect to win a protracted conflict. The unrealistic early Nazi assessments of the threat from America betrayed their overriding and immediate concern with establishing hegemony on the Continent. Here, the unrelenting pursuit of the critically important war in the east is the essential perspective from which to view the foreign policy leading up to it. The ideological ferocity engendered above all by the war with the USSR cannot simply be explained by strategic considerations alone, any more than opportunism can ever account for Hitler's armies installing themselves there in the first place.

Bibliographical Essay

Since the footnotes contain references to important early works, the following bibliographical essay confines itself to books published during the past fifteen years or so, including some of the major studies in the German language. The organization of the bibliographical essay accords roughly with the chapter sequence, with the exception of the 'general' and the 'foreign policy' sections.

A number of **general guides** can be consulted with profit. Bibliographical support for the Weimar Republic is provided by P. D. Stachura, *The Weimar Era and Hitler 1918–1933. A Critical Bibliography* (Oxford, 1978). It has interesting and idiosyncratic commentaries on key books. E. Kolb's *The Weimar Republic* (London, 1988) contains a reasonably full listing of work published after 1970 together with well-structured overviews of important debates about Germany during the 1920s. K. Hildebrand provides a comparable service for the 1930s, *The Third Reich* (London, 1984). J. Hiden and J. Farquharson, *Explaining Hitler's Germany. Historians and the Third Reich* (London, 2nd edition, 1989) tackle historiographical issues from the 1930s onwards and offer an extensive bibliography. However, they assume some background knowledge. I. Kershaw's *The Nazi Dictatorship. Problems, Perspectives and Interpretation*, currently in its third edition (London, 1993) is probably now the standard introductory guide in English, or indeed in any other language. It is remarkably full and fair minded in its analysis of the literature. Important new scholarship is highlighted by the regular surveys in the German periodical, *Vierteljahrshefte für Zeitgeschichte*, published in Munich. Also of value to the British reader is the *Bulletin* of the German Historical Institute in London. As well as listing new aquisitions to the Institute's outstanding library, the publication gives critical reviews of new books on German history. **Overviews of the Weimar Republic** are still relatively thin on the ground in comparison with those of the Third Reich. E. J. Feuchtwanger's *From Weimar to Hitler. Germany 1918–1933* (London, 1993) tries at least to shrug off some of the deterministic gloom surrounding the republic's history. A solid account in German is H. Schulze, *Weimar Deutschland 1917–1933* (Berlin, 1982), which is more readable than H. Köhler, *Geschichte der Weimarer Republik* (Berlin, 1981). H. A. Winkler's *Weimar 1918–1933. Die Geschichte der ersten deutschen Demokratie* (Munich, 1993) seems more thoughtful than either. R. Bessel and E. J. Feuchtwanger (eds), compiled a useful collection some time ago, *Social Change and Political Development in Weimar Germany* (London, 1981). M. Broszat, *Hitler and the Collapse of Weimar Germany* (Leamington Spa, 1987) is sparely written and focuses on the final years of the republic.

Turning to the Third Reich, it is impossible to overlook Broszat's classic study, *The Hitler State. The Foundations and Development of the Internal Structure of the Third Reich* (London, 1981). A number of British and German heavyweights debate domestic and foreign issues in G. Hirschfeld and L. Kettenacker (eds), *The 'Führer State': Myth and Reality* (Stuttgart, 1981). N. Frei's *National Socialist Rule in Germany. The Fuhrer State 1933–1945* (Oxford, 1993) is excellent. A brilliant but more individualistic account is that by the late D. Peukert, *Inside Nazi Germany. Conformity, Opposition and Racism in Everyday Life* (London, 1989). See also the tribute to a major German historian of Nazism by L. Niethammer and B. Weisbrod (eds), *Der Nationalsozialismus und die deutsche Gesellschaft. Ausgewählte Aufsätze. Hans Mommsen zum 60. Geburtstag* (Reinbek bei Hamburg, 1991). Also useful, H.-U. Thamer, *Verführung und Gewalt. Deutschland 1933–45* (Berlin, 1986). The three volumes of *Nazism, 1919–1945. A Documentary Reader* (Exeter, 1983–88), edited by J. Noakes and G. Pridham, are indispensable to the English reader. Beginners can profit from T. Kirk, *The Longman Companion to Nazi Germany* (London, 1995); M. Freeman, *An Atlas of Nazi Germany* (London, 1987); and the collection of essays from *History Today*, edited by R. Bessel, *Life in the Third Reich* (Oxford–London, 1987). For an overview of both Weimar and the Third Reich, G. Schulz, *Deutschland seit dem Ersten Weltkrieg 1918–1945* (Göttingen, 1985). Essays throwing *some* light on interwar Germany are to be found in D. Blackbourn, *Populists and Patricians. Essays in Modern German History* (London, 1987); J. Breuilly (ed.), *The State of Germany: The National Idea in the Making, Unmaking and*

Remaking of a Modern Nation-State (London, 1992); R. J. Evans, *Rethinking German History. Nineteenth Century Germany and the Origins of the Third Reich* (London, 1987); G. Eley, *From Unification to Nazism. Reinterpreting the German Past* (London, 1986); and finally, M. Hughes, *Nationalism and Society. Germany 1800–1945* (London, 1988). Turning to **Political and constitutional issues**, there is a dearth of recent general books in English on the **German revolution of 1918–1919**. (F. L. Carsten's earlier comparative study, *Revolution in Central Europe 1918–1919* (London, 1972), is all the more valuable.) Two good recent German studies are those by U. Kluge, *Die deutsche Revolution 1918–19. Staat, Politik und Gesellschaft zwischen Weltkrieg und Kapp-Putsch* (Frankfurt, 1985) and H. J. Bieber, *Bürgertum in der Revolution: Bürgerräte und Bürgerstreiks in Deutschland 1918–1920* (Hamburg, 1992). Regional aspects of the revolution are considered by H. Beyer, *Die Revolution in Bayern 1918–1919* (Berlin, 1982) and J. Tampke, *The Ruhr and Revolution. The Revolutionary Movement in the Rhenish–Westphalian Region 1912–1919* (London, 1979). There is valuable material in biographies of some of the major figures in the Republic's early political life, including R. König, (ed.), *Friedrich Ebert und seine Zeit. Bilanz und Perspektiven der Forschung* (2nd edn, Munich, 1991) and W. Wette, *Gustav Noske. Eine politische Biographie* (Düsseldorf, 1987). See also G. Schmidt, *Rosa Luxemburg. Sozialistin zwischen Ost und West* (Göttingen–Zurich, 1988) and F. L. Carsten, *Eduard Bernstein 1850–1932: Eine politische Biographie* (Munich, 1993). On the response of the trade unions, K. Schoenhoven (ed.), *Die Gewerkschaften in Weltkrieg und Revolution 1914–1919* (Cologne, 1985). The army's critical role can be followed in P. E. Guth, *Der Loyalitätskonflikt des deutschen Offizierkorps in der Revolution 1918–1920* (Frankfurt–Berne, 1983).

On the broader **constitutional setting** there is H. W. Koch's stolid *A Constitutional History of Germany in the Nineteenth and Twentieth Centuries* (London, 1984). This can be supplemented by L. Biewer, *Reichsreformbestrebungen in der Weimarer Republik* (Frankfurt–M, 1980) and by the splendid studies of G. Schulz, *Zwischen Demokratie und Diktatur. Verfassungspolitik und Reichsreform in der Weimarer Republik. Vol. 2, Deutschland am Vorabend der grossen Krise* (Berlin–New York, 1987); *Vol. 3, Von Brüning zu Hitler. Der Wandel des politischen Systems in Deutschland 1930–1933* (Berlin–New York, 1992). Some fascinating analyses of German democracy made in the late 1920s have been edited by K. Tribe, O. Kirchheimer, F. Neumann. *Social Democracy and the Rule of Law* (London, 1987). On the electoral processes, K. Rohe, *Wahlen und Wählertraditionen in Deutschland: Kulturelle Grundlagen* deutscher Parteien und Parteiensysteme im 19. und 20. Jahrhundert (Frankfurt–Main, 1992); J. W. Falter et al, (eds), Wahlen und Abstimmungen in der Weimarer Republik. Materialen zum Wahlverhalten 1919–1933 (Munich, 1986). K. D. Bracher and P. Mikat (eds), Staat und Parteien: Festschrift für Rudolf Morsey zum 65 Geburtstag (Berlin, 1992), is an ideal introduction to later detailed study of specific parties.

On the subject of **German political parties**, W. Ribhegge deploys arguments emphasizing the positive aspects of early Weimar democracy in Frieden für Europa. Die Politik der deutschen Reichstagsmehrheit 1917–18 (Berlin, 1988). The German socialists are treated in R. Breitman, German Socialism and Weimar Democracy (Chapel Hill, 1981) and W. L. Guttsman, The German Social Democratic Party, 1875–1933 (London, 1981). These books tend to focus on the top leadership. A broader picture is drawn in S. Miller and H. Potthoff, A History of the SPD from 1848 to the Present (Oxford, 1986). The fundamental dilemma of the German socialists is highlighted by H. A. Winkler, Klassenkampf oder Koalitionspolitik? Grundentscheidungen sozialdemokratischer Politik 1919–1925 (Heidelberg, 1991). How German socialists responded to National Socialists can be followed in W. Pyta, Gegen Hitler und für die Republik. Die Auseinandersetzung der deutschen Sozialdemokratie mit der NSDAP in der Weimarer Republik (Düsseldorf, 1989), and indeed in H. Gotschlich, Zwischen Kampf und Kapitulation. Zur Geschichte des Reichsbanners Schwarz-Rot-Gelb (Berlin, 1987). An excellent study in English is by E. Rosenhaft, Beating the Fascists? The German Communists and Political Violence 1929–1933 (Cambridge, 1983). C. Fischer, The German Communists and the Rise of Nazism (London, 1991) sees blurring of the lines between KPD and NSDAP activists. A relatively neglected aspect of the relationship between the SPD and the German communists is examined by G. Fuelberth, Die Beziehungen zwischen SPD und KPD in der Kommunalpolitik der Weimarer Periode 1918–19 bis 1933 (Cologne, 1985). More generally, see B. Fowkes, Communism in Germany under the Weimar Republic (London, 1984).

For the liberal parties see B. B. Frye, Liberal Democrats in the Weimar Republic. The History of the German Democratic Party and the German State Party (Carbondale, Ewardsville, 1985); K. Jarausch and L. E. Jones (eds), In Search of a Liberal Germany (New York–Oxford, 1990); L. E. Jones, German Liberalism and the Dissolution of the Weimar Party System (Chapel Hill–London, 1988); E. Demm, Ein liberaler in Kaiserreich und Republik. Der politische Weg Alfred Weber bis 1920 (Boppard, 1990). A general and readable account of the the Centre Party is that by E. L. Evans, The German Centre Party 1870–1933 (Illinois, 1981). For detail on its political role after 1918, K. Ruppert, Im Dienst der Staat von

Weimar. Das Zentrum als regierende Partei in der Weimarer Republik (Düsseldorf, 1992). By contrast, and very much not in the service of the Republic, see H. Holzbach, *Das System Hugenberg. Die Organization der bürgerlichen Sammlungspolitik vor dem Aufstieg der NSDAP* (Stuttgart, 1981) and U. Hoerster-Philipps (ed.), *Konservative Politik in der Endphase der Weimarer Republik. Die Regierung Franz von Papen* (Cologne, 1982). For insight into the sheer confusion and uncertainty in right-wing conservative circles, H. Weiss and P. Hoser (eds), *Die Deutschnationalen und die Zerstörung der Weimarer Republik. Aus dem Tagebuch von Reinhold Quaatz, 1928–33* (Munich, 1989) and G. Jasper, *Die gescheiterte Zähmung. Wege zur Machtergreifung Hitlers 1930–34* (Frankfurt, 1986).

Aspects of the NSDAP during the Weimar period are discussed in P. D. Stachura (ed.), *The Nazi Machtergreifung* (London, 1983). See also P. Fritzsche, *Rehearsals for Fascism. Populism and Political Mobilisation in Weimar Germany* (Oxford, 1990). For a comparative setting consult G. M. Luebbert, *Liberalism, Fascism or Social Democracy. Social Classes and the Political Origins of Regimes in Interwar Europe* (Oxford, 1991). For detailed analysis of the structure and composition of the NSDAP we have M. H. Kater, *The Nazi Party. A Social Profile of Members and Leaders 1919–1945* (Oxford, 1983) and P. Manstein's exhaustive *Die Mitglieder und Wähler der NSDAP 1919–1933. Untersuchungen zu ihrer schichtmässigen Zusammensetzung* (Frankfurt–M–New York, etc., 1988). A well-written and clear account following similar themes is that by D. Mühlburger, *Hitler's Followers. Studies in the Sociology of the Nazi Movement* (London, 1991). The scope of R. F. Hamilton's *Who voted for Hitler?* (New Jersey, 1982) is not as wide as the title suggests and the book should be used in conjunction with T. Childers, *The Social Foundations of Fascism in Germany, 1919–1933* (Chapel Hill–London, 1983). Childers brings out the way in which the National Socialist constituency was built up, on which process R. Koshar, *Social Life, Local Politics and Nazism. Marburg 1880–1935* (Chapel Hill, 1986) also throws light. Much detailed work has been done on the growth of the NSDAP to fill out the early studies (by, for example, J. Noakes, *The Nazi Party in Lower Saxony, 1921–1933*. (Oxford, 1971). Some of the more interesting recent books are E. Hennig (ed.), *Hessen untern Hakenkreuz. Studien zur Durchsetzung der NSDAP in Hessen* (Frankfurt–M, 1983); B. Mensing and F. Prinz, *Irrlicht im leuchtenden Muenchen? Der Nationalsozialismus in der 'Hauptstadt der Bewegung'* (Regensburg, 1991); and G. Paul, *Die NSDAP des Saargebietes, 1920–1930. Der verspätete Aufstieg der NSDAP in der katholisch-proletarischen Provinz* (Saarbrücken, 1987). On the SA's role in the party's growth, see C. Fischer, *Storm Troopers. A Social, Economic and Ideological Analysis 1929–1933* (London, 1983).

Insights into the **polycracy** which developed under **National Socialist rule after 1933** come from reading the masterly study by D. Rebentisch, *Führerstaat und Verwaltung im Zweiten Weltkrieg. Verfassungsentwicklung und Verwaltungspolitik 1939–45* (Stuttgart, 1989). There are a number of books about major organizations in the power game. These include R. L. Koehl, *The Black Corps. The Structure and Power Struggles of the Nazi SS* (Madison, 1993). This devotes relatively little attention to the period of war and occupation but see also B. Wegner, *The Waffen-SS. Organization, Ideology and Function* (London, 1988) and R. B. Birn, *Die Höheren SS- und Polizeiführer. Himmlers Verkehr im Reich und in den besetzten Gebieten* (Düsseldorf, 1986). The latter shows all too clearly how efficiently the system could pursue its priorities if need be. More on administration is to be found in H. J. Fischer, *Hitlers Apparat. Namen, Ämter, Kompetenzen: Eine Strukturanalyse des Dritten Reiches* (Kiel, 1988) and in P. Longerich, *Hitlers Stellvertreter. Führung der Partei und Kontrolle des Staatsapparatus durch den Stab Hess und die Partei-Kanzlei* (Munich, 1992). A valuable sectoral study of how the Third Reich functioned is that by L. Gruchmann, *Justiz im Dritten Reich 1933–1940. Anpassung und Unterwerfung in der Ära Gürtner* (Munich, 1988) and a regional dimension is added by R. Mann, *Protest und Kontrolle im Dritten Reich. Nationalsozialistische Herrschaft im Alltag einer rheinischen Grossstadt* (New York–Frankfurt, 1987). The role of personalities in the functioning of government can be traced in H. Peuschel, *Die Männer um Hitler. Braune Biographien: Martin Bormann, Joseph Goebbels etc.* (Düsseldorf, 1982), as well as in R. Smelser and R. Zitelmann, *The Nazi Elite* (London, 1993). On other individuals, see P. R. Black, *Ernst Kaltenbrunner. Ideological Soldier in the Third Reich* (Princeton, 1984) and S. Kuusisto, *Alfred Rosenberg in der nationalsozialistischen Aussenpolitik 1933–1939* (Helsinki, 1984). R. Overy's *Goering. The 'Iron Man'* (London, 1984) is not to be missed. On the most important personality, **Adolf Hitler**, there is so much that the reader is best advised initially to pick up I. Kershaws' compact introduction, *Hitler* (London, 1991). This could be read in conjunction with E. Jäckel's highly personal collection of essays, *Hitler in History* (Hanover–London, 1984).

Reliable **overviews of economic developments** include H. Boehme, *An Introduction to the Social and Economic History of Germany* (London, 1979) and K. Borchardt, *Grundriss der deutschen Wirtschaftsgeschichte* (Göttingen, 1985). An invaluable reference aid is provided by W. Steitz (ed.), *Quellen zur deutschen Wirtschafts- und Sozialgeschichte vom Ersten Weltkrieg bis zum Ende der Weimarer Republik* (Darmstadt, 1993). H. R. James develops a powerfully argued analysis of *The German Slump. Politics and Economics 1924–1936* (Oxford, 1984). The central problem of **reparations** during the Weimar period is described in B. Kent, *The spoils of war. The Politics, Economics and Diplomacy of Reparations 1918–1932* (Oxford, 1989). S. Schuker makes clear just how much worse things *could* have been for Germany in *American 'Reparations' to Germany 1919–1933. Implications for the Third-World Debt Crisis* (Princeton, 1988). O. Schötz, *Der Kampf um die Mark 1923/4. Die deutsche Währungsstabilisierung unter dem Einfluss der nationalen Interessen Frankreichs, Grossbritanniens und der USA* (Berlin, New York, 1987) shows how forceful British economic and monetary policy was towards Germany. E. E. Rowley considers *Hyperinflation in Germany* (London, 1994) and G. D. Feldman explores its wider ramifications in *Die Nachwirkungen der Inflation auf die deutsche Geschichte 1924–1933* (Munich, 1985). The conflict between central and local government over policy priorities emerges from P-C. Witt (ed.), *Wealth and Taxation in Central Europe. The History and Sociology of Public Finance* (Leamington Spa, 1987). For much more detail see G. Ambrosius, *Die öffentliche Wirtschaft in der Weimarer Republik. Kommunale Versorgsunternehmen als Instrumente der Wirtschaftspolitik* (Baden–Baden, 1982) and W. Heindl, *Die Haushalte von Reich, Ländern und Gemeinden in Deutschland von 1925 bis 1933. Öffentliche Haushalte und Krisenverschärfung* (Frankfurt–M, 1985).

On the Third Reich J. Overy's *The Nazi Economic Recovery 1932–1938* (London, 1982) is thoughtful, readable and concise. More extensive discussions of a number of controversial issues are to be found in his collected essays, *War and Economy in the Third Reich* (Oxford, 1994). Avraham Barkai's pioneering research on the nature of National Socialist economic policy, hitherto in German, can now be sampled by the English reader through his *Nazi Economics. Ideology, Theory and Policy* (New Haven, Conn.–Oxford, 1990). On **big business** and National Socialism H. A. Turner Jr, *German Big Business and the Rise of Hitler* (New York–Oxford, 1985) is now the standard account. The relationship between industry and the Hitler state is viewed in a sectoral setting by J. R. Gillingham, *Ruhr Coal, Hitler and Europe. Industry and Politics in the Third Reich* (London, 1985) while B. P. Bellon, *Mercedes in Peace and War. German Automobile Workers 1903–1945* (New York, 1990), traces the link between commercial success and compliance with the regime after 1933. What this meant for the workforce is further elaborated in K-J. Siegfried,

Rüstungsproduktion und Zwangsarbeit im Volkswagenwerk 1933–1945 (Frankfurt–M–New York, 1987). P. Hayes, *Industry and Ideology. IG Farben in the Nazi Era* (Cambridge, 1987) is in a class of its own. Other affinities between National Socialist ideology and industrial concerns are explored by C. Sachse, *Siemens, der Nationalsozialismus und die moderne Familie. Eine Untersuchung zur sozialen Rationalisierung in Deutschland im 20 Jahrhundert.* (Hamburg, 1990).

It is not always possible to separate economic issues from matters of **social history and policy.** Extensive consideration is given to a number of social issues by R. Bessel, *Germany after the First World War* (Oxford, 1994), although it does not go far beyond 1921 or so. No comparable recent general social history of the Weimar Republic comes to mind to match that offered for the Third Reich by N. Frei, *Nazi Germany. A social history* (London, 1992). On central concerns of Weimar social policy see W. Bogs, *Die Sozialversicherung in der Weimarer Demokratie* (Munich, 1981); K. C. Fuehrer, *Arbeitslosigkeit und die Entstehung der Arbeitslosenversicherung in Deutschland 1902–1927* (Bochum, 1990); and P. Lewek, *Arbeitslosigkeit und Arbeitslosenversicherung in der Weimarer Republik 1918–1927* (Stuttgart, 1992). For the Third Reich see M.-L. Recker, *Nationalsozialistische Sozialpolitik im Zweiten Weltkrieg* (Munich, 1985). Turning to the wider issue of German society, it is striking how much **workers and labour issues** have attracted historians. H. Grebing's *History of the German Labour Movement. A Survey.* (Leamington Spa, 1985) is highly rated but the working-class milieu is better described in R. J. Evans (ed.), *The German Working Class 1888–1933. The Politics of Everyday Life* (London, 1982). See too R. J. Evans and D. Geary (eds), *The German Unemployed 1918–1936* (London, 1987). P. D. Stachura's edited collection *Unemployment and the Great Depression in Weimar Germany* (London, 1987) has a narrower focus, but he has also produced *The Weimar Republic and the Younger Proletariat: An Economic and Social Analysis* (London, 1989). The modern reader can derive benefits from consulting a re-issue of a major older study, E. Fromm, *The Working Class in Weimar Germany. A Psychological and Sociological Study* (Oxford, 1984). Two well-written German accounts of trade unions are worth reading, M. Ruck, *Die Gewerkschaften in den Anfangsjahren der Republik 1919–1923* (Cologne, 1985) and, by the same author, *Freien Gewerkschaften im Ruhrkampf 1923* (Cologne, 1986). The relationship between workers and National Socialism touched on by Ruck is more fully elaborated in H. A. Winkler, *Der Weg in die Katastrophe. Arbeiter und Arbeiterbewegung in der Weimarer Republik 1930–33* (Berlin–Bonn, 1987) and V. Kratzenberg, *Arbeiter auf den Weg zu Hitler? Die NS*

Betriebszellen-Organisation. Ihre Entstehung, ihre Programmatik, ihr Scheitern 1927–34 (Frankfurt–M, 1987). The important contribution of the late T. Mason to work on labour in the Third Reich can be sampled in the expanded English introduction to his major collection of German documents, now issued as a separate volume, *Social Policy in the Third Reich. The Working Class and the 'National Community'* edited by J. Caplan (Providence–Oxford, 1993). One does not have to agree with all his findings to be stimulated by his wide-ranging arguments. A more pedantic but none the less thorough account is given by W. Zollitsch, *Arbeiter zwischen Weltwirtschaftskrise und Nationalsozialismus. Ein Beitrag zur Sozialgeschichte der Jahre 1928 bis 1939* (Göttingen, 1990). R. Smelser, *Robert Ley. Hitler's Labour Front Leader* (Oxford, 1988) gives a full picture of a central figure in labour policy (in spite of its often bizarre prose style). Some of the results of workers having to give up their traditional unions to become members of the Labour Front can be glimpsed in M. Linder, *The Supreme Labour Court in Nazi Germany. A Jurisprudential Analysis* (Frankfurt–M, 1987). What the regime did for wages and living standards can be seen in R. Hachtmann, *Industriearbeit im 'Dritten Reich'. Untersuchungen zu den Lohn- und Arbeitsbedingungen in Deutschland 1933–45* (Göttingen, 1989). On the question of foreign labour in the Third Reich see in particular U. Herbert, *Fremdarbeiter. Politik und Praxis des 'Ausländer Einsatzes' in der Kriegswirtschaft des Dritten Reiches* (Bonn–Berlin, 1985). Memories of forced labour can be read in C. U. Schminck-Gustavus (ed.), *Hungern für Hitler. Erinnerungen polnischer Zwangsarbeiter im Deutschen Reich 1940–1945* (Reinbek bei Hamburg, 1984).

Moving away from the factory, **agriculture and rural issues** surface in a number of well written recent English works. General overviews include R. G. Moellger (ed.), *Peasants and Lords in Modern Germany. Recent Studies in Agricultural History* (London, 1986) and R. J. Evans (ed.), *The German Peasantry. Conflict and Community in Rural Society from the Eighteenth to the Twentieth Centuries* (London, 1985). An entertaining account of the 1920s is R. Osmond's, *Rural Protest in the Weimar Republic. The Free Peasantry in the Rhineland and Bavaria* (London, 1993). For the Third Reich we have A. Bramwell, *Blood and Soil. Richard Walther Darre and Hitler's 'Green Party'* (Bourne End, 1985) and G. Corni, *Hitler and the Peasants. Agrarian Policy of the Third Reich 1930–1939* (A translation from the German original, New York–Oxford–Munich, 1990). (Neither of these two studies achieves as much as J. Farquharson's earlier book *The Plough and the Swastika. The NSDAP and Agriculture in Germany 1928–1945* (London, 1976).

The countryside embraced a wide social spectrum, thus facilitating the transition to books on the **middle classes** and the **German elites.** On the former the indefatigable R. J. Evans has edited, with D. Blackbourn, *The German bourgeoisie: Essays in the Social History of the German Middle Class from the Late 18th to Early 20th Century* (London, 1991). J. Kocka (ed.), *Angestellte in der deutschen Geschichte 1850–1980* (Göttingen, 1981) is to be recommended. English readers can now experience a classic book completed in 1932 which long remained unpublished thanks to Hitler's accession to power, H. Speier, *German White Collar Workers and the Rise of Hitler* (Yale, 1987). What became of middle-class expectations under National Socialist rule can be followed in M. Prinz, *Vom neuen Mittelstand zum Volksgenossen. Die Entwicklung des sozialen Status der Angestellte von der Weimarer Republik bis zum Ende der Nationalsozialismus* (Munich, 1986). Further reading on the German elites is suggested in the following section, but J. Caplan, *Government Without Administration. State and Civil Service in Weimar and Nazi Germany* (Oxford, 1990) provides an intelligent and challenging reconsideration of an important sector of German society. See also A. Kunz, *Civil Servants and the Politics of Inflation in Germany 1914–1924* (Berlin, New York, 1986).

The question of how the different sectors of German society fared after 1933 in Hitler's much vaunted **People's Community** is of course raised by the social histories already mentioned, but the amount of energy the regime was forced to devote to perpetuating the *idea* of a community can be gauged in D. Welch's admirable *The Third Reich. Politics and Propaganda* (London, 1993). H. Boberach (ed.), *Meldungen aus dem Reich. 1938–1945. Die geheimen Lageberichte des Sicherheitsdienstes der SS* (Herrsching, 1984) and T. Klein (ed.), *Die Lageberichte der Geheimen Staatspolizei über die Provinz Hessen-Nassau 1933–36* (Cologne, Vienna, 1986) confirm how attentive the regime was to 'public opinion'. I. Kershaw's penetrating study, *Popular Opinion and Political Dissent in the Third Reich. Bavaria 1933–1945* (Oxford, 1983), shows that the regime was right to be concerned, while at the same time the book raises harsh questions about the limits to popular resistance. The latter preoccupy R. Gellately, whose book *The Gestapo and German Society. Enforcing Racial Policy* (Oxford, 1990) asks how a relatively small police force *could* enforce the government's priorities without extensive compliance from the population at large. Other more indirect means of social control are indicated for example by J. Stephenson, *The Nazi Organization of Women* (London, 1980) and G. Kinz, *Der Bund Deutscher Mädel. Ein Beitrag über die ausserschulische Mädchenerziehung im Nationalsozialismus* (Frankfurt–M, 1992), or by F.

Kudlien (ed.), *Ärzte im Nationalsozialismus* (Cologne, 1985). How traditional authorities could be subverted to the 'community's' purpose is illustrated by R. Dreier and W. Sellert (eds), *Recht und Justiz im 'Dritten Reich'* (Frankfurt–M, 1989) and by M. Thielenhaus, *Zwischen Anpassung und Widerstand. Deutsche Diplomaten 1938–41* (Paderborn, 1985). The mistreatment of Jews prior to the war can be charted in A. Barkai, *Vom Boykott zur 'Entjudung'. Der wissenschaftliche Existenzkampf der Juden im Dritten Reich 1933–43* (Frankfurt, 1988).

The ever sensitive issue of why key German elites and leaders did less than they might have done to bring about **resistance to Hitler** naturally arises in relation to the armed forces. Earlier studies can now be augmented by two major works, the first a translation of the brilliantly argued short essays by K-J. Müller, *The Army, Politics and Society in Germany 1933–1945. Studies in the Army's Relations to Nazism* (Manchester, 1987), and the second a collection of writings edited by W. Deist, *The German Military in the Age of Total War* (Leamington Spa, 1985). K-J. Müller has also edited a comparative study, *The Military in Politics and Society in France and Germany in the 20th Century* (Oxford–Washington, 1995). Also of interest are W. Deist, *The Wehrmacht and German Rearmament* (London, 1986) and C. Hartmann, *Halder. Generalstabschef Hitlers 1938–1942* (Paderborn, 1991). A major new study is that by G. R. Uberschär, *Generaloberst Franz Halder. Generalstabschef, Gegner und Gefangener Hitlers* (Göttingen–Zurich, 1991). The role of the Church comes under rather harsh scrutiny in V. Barnett, *For the Soul of the People. Protestant Protest Against Hitler* (Oxford, 1992) and in R. P. Eriksen, *Theologians under Hitler* (New Haven, Conn., 1985). The English version of Volume 1 of K. Scholder's *The Churches and the Third Reich 1918–1934* (London, 1987) is immensely detailed. Wider issues of resistance are covered in P. Hoffmann, *German Resistance to Hitler* (Cambridge, Mass., London, 1988) and in F. R. Nicosia and L. D. Stokes (eds), *Nonconformity, Opposition and Resistance in the Third Reich* (Oxford, Washington, 1990). See also M. Balfour's penetrating and critical, *Withstanding Hitler in Germany 1933–1945* (London, 1988). Broader studies of note include M. Broszat and K. Schwabe (eds), *Die deutschen Eliten und der Weg in den Zweiten Weltkrieg* (Munich, 1989); D. L. Large (ed.), *Contending with Hitler. Varieties of German Resistance in the Third Reich* (Cambridge, 1992); and H. Bull (ed.), *The challenge of the Third Reich: The Adam von Trott Memorial Lectures* (Oxford, 1986). There is a moving biography of a key figure by W. Venohr, *Stauffenberg. Symbol der deutschen Einheit. Eine politische biographie* (Frankfurt–Berlin, 1986). The extent to which youth 'resisted' is considered by W. Breyvogel (ed.), *Piraten, Swings und Junge Garde. Jugendwiderstand im National-sozialismus* (Berlin, 1991). On youth see also J. von Lang, *Der Hitler-Junge. Baldur von Schirach: Der Mann der Deutschlands Jugend erzog* (Hamburg, 1991) and, more generally, P. D. Stachura, *The German Youth Movement 1900–1945. An Interpretative and Documentary History* (London, 1981).

The **foreign policy of Germany** after 1918 has spawned a vast literature. Bibliographical guidance to the interwar period is given in J. W. Hiden, *Germany and Europe 1919–1939* (2nd edn, London, 1993). As to the **Weimar Republic's foreign relations,** M. Lee and W. Michalka, *German Foreign Policy 1917–1933* (Leamington Spa, 1987) fail to do sufficient justice to the complexity of issues. However, they give full coverage to major arguments between German historians. Some re-thinking is accomplished in R. Davin-Luetgemeier, *Pazifismus zwischen Kooperation und Konfrontation. Das deutsche Friedenskartell in der Weimarer Republik* (Cologne, 1982). On the all-important question of foreign trade policy after 1919 see J. Bellers' comparative study, *Aussenwirtschaftspolitik und politisches System der Weimarer Republik und der Bundesrepublik* (Münster, 1988). The most important general study of Weimar foreign policy remains that by P. Krüger, *Die Aussenpolitik der Republik von Weimar* (Darmstadt, 1985), which manages to escape many of the clichés about German revisionism after 1919. See also his shorter *Versailles. Deutsche Aussenpolitik zwischen Revisionismus und Friedenssicherung* (Munich, 1986). A reliable but rather predictable narrative account is that by R. Henig, *Versailles and after. Europe 1919–1933* (London, 1984). Little attempt can be made here to grapple with the Stresemann literature. R. P. Grathwol, *Stresemann and the DNVP. Reconciliation or Revenge in German Foreign Policy 1924–1928* (Lawrence, Kansas, 1980) poses a somewhat illusory choice. A better introduction is that by W. Michalka and M. M. Lee (eds), *Gustav Stresemann* (Darmstadt, 1984). B. Schot's *Stresemann, der deutsche Osten und der Volkerbund* (Wiesbaden, 1984) is an original contribution which should by now have transformed views on Stresemann's policy on German minorities abroad. A rather moving book is that by the German foreign minister's son, W. Stresemann, *Mein Vater Gustav Stresemann* (Frankfurt–Berlin–Vienna, 1985). V. Torunsky, *Entente der Revisionisten? Mussolini und Stresemann 1922–1929* (Cologne–Vienna, 1986) is justifiably sceptical about the extent to which Stresemann was prepared to co-operate with fascist Italy. Finally there is M. Berg, *Gustav Stresemann. Eine politische Karriere zwischen Reich und Politik* (Göttingen–Zurich, 1992). The foreign minister who came after Stresemann had a difficult time to judge from W. Ratliff, *Faithful to* *the Fatherland. Julius Curtius and Weimar Foreign Policy* (New York, 1990).

The **foreign policy of the Third Reich** is best approached through the solid diplomatic studies of G. Weinberg, whose second volume, *The foreign policy of Hitler's Germany. Starting World War II* (Chicago–London, 1980) takes up the story around 1936. (The first volume, *The Foreign Policy of Hitler's Germany. Diplomatic Revolution*, appeared in 1970.) The wider setting of German policy can be viewed in W. J. Mommsen and L. Kettenacker (eds), *The Fascist Challenge and the Policy of Appeasement* (London, 1983). The prolific German historian, K. Hildebrand, has some reflective and indeed provocative essays in his *German Foreign Policy from Bismarck to Adenauer. The Limits of Statecraft* (London, 1989). It is well worth comparing this with C. Bloch's highly personal and thoroughly entertaining *Le IIIe Reich et le monde* (Paris, 1986). A convenient introduction to the often tortuous debate on Hitler's policy views is the book by G. Stoakes, *Hitler and the Quest for World Dominion. Nazi Ideology and Foreign Policy in the 1920s* (London, 1986). On the strategic issues and their relationship to foreign policy, W. Murray's attractively written and well argued comparative study, *The Change in the European Balance of Power 1938–1939. The Path to Ruin* (Princeton, 1984), is essential reading. Books dealing with German and British differences over eastern Europe are M.-L. Recker (ed.), *From Competition to Rivalry. The Anglo-German Relationship in the Countries at the European Periphery 1919–1939* (Stuttgart, 1986) and A. J. Prażmowska, *Britain, Poland and the Eastern Front 1939* (Cambridge, 1988). These can be supplemented by R. Ahmann's highly original study, *Nichtangriffspakte: Entwicklung und operative Nutzung in Europa 1922–1939* (Baden-Baden, 1988) and by D. M. Crowe, *The Baltic States and the Great Powers: Foreign Relations 1938–40* (San Francisco–Oxford, 1992). On the war itself, three volumes of the prestigious German series on Germany and the Second World War have been translated. These are, Vol. 1: *The build-up of German Aggression*, Vol. 2: *Germany's Initial Conquests in Europe* and Vol 3: *The Mediterranean, South-East Europe and North Africa 1939–1941* (Oxford, 1994).

On the war in the east, G. R. Ueberschär and W. Wette (eds), *'Unternehmen Barbarossa'. Der deutsche Überfall auf die Sowjetunion 1941* (Paderborn, 1985). The growing critical attention to the conduct of the German army during this grim conflict is reflected in O. Bartov, *The Eastern Front, 1941–1945. German Troops and the Barbarisation of Warfare* (London, 1986). For a further development of O. Bartov's powerful, emotional arguments see his *Hitler's Army. Soldiers, Nazis and*

War in the Third Reich (Oxford–New York, 1991). Important, too, is T. Schulte's study of the rank and file in two army rear areas on the middle sector of the eastern front, *The German Army and Nazi Policies in Occupied Russia* (Oxford, 1989). German troop reactions against brutality can be sampled in the publication based on Soviet archives, A. Golovchansky and V. Osipov, *'Ich will raus aus diesem Wahnsinn'. Deutsche Briefe von der Ostfront 1941–1945. Aus sowjetischen Archiven* (Wuppertal, 1991, 2nd edn). However, one returns to the stark reality underlined by C. Browning, *Ordinary Men. Reserve Police Battalion 101 and the Final Solution in Poland* (New York, 1993). More generally, see C. Browning, *The Path to Genocide. Essays on Launching the Final Solution* (Cambridge, 1992); R. Hilburg, *The Destruction of the European Jews* (Leicester, 1986); and G. Hirschfeld (ed.), *The Policies of Genocide. Jews and Soviet Prisoners of War in Nazi Germany* (London, 1986). Forceful, interesting but by no means undisputed arguments relating population economics to genocide can be found in G. Aly and S. Heim, *Vordenker der Vernichtung. Auschwitz und die deutschen Pläne für eine neue europäische Ordnung* (Franfurt–M, 1993). Broader settings for the policies of mass murder are depicted in J. P. Fox, *Adolf Hitler and the Jewish Question. A Study in Ideology and Policy* (London, 1986); H. Graml, *Anti-Semitism and its Origins in the Third Reich* (London, 1992); and P. Pulzer, *Jews and the German State. The Political History of a Minority 1848–1933* (London, 1992). The sensitive issue of how Germans reacted to genocide is handled by D. Bankier, *The Germans and the Final Solution. Public Opinion under Nazism* (London, 1991) and by S. Gordon, *Hitler, Germans and the 'Jewish Question'* (Princeton, 1984). R. Plant's book, *The Pink Triangle. The Nazi War against Homosexuals* (New York, 1986), provides reminders that not only Jews were killed, while the killing of Germans by Germans, as well as the links between 'medicine' and genocide, are treated in R. J. Lifton, *The Nazi doctors. Medical Killing and the Psychology of Genocide* (London, 1987); in G. Aly, P. Chroust and C. Pross, *Cleansing the Fatherland* (Baltimore, 1994), and in M. Burleigh's powerful and depressing *Death and Deliverance. 'Euthanasia' in Germany 1900–1945* (Cambridge, 1995). The trauma in coming to terms with this past is handled in G. Hartman, *Holocaust Remembrance. The Shapes of Memory* (London, 1993) and by H. Mommsen, *From Weimar to Auschwitz* (Princeton, 1991). R. J. Evans's crisp account of historical controversies about the nature of the Holocaust, *In Hitler's Shadow. West German Historians and the Attempt to Escape from the Nazi Past* (New York, 1989), is eminently readable and fair.

Index